A Second Chance for Justice

A Second Chance for Justice: The Prosecutions of Gabe Watson for the Death of Tina Thomas

By

Asher Flynn and Kate Fitz-Gibbon

CAMBRIDGE
SCHOLARS
PUBLISHING

A Second Chance for Justice:
The Prosecutions of Gabe Watson for the Death of Tina Thomas,
by Asher Flynn and Kate Fitz-Gibbon

This book first published 2013

Cambridge Scholars Publishing

12 Back Chapman Street, Newcastle upon Tyne, NE6 2XX, UK

British Library Cataloguing in Publication Data
A catalogue record for this book is available from the British Library

ISBN (10): 1-4438-4202-8, ISBN (13): 978-1-4438-4202-0

Table of Contents

List of Tables vii

Foreword viii

Acknowledgements xii

About the Authors xv

Introductory Note xvi
22 October 2003 — 23 February 2012

Introduction 1
The *Watson* Case

Part I: Justice in Queensland

Chapter One 14
Operation Charlie Oswald

Chapter Two 40
Delaying Justice? The Prolonged Police Investigation

Chapter Three 57
"Dealing" with Gabe

Chapter Four 85
"Bargaining" with the Thomas Family

Part II: Justice in Alabama

Chapter Five 112
Prosecuting Gabe … Again

Chapter Six 135
Murder for Money: Proving the Motive

Chapter Seven 152
The Fatal Dive

Chapter Eight 183
Judging "the Character" of Gabe

Part III: Achieving Justice

Chapter Nine 200
Gabe's Acquittal

Chapter Ten 212
(In)Justice for Tina? (In)Justice for Gabe?

Chapter Eleven 237
A Second Chance for Justice

Reference List 251

Appendix A 262
Chapter Overviews

LIST OF TABLES

1-1 Timeline of Events Pertinent to the Legal Proceedings in *Watson*

1-2 Interview Participants

5-1 The Prosecution Pecuniary Gain Witness List

7-1 The Prosecution Fatal Dive Witness List

FOREWORD

> Bring someone to justice: arrest someone for a crime and ensure that they are tried in court: Everything will be done to bring those responsible to justice.
>
> —Oxford Dictionary

It was on the night of 21 October 2003 that I first met Gabe and Tina Watson. They were on their honeymoon. Tina was bubbly, energetic and personable, while Gabe seemed to be the more serious of the two—but nothing that does not make up the mix of a normal couple. I was the trip director and dive master on board the *Spoilsport*, which was taking scuba divers from around the world, including Gabe and Tina, on a seven-day expedition. Our first dive was to be the *SS Yongala* wreck. Part of my role included conducting interviews with the guests about their diving experiences and what they wanted to get out of the expedition, as well as performing the many detailed dive safety briefings. In speaking with Gabe and Tina, due to her limited diving experience, I recommended that Tina have an initial orientation dive to make sure she was comfortable in the water. This offer was extended to Gabe as the accompanying dive buddy, as some people prefer to dive with their partners. Tina and Gabe both turned down the offer. Gabe stated that he was a rescue diver and he was comfortable with the dive and with accompanying Tina on the dive, while Tina explained that she was comfortable just diving with Gabe. The offer of an orientation dive was made a second time during the interview and then again the following morning, but these offers were met with the same response. Before they headed off on their dive on 22 October 2003, Tina hugged me. The next time I saw Tina, I was attempting to rescue her from where she lay unconscious under water, with her eyes open and all her scuba diving equipment in place.

While leading my orientation dive group down towards the *SS Yongala* just after 10am or so on 22 October 2003, I saw a person lying unresponsive a bit off from the wreck. I immediately began a rescue dive. When I reached the diver, I saw that it was Tina. Gabe was nowhere in sight. I grabbed Tina and we quickly ascended to the surface and I did everything I could to ensure every chance of her survival. Despite our best efforts, including around 40 minutes of resuscitation attempts, Tina passed away on board a second dive vessel, the *Jazz II*, at 11:21am. This tragic moment formed the beginning of almost nine years of legal proceedings, and the beginning of my realisation that justice is not what it seems.

A Reflection on Justice

Over the course of the legal proceedings in the *Watson* case, I have provided statements to the Queensland Police Service about the events that occurred on 22 October 2003, assisted in the collation of evidence as part of the dive re-enactment tests carried out by the police, and testified as a prosecution witness at the capital murder trial of Gabe Watson in Alabama. Until having these experiences with the law, I had always held the belief that justice was about correcting wrongs and bringing right to those who had been wronged. It may have seemed an innocent way to think of justice, maybe even naive, but then again, shouldn't something like right and wrong be simple in principle? Is it wrong to expect that when they say justice is to be done, that justice will be done? The simplest of concepts: who is right and who is wrong? Who did right and who did wrong? I had always held the belief that justice entailed finding the truth, regardless of what "need" or "cost" it took to get there.

A business is focused on the bottom line: what have I got to sell, who wants to buy, and how can I get more people to buy what I am selling? What does this have to do with justice? I have come to realise, a great deal. The prosecutors, the defence lawyers and their clients are all in the business of selling. They are trying to sell their version of events to the judge, the public and the jury—if the case is "lucky" enough to get to a jury trial. The better that they can do this, the better chance that team will have of winning their case. Justice is not about the facts or the truth; it's about how and who best sells their story. In the *Watson* case, this was no different—it was just that selling your story was based solely on what money and resources you had available.

Money doesn't just make the world go around, money makes justice viable or out of reach. In Queensland, getting justice in the *Watson* case was subject to the restriction of cost. Early on in Queensland, it was made clear in the many challenges blocking the police investigation, and in the prosecution's decision to forego a murder trial, that the matter—for a reason that has never been made clear—needed to be wrapped up as quickly as possible. Justice was to be obtained swiftly, with the "added" benefit of not expending "unnecessary" costs. The cost of justice again became an issue when the case made its way to Alabama, with even the trial being postponed because of budgetary cuts. Nine months further down the track, when the case was finally heard, the state-funded prosecution was limited in the resources they had, and could only call a handful of the important witnesses needed to fully present its case. In both Queensland and Alabama, justice was limited by what the state was able and willing to pay. And in this case, that figure was not much at all.

A Second Chance for Justice?

In *A Second Chance for Justice*, Asher Flynn and Kate Fitz-Gibbon examine the different ways in which the Queensland and Alabama criminal justice systems responded to Tina's death, and how resource and efficiency issues can shape perceptions and outcomes of justice. The authors provide a unique insight into the ways in which justice was sought and denied—subjectively, substantively and procedurally—in both countries. And despite the different approaches used by the two legal systems, they find a similar pattern emerging from both prosecutions of Gabe Watson: that justice was decided by resources and the voice of one.

This book is split into three parts, each addressing the moments in which justice had the opportunity to be achieved. The analysis follows the case from 2003 until its conclusion, at least in a legal sense, in Alabama in February 2012. Across the three parts, this captivating book takes readers on a journey through some of the key, contentious legal issues, injustices and obstacles that emerged throughout the Queensland and Alabama legal responses to the *Watson* case, and leaves readers asking significant questions of the Queensland and Alabama justice systems, including: what does justice look like in a resource-starved, efficiency-driven legal system? Can the decision of one reflect justice? Do we accept the changing face of justice? How many other cases have faced the same or similar injustices?

Although this book focuses primarily on the *Watson* case, it contains much discussion that will be of interest to those unfamiliar with the case, and for those interested in justice—something that should be considered of vital importance for all members of society. In recognising the significant contributions of their participants, the authors provide a generous voice to the perspectives of those most involved in the case, including the police investigators, prosecutors, defence lawyers and members of the Thomas and Watson families. This offers readers a truly unique insight into the very real consequences that arise from experiences of justice and injustice.

At the conclusion of this book, readers will have gained a broader perspective on how "justice" truly operates within the Queensland and Alabama legal systems. Beyond this, readers will also have gained a unique insight into and appreciation of the practical operation of the justice system. As someone directly affected by this case, I cannot emphasise the importance and significance this book provides in shedding light on how the "justice" system really works.

Final Thoughts

I am no longer a dive master or instructor. I work as an Advanced Care Paramedic with the Queensland Ambulance Service in Brisbane, Australia. I have contributed to this book as a person not intimately knowledgeable, but intimately involved in the almost nine-year legal proceedings surrounding Tina's death. I no longer believe that justice is about proving right from wrong. Rather, it all comes down to who can afford the resources to best "sell" their story. So, should I ever seek justice from the law, I hope that I have the state-funded side up against me, because as long as justice comes at a cost, my chances of attaining some version of it are far higher as the one accused, than as the victim.

Wade Singleton

ACKNOWLEDGEMENTS

When we first envisaged writing this book, we were driven by the obscure concept of justice and a desire to understand the many contentious legal decisions that have surrounded the *Watson* case since October 2003. Along the way, we have met a range of people who have been affected by this case—personally, emotionally, financially and legally. We found that they were also driven by this obscure notion of justice and a desire to understand why and how this case was able to proceed in the manner that it had for almost nine years. We hope this book will provide some insight and answers to these issues.

We would like to thank the following people for their support, participation and guidance—without them, this book simply could not have been written. First and foremost, we would like to thank the individuals who shared their stories, experiences and invaluable memories with us. We feel incredibly privileged for the generosity that these individuals showed in speaking with us, often at a very difficult time in their lives. We are very grateful that we have been given the opportunity to gain some understanding of their experiences of justice in the Queensland and Alabama legal systems.

To Tommy and Cindy Thomas, we are deeply sorry for the loss of your beautiful, energetic and bubbly daughter Tina. Thank you for sharing your memories of Tina with us and for allowing us such a personal insight into how your lives have changed and what you have experienced since 22 October 2003. Our discussions with you were invaluable in helping decipher what really happened in the justice systems of both countries.

To Lieutenant Brad Flynn and Detective Senior Constable Kevin Gehringer, thank you for sharing your expertise and for providing us with a personalised insight into the difficult and prolonged experiences that both of you have had in understanding and working within the constraints imposed by the resources, decisions and obstacles thrown up in the Queensland and Alabama legal systems. We are indebted to you for the generosity you both showed in the time that you spent with us, in your willingness to answer our questions and in your very kind spirits. To Commissioner David Glasgow, we thank you for your generous contribution to our book, for sharing your views, and for providing us with a glimpse into the significant problems that exist within the resource-starved climate of the Queensland criminal justice system. Thank you for your time and support. To Alabama Assistant Attorney-General Don Valeska, thank you for supporting this book from the outset and for your willingness to share with us an understanding of your experiences prosecuting a case that has raised so many unique questions.

To David Watson and Bob Austin, we thank you for sharing your perspectives and the experiences of what your son and friend, Gabe Watson, endured throughout this emotional, challenging and exhausting nine years. We value your support and contribution in providing us with an understanding of the effects of the legal processes on your family. To Brett Bloomston and Jo Basgier, thank you for sharing your astute perspectives on a case that clearly meant a lot to both of you. We appreciate your guidance and thank you for allowing us access to what has remained the hidden side of this case—the defence. Thank you also for your support of the book and for providing us with various materials to contribute to its accuracy.

We are very thankful to Wade Singleton who contributed the foreword to this book and provided a reflection on his experiences with, and changing perceptions of, justice. Wade is a remarkable person and remains to many, including the Thomas family, a true hero.

We would also like to thank the following individuals for their support, guidance and/or contributions to the book: Tina Coker Hammonds, Andrew Arrington and John Hensley from the Office of the Alabama Attorney-General; Michael Hanle, Garner Thompson and Ashley from the defence team in Alabama; Detective Senior Sergeant Gary Campbell; Andy Toulson; Mel Flynn; Linda Valeska; Lyn Lewis; Eric Velasco; Tuck Thompson; Butch Dill; Chief Doug Jones; Judge Tommy Nail; and the court staff and security personnel at Jefferson County Courthouse.

We are also very grateful for the ongoing support and guidance that we have received from our colleagues at Monash University and Deakin University. We are particularly thankful to Professor Jude McCulloch, who on a rainy day in San Francisco encouraged us to turn the questions we were asking about this case into a book. Thank you also to Michael Flynn and to Pamela and Allen Bowles for your invaluable feedback and guidance on earlier drafts—your encouragement (as always) and belief in the project was instrumental in the completion of this book. We would also like to thank Julia Farrell for her assistance in proofreading the final manuscript and Cambridge Scholars Publishing for their interest in the research and their support throughout the publishing process.

Finally, to our incredible families and our wonderful partners—Mark and Mick—thank you for your continual love and support.

Our purpose in writing this book has been to provide a better understanding of the Queensland and Alabama legal systems' responses to the fatal dive that occurred on 22 October 2003, and we hope that we will have shed some much-needed light on the problems that exist within the resource-starved climates in which justice is determined. The legal issues that are examined in this book are reflective of the problems confronting criminal justice systems globally, and we hope that our analysis propels a discussion as to how we can attempt to address these concerns. Most importantly, we hope that this book honours Tina's memory.

ABOUT THE AUTHORS

Dr Asher Flynn is a Lecturer and Researcher in Criminology at Monash University, Victoria, Australia. Her research encapsulates a diverse range of socio-legal and critical criminology concerns, with a particular focus on plea bargaining, sentencing, criminal prosecutions and the criminal justice system. Asher has published in a range of high quality, high impact criminology, socio-legal and law journals. *A Second Chance for Justice* is her first book.

Dr Kate Fitz-Gibbon is a Lecturer and Researcher in Criminology at Deakin University, Victoria, Australia. She researches in the area of the law's response to lethal intimate partner violence and the effects of law reform in Australian and international jurisdictions. Dr Fitz-Gibbon has published on the operation and effects of homicide law and sentencing reform with a key focus on gender and justice.

INTRODUCTORY NOTE

22 OCTOBER 2003 — 23 FEBRUARY 2012

> A person who was full of life and energy. She was the type of person who walked into a room and lit it up ... People didn't forget her. She was my big sister and we would talk just about every day either on the telephone or in person. We worked together and spent a lot of our time together. It was like us against the world. We talked about everything together. We talked about our work lives, our private lives, our relationships and our future plans ... We even talked about being in the same nursing homes together as roommates. Tina was a bubbly person … [She] was a true romantic.[1]
>
> —Tina's sister, Alanda Thomas

Christina Mae Thomas Watson (Tina Thomas) had a smile that exhumed warmth and happiness. She had a cheeky sense of humour and a kind spirit. Tina was one of those special people, who was so bright and bubbly that you couldn't help but get captured in her aura. Tina loved animals, college football and shopping. Her favourite movie was *Gone with the Wind* and over the years, with the help of her parents, Tommy and Cindy, she had collected a range of memorabilia, including figurines and posters. During high school, Tina would join as many extra-curricula classes and clubs as possible, usually alongside her best friend Amanda Phillips, mostly so they would have lots of pictures in the year book. When the end of each year arrived, Tina would sit with her mum, Cindy, laughing as they went through all the pictures, and reading all the comments and signatures that people had written in Tina's book. At Christmas time, Tina would hand out the presents. She would count each present, because Tina and her sister, Alanda, had to receive the same amount, so they could be exactly the same. For her 18th birthday, Tina's parents bought her diamond earrings and wrapped them in multiple boxes—starting with a really big box, then a slightly smaller box, then an even smaller box and a smaller box. This game continued for some time. Tina loved these types of surprises, where she would be laughing and

[1] Alanda Thomas, witness statement, 30 April 2007.

guessing what the present could possibly be and when she would finally get to it.

Tina met David Gabriel Watson (Gabe Watson) when they were both students at the University of Alabama, Birmingham campus. They began dating in 2002 and on 11 October 2003, Tina married Gabe at the Southside Baptist Church in Birmingham, Alabama. For their honeymoon, Gabe had planned a trip to Australia and they arrived in Sydney in the state of New South Wales on 17 October 2003 to begin their lives together as husband and wife. After a few days spent visiting sites like Taronga Zoo, where they took photographs cuddling koalas, and the Opera House, Tina and Gabe arrived in Townsville in the state of Queensland and boarded the *Spoilsport*, a dive vessel that would take them on a seven-day scuba diving expedition to the Great Barrier Reef, the Coral Sea and the historic *SS Yongala* wreck.

On 22 October 2003, the first day of their diving expedition, and five days into their honeymoon, Tina entered the water twice with Gabe. On their first dive attempt, Tina and Gabe resurfaced after descending just one to two metres, as Gabe had complained of a fault in his dive computer. In order to rectify the problem, which Gabe has claimed was the result of an incorrectly inserted battery, Tina and Gabe reboarded the *Spoilsport*. After fixing the dive computer battery and returning to the diver's drop point, Gabe and Tina entered the water for the second and final time together. Within minutes of descending, Gabe has claimed that Tina gestured to him with her thumb pointing behind her shoulder, to indicate that she wanted to go to the surface. From this point, Gabe has provided approximately 16 varying accounts of what happened next. These accounts have been given to a range of people, including the police, fellow divers on the *Spoilsport*, members of Tina's family and as part of a sworn declaration made in conjunction with a civil lawsuit in the United States (US). There are some slight and some significant variations among the 16 accounts that Gabe has provided. However, across these statements, as noted by the Queensland Assistant Director of Public Prosecutions, Brendan Campbell SC, Gabe has:

> consistently claimed that … [Tina] indicated that she was in difficulty … [and] they attempted to return to the access line. He was assisting her by holding her … There was then an incident where his mask and regulator were dislodged and [Tina] … sank away from him and he then decided to surface.[2]

[2] Brendan Campbell, sentencing hearing, 5 June 2009.

Gabe has claimed that after Tina gestured to him underwater, he began towing her by her arm, and/or her dive vest, and/or her hand, against the current, back towards the access line of the *Yongala* (the rope line used by divers to descend and ascend from the *Yongala* to the ocean's surface). Gabe has explained that he turned and indicated for Tina to inflate her buoyancy control device (BCD) by pressing a button located on her scuba diving vest, which would enable her to quickly ascend to the surface, but for unknown reasons she failed to do so. Gabe has claimed that at some point he turned towards Tina and she either grabbed hold of his mask, or knocked his mask, or knocked his mask and regulator ajar, at which stage he let go of her to clear and readjust his mask and regulator, or to clear and readjust his mask and put his alternate regulator in, referred to as the "safe second". It was at this point that Gabe has said that Tina began sinking downwards towards the ocean floor. He has explained that she was facing upwards, with her eyes open and her arms stretched outwards towards the surface. Gabe has claimed that Tina was somewhere between two and four metres, five to ten feet, or at least out of arm's reach away and below him. He has described her as sinking at a pace which despite wearing flippers, meant he was unable to reach her.

Gabe has suggested to some that he attempted to swim after Tina, but the pressure in his ears caused too much pain for him to continue; while to others, he has explained that when swimming after Tina, as fast as he was attempting to reach her, she was sinking at a quicker rate. In other versions, Gabe has suggested that despite thinking of the various ways he could assist his wife—including removing Tina's weights, and inflating his and/or her BCD which would enable them both to ascend to the ocean surface quickly—he ultimately felt there was nothing further he could do to help Tina, so he decided to leave her and begin ascending alone to seek help.

During his ascent to the surface, Gabe initially claimed that he approached two other divers, possibly of Asian descent, on the access line and attempted to seek their assistance, without success. However, given the location of where Gabe ultimately resurfaced, and that no witnesses support this version of events, it is now accepted that this did not occur. Upon resurfacing, Gabe was seen signalling for help and was overheard saying, "she's gone to the bottom and she's disappeared. She's in trouble".[3]

Within approximately two and a half minutes of Gabe resurfacing alone, the *Spoilsport* dive master and trip director, Wade Singleton—the

---

[3] Craig Haslett, witness statement, 22 October 2003.

man in charge of the dive expedition—surfaced holding Tina in his arms. Singleton has claimed that while underwater he sighted a diver motionless at the bottom of the ocean and upon reaching her, identified the diver as Tina. He has also noted that her eyes were open, her mask and regulator were in place, but she was not breathing. To immediately ascend with Tina, Singleton has explained that he removed his weight belt and successfully inflated Tina's BCD. During the ascent, he then forced air into her regulator, referred to as "purging her regulator", in an attempt to provide her with oxygen to enable her to breathe. Singleton's ability to do this indicated that there was air remaining in Tina's tank, and that her equipment was working, including the BCD that Gabe had earlier said she could not inflate. Upon reaching the surface, and placing Tina onto a second dive vessel, the *Jazz II*, which was at the *Yongala* site for a daytrip, resuscitation attempts were made to revive Tina for approximately 40 minutes. Tina was pronounced dead at 11:21am on 22 October 2003, 11 days after her wedding.

Initially, Tina's death was considered a tragic accident. It was only after preliminary police investigations revealed Gabe's rescue diving accreditation levels; the various inconsistencies and perceived implausibility in his version of events; his seemingly bizarre conduct, including his actions towards Tina's family in the days, months and years following her death; and the emergence of evidence suggesting a financial incentive and Gabe's perceived controlling and jealous character, that the investigation shifted towards a potential homicide inquiry. Over the next four to five years, the police investigation which began with the Townsville Water Police Division and the Townsville Criminal Investigation Branch (CIB) spread to the US, to include members of the Helena Police Department, located in the state of Alabama, and the Federal Bureau of Investigation. Through this multi-agency investigation, the CIB collected evidence which would later be used for two prosecutions of Gabe Watson for the death of Tina Thomas.

In response to the initial police investigation, a coronial inquest was held in Townsville, Queensland, to determine the cause and circumstances of Tina's death. The inquest commenced over four years after Tina's death on 13 November 2007 before Coroner David Glasgow. The hearing lasted 24 days, but was spread over seven months. Gabe did not provide evidence or attend the inquest. On 20 June 2008, after 64 oral and written statements had been given by witnesses located across eight countries, Coroner Glasgow found that there was "evidence of sufficient reliability which … satisfy me, that a properly instructed jury could make a finding of guilt against David Gabriel Watson on a charge of murder".[4] Coroner Glasgow then committed Gabe to stand trial for murder in Queensland and issued a warrant for his arrest. Gabe remained in Alabama when this finding was delivered.

Just over five months later, on 28 November 2008, the Queensland Office of the Department of Public Prosecutions (ODPP) presented the Brisbane Supreme Court with an indictment, charging Gabe Watson with the murder of Tina Thomas. Gabe was initially indicted to attend court on 3 February 2009; however, this date was later adjourned as both the prosecution and defence requested additional time to prepare their cases.

Throughout the five-year police and coronial investigation, Gabe continually denied any involvement in his wife's death, until a plea bargain agreement was reached with the Queensland ODPP which included, among other concessions, the withdrawal of the murder charge. After voluntarily returning to Australia on 13 May 2009 and spending 23 days in custody, Gabe was officially indicted before the Honourable Justice Lyons at the Brisbane Supreme Court on 5 June 2009, where he pleaded guilty to manslaughter by criminal negligence. Under s 290 of the *Criminal Code 1899* (Qld), manslaughter carries a maximum penalty of life imprisonment. However, informed by the agreed statement of facts prepared by the prosecution and defence as part of the plea bargain agreement that was reached, Gabe was sentenced to a maximum term of four and a half years imprisonment, which was to be fully suspended after 12 months, including the time he had already served. This meant that Gabe would serve a further 11 months and seven days imprisonment for his negligent role in Tina's death.

In response to a bevy of national and international backlash, alongside strong pressure from the then Alabama Attorney-General Troy King, the (former) Queensland Attorney-General, Cameron Dick, lodged an appeal against the manifest inadequacy of Gabe's sentence. This matter was heard on 17 July 2009. On 18 September 2009, in a two-to-one decision, the Queensland Court of Appeal found in favour of the prosecution and determined that Gabe's maximum sentence should remain at four and a half years, but that the period of suspension was to be increased from 12 months to 18 months, including time already served.

On 22 October 2010, seven years to the day that Tina died, Gabe was serving the last 20 days of his sentence in Borallon Correctional Centre in Queensland. On another continent, in the city of Birmingham, Alabama, a

---

[4] Transcript of Proceedings, *Inquest into the death of Christina Mae Watson* (20 June 2008) 64 (Coroner David Glasgow).

grand jury of 18 was listening to Alabama Assistant Attorney-General Don Valeska and Tina's father, Tommy Thomas, present evidence to indict Gabe for Tina's murder. Within five hours, the grand jury indicted Gabe on two charges of capital murder—capital murder for pecuniary gain and capital murder by kidnapping—both of which carry a potential death sentence.

As a general principle, Australia does not condone the implementation of capital punishment. Accordingly, under ss 22(3)(c) and 25(2)(b) of the *Extradition Act 1988* (Cth), Australia's federal Attorney-General can refuse to authorise the extradition of an individual facing a capital offence, unless the extradition country provides an undertaking that the person will not be tried; or if they are tried for the offence, that the death penalty will not be imposed; or if the death penalty is imposed, that it will not be carried out. While Australia was able to deport Gabe at the conclusion of his sentence, meaning that technically these extradition protections did not extend to his situation, the Australian Government refused to deport Gabe to the US until it received a written undertaking that the death penalty would not be imposed if he were found guilty of either, or both, of the capital murder charges. As a consequence, upon his release from prison on 11 November 2010, Gabe was escorted by immigration officials to Melbourne in the state of Victoria. Once in Melbourne, Gabe was held in an immigration detention centre until an official written statement confirming that he would not face the death penalty if convicted was received by Australian authorities eight days later.

On 25 November 2010, Gabe was deported to the US where he remained in custody until his bond hearing in the Jefferson County Courthouse in Birmingham, Alabama, on 14 December 2010, at which point he was released on a $100,000 bond by Judge Tommy Nail. The bond included additional conditions requiring Gabe to wear an electronic monitoring device and obey evening curfews. At the same hearing, Judge Nail scheduled Gabe's murder trial to commence on 23 May 2011. However, due to resource constraints, including the justice budget of the State of Alabama being stripped by approximately $120 million,[5] Gabe's murder trial was delayed because the courthouse could not be properly resourced with adequate security staff to run the trial. The trial was consequently delayed by almost nine months, with a new start date of 13 February 2012.

---

[5] National Centre for State Courts, *Alabama Overview* (2012) <http://www.ncsc.org/information-and-resources/budget-resource-center/states-activities-map/alabama.aspx>.

On the morning of 13 February 2012, Gabe's capital murder trial began with the prosecution withdrawing one of the charges—capital murder by kidnapping—and proceeding only on the capital murder for pecuniary gain charge. After nearly a day and a half of pre-trial arguments and an extensive jury selection process, the prosecution began presenting its case. On Thursday 23 February 2012, after six and a half trial days, during which 22 witnesses testified for the prosecution, the defence put forward a motion for a judgement of acquittal, claiming that the prosecution had failed to provide sufficient evidence to sustain a conviction for the capital murder offence. At approximately 1:50pm on 23 February 2012, Judge Tommy Nail granted the defence's motion and acquitted Gabe of the capital murder charge.

As enshrined in the Fifth Amendment of the *Constitution of the US* and based on US Supreme Court case law,[6] Judge Tommy Nail's decision can never be appealed. Consequently, after almost nine years of investigations, prosecutions and intense media and public scrutiny, the case against Gabe Watson officially ended, at least within the context of the criminal justice system.

Table 1-1: Timeline of events pertinent to the legal proceedings in the *Watson* case

Date	Event
11 October 2003	Gabe and Tina marry in Alabama.
17 October 2003	Gabe and Tina arrive in Australia for their honeymoon.
21 October 2003	Gabe and Tina arrive in Townsville, Queensland, and board the *Spoilsport* for a seven-day diving expedition.
22 October 2003	Gabe and Tina have two dive attempts on the *SS Yongala* wreck. Tina is pronounced dead at 11.21am.
22 October 2003	Gabe provides his first statement to the Townsville police. The statement is taken by Detective Senior Constable Kevin Gehringer. Gabe has a support person present for the statement, Mrs Paula Snyder, a fellow diver from the *Spoilsport*.
27 October 2003	At his own request, Gabe provides a second statement to the Townsville police. The statement is taken by Detective Senior Constable Kevin Gehringer and Senior Constable Glen Lawrence.

6 See *United States v Martin Linen Supply Co.* 430 U.S. 564 at 570-572 (1977); *Sanabria v United States* 437 U.S. 54 at 63-65 (1978).

	Gabe's mother, Glenda Watson, is also present as Gabe's support person.
October 2003	The Townsville Water Police Division take carriage of the investigation.
July 2004	The investigation is moved from the Townsville Water Police Division to the Townsville CIB.
August 2004	The Helena Police Department in Alabama is contacted by the Townsville CIB and its assistance is sought in the investigation, namely to assist with collecting witness statements.
April 2007	Detective Senior Sergeant Gary Campbell, lead investigator on the case, travels to the US to meet with the Alabama police investigators, interview various witnesses and collect evidence.
13 November 2007	The coronial inquest commences in Townsville, Queensland, before Coroner David Glasgow.
20 June 2008	Coroner David Glasgow charges Gabe with murder, which includes committing him to stand trial and issuing a warrant for his arrest.
28 November 2008	The Queensland ODPP presents the Brisbane Supreme Court with a murder indictment against Gabe Watson for the premeditated homicide of Tina Thomas.
27 January 2009	A video conference with several people from the ODPP and Queensland Police Service (QPS), including the Assistant ODPP Director and crown prosecutor in charge of the case, Brendan Campbell SC, ODPP Director Anthony Moynihan SC and the QPS Deputy Commissioner Ian Stewart, is held with Detective Senior Sergeant Gary Campbell and Detective Senior Constable Kevin Gehringer, to discuss the possibility of withdrawing the murder charge and accepting a manslaughter plea in the *Watson* case.
Late January 2009	Gabe's Australian lawyers travel to the US to meet with him.
3 February 2009	Gabe's arraignment date is rescheduled, with both the defence and prosecution requesting additional time.
13 May 2009	Gabe voluntarily returns to Australia and is remanded in custody.
14 May 2009	Crown prosecutor Brendan Campbell, along with Detective Senior Sergeant Gary Campbell and an ODPP media representative, travel to Alabama to meet with the Thomas family.

16–17 May 2009	Assistant ODPP Director and crown prosecutor in charge of the case, Brendan Campbell SC, meets with the Thomas family and Lieutenant Brad Flynn (Helena Police Department) in Alabama to discuss the Australian trial process and the possibility of a plea deal occurring in which Gabe would plead guilty to manslaughter.
May 2009	Assistant ODPP Director and crown prosecutor in charge of the case, Brendan Campbell SC, informs Tommy Thomas that a plea deal has been reached between the ODPP and Gabe. The deal involves the murder charge being withdrawn and Gabe pleading guilty to manslaughter by criminal negligence.
3 June 2009	Assistant ODPP Director and crown prosecutor in charge of the case, Brendan Campbell SC, meets with members of the Thomas family, Lieutenant Brad Flynn, Detective Senior Sergeant Gary Campbell and Detective Senior Constable Kevin Gehringer in Brisbane, Queensland, to discuss the sentencing hearing and reveals information about the plea deal which implies some inaccuracies in the information he provided to them 18 days earlier.
5 June 2009	Gabe pleads guilty to manslaughter by criminal negligence in the Queensland Supreme Court and is sentenced to four and a half years imprisonment, fully suspended after 12 months, including time served.
17 July 2009	An appeal against the manifest inadequacy of Gabe's sentence, lodged by the (former) Queensland Attorney-General Cameron Dick, is heard in the Queensland Court of Appeal.
18 September 2009	The Queensland Court of Appeal increases the suspension period of Gabe's sentence to 18 months, including time served, but the head sentence remains at four and a half years.
22 October 2010	An Alabama grand jury indicts Gabe on two counts of capital murder – murder for pecuniary gain and murder by kidnapping.
11 November 2010	Gabe is released from Borallon Correctional Centre and escorted to an immigration detention centre located in Melbourne, in the state of Victoria.
19 November 2010	Australian authorities receive a written guarantee from the US that the death penalty will not be sought if Gabe is convicted of a capital murder offence.
25 November 2010	Gabe is deported to the US.

14 December 2010	The Alabama bond hearing commences and Judge Tommy Nail releases Gabe on a $100,000 bond with some restrictive conditions, including that he must wear an electronic monitoring device and adhere to an evening curfew. The trial date is set for 23 May 2011.
8 April 2011	Gabe's original trial date is rescheduled from 23 May 2011 to 13 February 2012 due to resource constraints and a lack of adequate security personnel to staff the Jefferson County Courthouse.
13 February 2012	Gabe's capital murder trial commences on what would have been Tina's 35th birthday.
23 February 2012	The prosecution rests its case and the defence files a motion for judgement of acquittal. Judge Tommy Nail acquits Gabe of the capital murder charge.

INTRODUCTION

> Justice embodies notions of fairness to all members of the community, including victims and offenders, and striking a balance between their competing interests is the cornerstone of current criminal justice policy. But it also assumes a consensus on what constitutes justice, and achieving justice.[1]
>
> —Dr Susan Easton and Professor Christine Piper

Justice is a peculiar concept. Its meaning is subjective, and obscure. It is arguably illusive, and as the theories underpinning research in the field of justice suggest, it may be that in any particular case one person perceives justice as prevailing, while another disputes its existence.[2] As Dr Susan Easton and Professor Christine Piper explain, "the notion of justice is not clear-cut … justice is a slippery concept".[3] Perceptions of justice depend on how an individual understands or defines a situation in terms of "maximizing their self-interests; their needs for status and inclusion; or questions of basic moral right and wrong".[4]

Within the process of the law, the definitive outcome is the attainment of justice. But what does justice mean and look like? The law is a system of truth and knowledge based on reason, abstraction, neutrality, rationality and objectivity. It is a system of shared consensual social values within society, which serves as a check on governmental power, and operates on the basis of equality for all. It is, at times, criticised as the prize of the powerful, as a patriarchal institution, and as a discourse of power and knowledge. Yet, within a democratic society, like that of Australia or the United States (US), the law and the legal system stand as the fundamental

---

[1] Susan Easton and Christine Piper, *Sentencing and Punishment: The Quest for Justice* (Oxford University Press, 3rd Edition, 2012) 7.

[2] Linda Skitka, "Exploring the 'Lost and Found' of Justice Theory Research" (2009) 22 *Social Justice Research* 98; Linda Skitka, Christopher Barman and Elizabeth Mullen, "Morality and Justice: An Expanded Theoretical Perspective and Review", in Karen Hedtvedt and Jody Clay-Warner (eds), *Advances in Group Processes* (Vol. 25, Emerald Group Publishing, 2008) 1–27.

[3] Easton and Piper, above n 1, 36.

[4] Skitka, above n 2, 99.

mechanism through which one can attain traditional, procedural and substantive forms of justice.

In the legal setting, justice is traditionally equated with fairness, equality of treatment, and respect for individual rights. Justice is generally considered to sit under the rule of law, which encompasses procedural and substantive justice ideals. Procedural justice is measured by perceptions of fairness within the legal *processes* that are used to resolve disputes, while substantive justice is measured by perceptions of fairness in the *outcomes* of those legal processes. As identified by the Honourable Martin Moynihan in his review of Queensland's criminal and civil justice systems, the values reflected in the rule of law require that a legal system "provide equal justice for all according to the law … by disposing of cases impartially, fairly, expeditiously, with the minimum unavoidable delay and with the minimum, but necessary, use of public resources".[5]

Within legal proceedings a number of strict rules of evidence and procedure have been put in place to provide protections for those accused of criminal misconduct, and for those who have fallen victim to such conduct. In this sense, the criminal justice systems in Australia and the US operate within a due process framework, the underlying principle of which is equality for all who come before the law, regardless of their financial means, race, religion, gender, age or sexuality. Examples of due process are evident on a global scale, where the right to a fair trial is enshrined in Article 11 of the *Universal Declaration of Human Rights 1948*, and the right to equality before the law is enshrined in Article 14 of the *International Covenant on Civil and Political Rights 1966*. Due process is also evident at the local level, where the right to a fair trial before an impartial jury is a fundamental right that each state of the US is required to provide, as guaranteed by the Sixth and Fourteenth Amendments of the *Constitution of the US*. Variations of this right similarly exist in Queensland, guided by s 80 of the *Australian Constitution* and s 604 of the *Criminal Code 1899* (Qld), except in the rare event where a trial by judge alone is requested by the accused and supported by the prosecution and the court under s 614 of the *Criminal Code 1899* (Qld).

Professor Austin Sarat argues that due process lies at "the heart of our conceptions of fairness and justice … [It is] the right to one's day in court, the right to be heard, the right to take part in procedures through which

---

[5] Honourable Martin Moynihan AO QC, *Review of The Civil And Criminal Justice System in Queensland* (Queensland Government, 2008) 23, 29.

one's fate is determined".[6] On this basis, the justice systems central to the *Watson* case—those of Queensland and Alabama—are built on adversarial frameworks that are designed to provide justice, within a context requiring "that the state proves its case against the accused … and that the accused be given a meaningful opportunity to contest the case against him or her".[7] The underlying basis of this system, as identified by the Honourable Martin Moynihan, is that a "conviction of a criminal offence should be the result of a 'fair trial' in which an accused has the opportunity to know and to meet the case made against them, with proper legal representation".[8]

Within this context, the jury trial is seen as the "focal point", the stage "at which all the relevant issues can be examined and adjudicated",[9] with the jury acting "as the ultimate arbitrator of fact".[10] Thus, substantive and procedural justice, due process and the rule of law are underpinned by a perception that justice equates with a trial by jury. Even subjectively, the concept of justice is strongly linked to a jury trial, on the basis that determining whether an outcome is just is not merely informed by what that outcome is, but also by the process through which that outcome is attained.[11] The jury trial is subsequently held up as the pinnacle of our legal systems— a process that is used to incorporate community input and a social moral consensus; one that keeps the legal process in line with community expectations and values; and one that provides an essential link between "the law" and society.

---

[6] Austin Sarat, "Going to Court: Access, Autonomy and the Contradictions of Liberal Legality", in *The Politics of Law: A Progressive Critique*, ed. David Kairys (Basic Books, 3rd Edition, 1998) 103.

[7] John Jackson, 'The Adversary Trial and Trial By Judge Alone' in Michael McConville and Geoffrey Wilson (eds) *The Handbook of the Criminal Justice Process* (Oxford University Press, 2002) 336.

[8] Moynihan, above n 5, 28.

[9] Jackson, above n 7, 336–7.

[10] Moynihan, above n 5, 28.

[11] Allan Lind and Tom Tyler, *The Social Psychology of Procedural Justice* (Plenum Press, 1988); John Thibut and Laurens Walker, *Procedural Justice: A Psychological Analysis* (Erlbaum, 1975); Tom Tyler and Steven Blader, "The Group-Engagement Model: Procedural Justice, Social Identity and Co-Operative Behavior" (2000) 7 *Personality and Social Psychology Review* 249; Tom Tyler, Robert Boeckmann, Heather Smith and Yuen Huo, *Social Justice in a Diverse Society* (Westview Press, 1997); Linda Skitka and David Houston, "When Due Process Is of No Consequence: Moral Mandates and Presumed Defendant Guilt or Innocence" (2001) 14 *Social Justice Research* 305.

In recognising that the jury trial underpins the foundation of attaining justice, Associate Professor Albert Dzur describes the use of a jury as a process that:

> Allows both formal legal rules and community norms to affect judgments, through a setting that keeps decision makers alert to the complexity of context, and the peculiarity of concrete details. In other words, the trial ideally holds open the tensions between formal and informal, system and life-world, citizen and official, and does not allow one side to dominate.[12]

Professor Dzur expands upon this argument by claiming that the jury trial plays an important role in "holding citizen-jurors accountable for laws and their enforcement",[13] noting that "the existence of the jury in a criminal trial means that punishment is effectuated through lay people … Jurors leave the courtroom with an expanded interest in the public sphere and a greater sense of civic responsibility".[14] In relation to Queensland's justice system, the Honourable Martin Moynihan expresses a similar view:

> There is much to be said in support of the jury system which involves citizens drawn from the community, to determine whether or not the prosecution has proved guilt beyond reasonable doubt, before delivering a verdict of guilty. Jury duty is one of the few civic obligations directly discharged by citizens, rather than by elected representatives or by executive government acting through employed public servants ... There is no doubt the jury franchise should be wide … and supported.[15]

Thus, justice within the legal setting can be viewed procedurally, substantively and even subjectively as being represented by a trial before an independent adjudicator, in which two sides—one representing the state, and to a lesser extent, the victim; and one representing the accused—present their evidence of guilt and innocence, which is debated and tested before a jury comprising 12 members of the community, tasked with determining the culpability of the accused. On this basis, the *Watson* capital murder trial in Alabama arguably provided the opportunity for procedural, subjective and substantive justice to be attained, even within a due process framework.

Specifically, the second prosecution of Gabe Watson for the death of Tina Thomas provided those most intimately involved in the case with the

---

[12] Albert Dzur, 'Why American Democracy Needs the Jury Trial' (2011) 5 *Criminal Law and Philosophy* 87, 88.

[13] Ibid, 89.

[14] Ibid.

[15] Moynihan, above n 5, 30.

opportunity to experience a second chance for justice. A jury trial in Alabama could have provided Gabe with the opportunity to prove that, while he may have admitted to being negligent in his role as Tina's "dive buddy" in Australia, he did not intentionally plan and carry out the murder of his wife of 11 days. Furthermore, it could have offered Gabe the opportunity to "clear" his name, to leave behind eight years and four months of speculation, to reopen his civil lawsuit against the Old Republic travel insurance company and to win the right to control Tina's property and have the determinative say on where she will remain buried.

At the same time, a jury trial, regardless of the verdict, could also have offered the Thomas family closure and the opportunity to finally have all the evidence surrounding Tina's death exposed and tested within the confines of the rules of evidence that are applied to a criminal trial. Importantly, the trial offered the possibility for a jury of 12 members of the Alabama community to decide whether Gabe was guilty, as opposed to a decision regarding his culpability and involvement being made by a couple of Queensland lawyers. If after having heard all of the evidence the jury were to return with a guilty verdict, the trial would offer the Thomas family definitive evidence that their quest to see Gabe tried for his involvement in Tina's death was justified. Significantly, even if a not guilty verdict was returned, the trial still provided justice for the Thomas family, as the evidence in this case could finally be publicly revealed, tried and debated, and on that basis, 12 independent citizens would have determined that Gabe was not guilty of Tina's murder. Regardless of the outcome, a jury trial would provide the Thomas family with the opportunity to see the evidence scrutinised within a court of law, thereby receiving a just process and outcome according to "the law".

Thus, Monday 13 February 2012 will forever mark the 35th anniversary of Tina Thomas's birth, eight years, three months and 22 days since her death, and the date on which a second chance for justice could unfold ... or could it?

Our Story

Since October 2003, numerous theories and questions have emerged surrounding the death of Tina Thomas. International media outlets, as well as social media networks, have either condemned or sympathised with the man twice accused of Tina's murder, while a great deal of sadness and empathy has been expressed for the Thomas family. Even following the (contentious) legal acquittal of Gabe, theories about how Tina died continue to be publicly proposed, and speculation and conjecture as to who is to blame persist, including repeated accusations against Gabe.

Our discussion does not attempt to attribute blame or make a determination of guilt or innocence over what occurred underwater between Gabe and Tina, 16 metres beyond the *SS Yongala* wreck on 22 October 2003. As highlighted in Judge Tommy Nail's acquittal of Gabe in February 2012, due to the way the trial ended, without the defence evidence being exposed or tested, "I don't think anyone knows for sure what happened in the waters down there and they probably will never know".[16] What the following discussion seeks to explore are perceptions of justice, and where these fit in relation to the seemingly conflicting decisions and approaches adopted by the Queensland and Alabama criminal justice systems in responding to Tina's death. We seek to identify what justice looked like in this case, and whether perceptions and understandings of justice are outdated in the resource-driven climates that now confront, and arguably control, the procurement of justice in many legal systems around the globe – a factor that featured heavily in the handling of this case in both jurisdictions.

Significantly, in exploring concepts and perceptions of justice, we critically analyse the legal aftermath of this highly controversial case by examining the conduct of those involved in the case, and the legal processes that were used in both jurisdictions – processes that were used, and according to some, abused, over a nearly nine-year period. Indeed, the difference in the approaches utilised by the two jurisdictions raises a number of questions regarding traditional understandings of due process and the basic rule of law principles that underpin this concept – factors that we believe hindered the potential for justice to ever be achieved in this case. Specifically, given the contentious resolution of the case by plea bargain in Queensland in 2009, we challenge the perspective that justice could ever have been attained in this case by running a trial in 2012 in Alabama. Using a procedural justice framework, which suggests that it is the *process* of getting to the outcome, as opposed to the outcome alone, that is the key determinant of justice, we seek to highlight the injustices that occurred throughout the various stages of the legal process in both Queensland and Alabama, up to and including the February 2012 acquittal, which prevented the attainment of substantive, procedural or subjective justice, and in turn, closure, in this case.

---

[16] Judge Tommy Nail, court observations, 23 February 2012.

Our Approach

In order to provide a true and full reflection of the case, and the impacts arising from the manner in which it was legally approached, handled and finalised in both countries, we attended and observed every day of the somewhat abrupt capital murder trial in Alabama from 13–23 February 2012. Additionally, we examined the magnitude of legal documents compiled over the nearly nine-year period in which the case was handled in Australia and the US. Importantly, we also sought participation from those people who had a significant and intimate involvement in the case in either, or both, jurisdictions. The analysis that follows is thus informed by in-depth interviews and discussions with representatives of almost all parties involved in and affected by the investigation and double prosecution of Gabe Watson for the death of Tina Thomas. The interviews were conducted prior to and following Gabe's acquittal in Alabama, and ranged in duration from 1.5 to 4 hours. As shown in Table 1-2 below, the interviews were conducted with ten key participants.

We also engaged in several discussions and informal interviews with members of the Australian and US media, some of whom were involved in the case since 2003; US prosecutors and defence attorneys who attended the trial; members of the Queensland police who testified at the trial; Jefferson County Courthouse staff; and support persons from the Watson and Thomas families. This level of participant involvement was quite significant, not only in terms of the quality and quantity of the data, but also because several of the participants, including those representing the Townsville Criminal Investigation Bureau (CIB), the Helena Police Department and the Office of the Alabama Attorney-General, have denied all other requests for interviews since Gabe's acquittal.

We are extremely grateful and indebted to all of the people who shared their stories and offered their memories, reflections and insight. These perspectives have enabled us to gain a unique and invaluable understanding of this case. In order to provide credence to the participants and their views, at times throughout the book we chose to include lengthy excerpts from our discussions. We have chosen to do this because we believe it is vital that the meaning and content of our participants' comments are accurately represented. The participants' voices bring truth and meaning to this book, and to our understanding of the law's response to Tina's death. By drawing heavily from the interviews and discussions, we allow our analysis to be informed by these important voices.

Table 1-2: Interview participants (alphabetical order)

Name and title	Referred to as	Role in the *Watson* case
Mr Bob Austin	Austin	Gabe's family and civil attorney in Alabama, also family friend of the Watsons.
Mr Jo Basgier of Bloomston & Basgier	Basgier	Attorney in Gabe's US defence team in the *Watson* capital murder trial in Alabama in February 2012.
Mr Brett Bloomston of Bloomston & Basgier	Bloomston	Gabe's primary defence attorney in the *Watson* capital murder trial in Alabama in February 2012.
Lieutenant Brad Flynn	Flynn	Member of the Helena Police Department in Alabama; one of the primary police members involved in the investigation of the death of Tina Thomas from December 2004; subpoenaed as a defence witness in the *Watson* capital murder trial in Alabama in February 2012.
Detective Senior Constable Kevin Gehringer	Gehringer	Member of the Townsville CIB in Queensland; one of the primary police members involved in the investigation of the death of Tina Thomas from October 2003; prosecution witness in the *Watson* capital murder trial in Alabama in February 2012.
Coroner David Glasgow	Glasgow	Coroner for the inquest into the cause and circumstances of Tina's death in Townsville, Queensland, from 13 November 2007 to 20 June 2008.
Mrs Cindy Thomas	Cindy	Tina's mother; rebuttal witness for the prosecution in the *Watson* capital murder trial in Alabama.
Mr Tommy Thomas	Tommy	Tina's father; prosecution witness in the *Watson* capital murder trial in Alabama in February 2012.
Alabama Assistant Attorney-General Don Valeska	Valeska	Lead prosecutor in the *Watson* capital murder trial in Alabama in February 2012.
Mr David Watson	David	Gabe's father.

Our requests for discussions were not always met with acceptance, and we acknowledge that there are three main perspectives absent from this analysis. The first is that of Gabe Watson. While Gabe declined to participate, we were able to gauge insight into his experiences, and the emotional, financial and physical impacts that the investigation and double prosecution had on him, from the voices of his father, David Watson; his family and civil attorney, Bob Austin; and his two primary US defence attorneys, Brett Bloomston and Jo Basgier. We have also collected copies of any interviews that Gabe's family and legal team have provided to the media, and have obtained the transcripts of Gabe's only two televised interviews, conducted after his acquittal in 2012, with the Australian Nine Network's *60 Minutes* program, and the US ABC network's *20/20* program. The transcripts have allowed us to gain further insight into Gabe's perspective on the case including the legal processes and outcomes that he endured.

The second key perspective absent from this analysis is that of Judge Tommy Nail, who oversaw the Alabama trial, pre-trial arguments and bond hearing. While Judge Nail initially consented to participate in an interview, on the morning that he acquitted Gabe, prior to the prosecution resting its case and the defence submitting its motion for a judgement of acquittal, Judge Nail's associate informed us that the judge would no longer be available for an interview. Although we appreciate that this decision was made in accordance with Judge Nail's resolution not to provide any public commentary regarding his decision to acquit Gabe, outside his in-court verbal statement, we believe that the timing at which he changed his mind about talking to us is significant. Questions surrounding this timing and its implications are explored in more detail in Chapter Six. While the judge's direct perspective is absent, our observations of his conduct and comments throughout the trial and included in the transcripts of earlier hearings relating to this case provide significant insight into his perspective, and as such, still contribute strongly to our analysis.

Perhaps the most pressing direct perspective that is absent from our analysis is the voice of the Queensland Office of the Director of Public Prosecutions (ODPP), in particular that of the Director of the ODPP, Anthony Moynihan SC, and the Assistant Director of Public Prosecutions and crown prosecutor in charge of this case in Queensland, Brendan Campbell SC. Neither Director Moynihan nor Brendan Campbell were willing to engage in an interview prior to or following the conclusion of Gabe's capital murder trial in Alabama, on the basis that discussing case details would conflict with ODPP policy.

We initially requested a discussion with both Brendan Campbell and Director Moynihan by email on 11 April 2011, to which we received the following two emailed responses three days later:

Brendan Campbell:	Thank-you for your email. I do not wish to make any comment about this matter at this time.[17]
Director Moynihan:	Thank-you for your email below. The Director does not intend to make any public comment in relation to this matter.[18]

Further requests for interviews and written comments were sent via email on 27 March 2012, 30 March 2012, 2 April 2012 and 15 April 2012, after the Alabama trial had concluded. In these emails, we explained that in conducting our research, we had spoken with a range of people involved in the case and several comments had been made pertaining to the conduct of those working within the Queensland ODPP. We clarified that in writing the book, we could only draw on the data that we had collected from our interviews, court observations and the thousands of primary source documents we had obtained from the Queensland coronial inquest, the transnational police investigation, and various court transcripts and legal documents obtained in both Australia and the US. We explained that, for this reason, if the ODPP would not provide any comments in relation to the case or the issues we had identified in our data, we would have to rely solely upon our expansive existing material to provide our case analysis. We also noted that we would include a statement in the book explaining that we had attempted to discuss these matters with Director Moynihan and Brendan Campbell. In response, we received the following three emails from Brendan Campbell:

> I have discussed your request with the Director of Public Prosecutions, Mr Anthony Moynihan SC. We consider it remains inappropriate to comment in relation to this matter.[19]

> We understand the nature of your request and do not consider it is appropriate to make any comment about the *Watson* matter.[20]

[17] Email from Brendan Campbell, 14 April 2011.
[18] Email from Pia Gillespie, Executive Secretary to Director Anthony Moynihan, 14 April 2011.
[19] First email from Brendan Campbell, 30 March 2012.
[20] Second email from Brendan Campbell, 30 March 2012.

> It remains our position, in accord with the usual practice of this Office that we do not intend to make further comment in relation to this matter.[21]

The lack of participation and cooperation from Brendan Campbell and Director Moynihan is both unfortunate and problematic. It leaves unanswered many questions pertaining to the decisions and motivations underpinning the plea bargain agreement reached in Queensland, and around Brendan Campbell's conduct leading up to and immediately following the deal. As a consequence, and as clearly stated in our correspondence with the ODPP representatives, our analysis of the plea deal and the conduct of those involved in making the deal is based on the only official public statement about the plea deal made by Director Moynihan in 2009; court, police, coronial and other relevant legal documentation; and the perspectives of representatives from the Townsville CIB and Helena Police Department, the Office of the Alabama Attorney-General, members of the Thomas and Watson families, members of Gabe's US defence team, and Gabe's civil and family attorney. By drawing from this range of data, we believe that the missing voice of the ODPP is compensated for in our analysis.

[21] Third email from Brendan Campbell, 15 April 2012.

PART I

JUSTICE IN QUEENSLAND

CHAPTER ONE

OPERATION CHARLIE OSWALD

> A close examination of the complex evidence shows that police made a crucial oversight and a fundamental mistake early in the investigation … The mistake has had profound ramifications on the course and conduct of the police investigation and the fate of [Gabe] Watson.[1]
>
> —Australian Journalist Hedley Thomas

The police investigation into the death of Tina Thomas was known by the codename *Operation Charlie Oswald*. During the initial stages of the investigation, there was no suggestion that it would be the beginning of an almost nine-year global search for justice, or that the evidence obtained would form the basis for the prosecution of Gabe Watson in both Australia and the US.

It was around 4pm on Wednesday 22 October 2003 when Detective Senior Constable Kevin Gehringer of the Townsville CIB began his shift. The Townsville CIB was unusually crowded, and Gehringer was soon informed by Detective Senior Sergeant Joe Kitching that there had been an incident at the *Yongala* dive site which had resulted in a fatality. Kitching informed Gehringer that the matter involved a young couple from the US, and as Gehringer explained, the preliminary thoughts were that the deceased "had some sort of a medical condition that's caused her to drown, or it may be related to some equipment type failure, but he [Kitching] definitely said, as far as they thought, well as far as initial reports were concerned, it was just an accidental drowning". Gehringer was given the task of collecting a statement from the deceased's husband, Gabe Watson.

At approximately 6:30pm, Gehringer began taking Gabe's statement in the presence of his support person, Mrs Paula Snyder, a fellow diver from the *Spoilsport* whom Gabe had met aboard the boat with Tina the previous night. In later describing his primary purpose in obtaining this statement, Gehringer explained:

---

[1] Hedley Thomas, "Early Error Blinded Police on Dive Death", *The Australian* (Australia), 11 December 2010.

> I wanted to get a statement off him [Gabe] in as much detail as I could as to what happened … Because I wasn't a diver … [I was] trying to get my head around what diving's about and what I thought would be important to put in the statement … That's why I was trying to cover absolutely everything that I could think of on the spot to think, well, what's relevant about a diving death, what would you want to know, what's important? With most investigations, they always cover different topics and I'm not an expert in any number of those topics. So all you're trying to do is get the witness to give you as much detail as you possibly can … [So] I say to tell me what happened and I try and get [the person] to just give me a version without interrupting ... And I'll take that statement down and then once the statement's down, I'll go back and then we'll just sit down together, read through it and I'll sort of pick out—well, what can you tell me a bit more about this part? Can you tell me a bit more about that part? And that's essentially what I was doing with Gabe on that night.

At approximately 10:25pm, almost four hours later, Gabe finished providing what would be the first of two official statements given to the Townsville CIB. In reflecting on his perceptions of Gabe at this time, Gehringer acknowledged that he "certainly wasn't looking at Gabe as a suspect or someone who had done anything wrong". In fact, when providing a copy of the statement to his senior officer, Gehringer recalled commenting that:

> If it was my wife, I would like to think that I would have maybe gone down and brought her up ... but I was actually thinking, well yes, if he did panic, maybe he did panic, and it wasn't the right thing to do, but that's what he's done. So that's what I'd … told my superior after I'd finished taking the statement.

The next encounter between Gehringer and Gabe occurred two days later, on 24 October 2003, at the viewing of Tina's body at the Townsville Hospital. During this interaction, Gabe indicated that he wanted to clarify a couple of issues raised in his initial statement in response to comments about the diving conditions that he had read in a newspaper article that had appeared that morning in the *Townsville Bulletin*.[2] The key statements that Gabe wanted to respond to were made by the general manager of Mike Ball Dive Expeditions (Mike Ball), Mr Stan Kielbaska, who was quoted as saying that "the diving conditions were near-perfect",[3] and that Tina's death "has us stumped and baffled, because it does not appear to be dive-

---

[2] Andy Toulson, "Diver on Honeymoon: Husband Rocked by Tragic Death", *Townsville Bulletin* (Queensland), 24 October 2003.

[3] Stan Kielbaska, cited in Toulson, above n 2.

related".[4] Gehringer described being pleased to have the opportunity to discuss these issues and revisit Gabe's initial statement because, as he explained, "I wasn't too sure whether there was other things we needed to clarify from the diving aspect and the equipment aspect, and had we asked all the questions that we needed to about covering the malfunction of equipment"? It was therefore decided that Senior Constable Glen Lawrence, who was a scuba diver and member of the Townsville Water Police Division, would also be present at Gabe's second police statement, as he could clarify with Gabe any relevant diving technicalities that arose in the interview.

Gabe began giving his second statement at the Townsville CIB at 5:21pm on 27 October 2003. In addition to Gehringer, Gabe and Lawrence, Gabe's mother, Glenda Watson, who had flown to Australia upon hearing of Tina's death, was also present. Gehringer claimed that the opportunity to acquire a second statement allowed him to clarify details of Gabe's account of the fatal dive. As he explained, "at that stage, it was really just a case of gathering as much information as we could about the particular dive". Gabe's second statement was finalised approximately two and a half hours later at 7:44pm. Gehringer noted that at this point in the police investigation, Gabe was not considered a suspect, and the death was being treated as an accidental drowning. As Gehringer noted, "when he gave that second statement, again he wasn't being treated as a suspect … Our opinion then was the fact that yes this was going to be a [accidental] death". Because this was the perception of the police at the time, as a member of the Townsville Water Police Division, Lawrence was given carriage of the file.

Lawrence initially had some concerns regarding the plausibility of Gabe's second police statement, but it was only during the course of his investigation that he became increasingly suspicious of various elements of Gabe's accounts of the dive. In particular, Lawrence questioned the inconsistencies between Gabe's first and second police statements, his version of events as contrasted to other witness statements, and his general descriptions of what happened underwater, which contradicted Lawrence's understanding and personal experiences of scuba diving. Lawrence thus began to query whether there was something more to Tina's death than a tragic accident. As he recalled in a later statement to the CIB police investigators:

> Through reading the witness statements and associated reports ... I became aware of inconsistencies in many areas of the investigation. I reported

---

[4] Ibid.

> these inconsistencies to [the] CIB and my supervising inspector. As a result of this report, I made a presentation outlining my concerns in relation to these issues.[5]

In response to Lawrence's presentation, and because the expertise and resources required to conduct an in-depth criminal investigation fell outside the capacity of the Water Police Division, in July 2004, the brief of evidence file was returned to the Townsville CIB. At this stage, Detective Senior Sergeant Gary Campbell began leading the investigation into the death of Tina Thomas, and as second in command, Gehringer was again assigned to the case.

Upon reading the brief of evidence prepared by Lawrence, Campbell and Gehringer became aware of the need to locate a number of witnesses to collect additional statements, some of which would be collected for the first time – for example, from Gabe and Tina's certified diving instructor, Tom Jackson, and members of Tina's family. Other witnesses were also needed to provide follow-up statements, including passengers on the two boats who were present when Tina died, the *Spoilsport* and the *Jazz II*, the latter being the diving vessel on which resuscitation attempts were made. One of the primary statements that Campbell and Gehringer specifically wanted to clarify was that of Dr Stanley Stutz, a diver aboard the *Jazz II*, who was the only person who directly witnessed an underwater interaction between Gabe and Tina before she died. As Gehringer explained:

> Gary and I have just started reading through the brief looking at what information had been gained … [and we] read Stutz's statement … [Gary] said ... he's [Stutz has] seen something … All of a sudden there's our one and only eyewitness to some interaction of these two divers and at that stage, all we knew was what was in Stutz's original statement. So then it was a case of trying to track down Stutz ... It took us several weeks before we actually got in contact … and because he was an ER [emergency room] doctor, it was just near on impossible to try and catch up. But we eventually made contact with him. Then there were email exchanges and then, that must have been when [Lieutenant] Brad [Flynn] became part of the investigation.

Given the financial and geographical difficulties created when the investigation became transnational, the Townsville CIB had become reliant upon the assistance of a US investigator to help collect witness statements and collate evidence. Gehringer explained that the Townsville CIB first began communicating with the Helena Police Department in

---

[5] Senior Constable Glen Lawrence, witness statement, 25 February 2005.

Alabama around August 2004. This supports the police documentation of the investigation, dated 27 August 2004, which states that "a number of inquiries have also been initiated that need to be made in the US".[6] Under s 2 of the *Mutual Assistance in Criminal Matters (United States of America) Regulations 1999*, Australia can request international mutual assistance in criminal matters from the US, including:

> Taking the testimony or statements of persons; providing documents, records and other articles of evidence; servicing documents; locating or identifying persons ... executing requests for searches and seizures ... and any other form of assistance not prohibited by the laws of the Requested States.

On the basis of this agreement, and with the support of Interpol, Lieutenant Brad Flynn of the Helena Police Department became involved in *Operation Charlie Oswald* in December 2004, at the request of his Department Chief, Doug Jones. Flynn recalled that Jones called him into his office to say that "we've had some phone calls with some Australian police officers and they're in reference to a girl from Helena that had died in Australia, and I want you to help them". Thus, over 12 months after Tina's death, *Operation Charlie Oswald* became a transnational investigation aimed at determining what happened 16 metres off the *SS Yongala* wreck in Queensland on 22 October 2003.

From Accident to Homicide: A Quick Judgement?

A significant level of scepticism has been directed at *Operation Charlie Oswald*, perhaps somewhat understandably by Gabe's Australian and US defence teams, but also by several media commentators, including, perhaps most vocally, the work of Hedley Thomas (hereafter H. Thomas – no relation to Tina), *The Australian* newspaper's national chief correspondent. One of the most prominent concerns surrounding the police investigation centres on the point at which Gabe was identified as a murder suspect, and specifically, what led the police to this belief. In particular, accusations have been levied publicly, and during the progress of legal proceedings in both Queensland and Alabama, that the police first determined that Gabe was guilty, and then sought to locate the evidence that would support their hypothesis, as opposed to the evidence leading the

[6] Queensland Police Service, "Investigation into the Death of Christina Mae Watson nee Thomas whilst Scuba Diving off Townsville—22nd October 2003—Operation Charlie Oswald", *QPS Report* (Townsville) 27 August 2004.

police to view Gabe as a suspect. As H. Thomas claimed in an article entitled "Error blinded police on dive death", the police became "convinced [Gabe] Watson was a liar … and their investigation proceeded accordingly".[7]

The perception that the police had tunnel vision of Gabe's guilt, which then fuelled the investigation, was a common belief shared by members of Gabe's family and his Australian and US defence teams. Indeed, the view that the police investigation was erroneous and biased was a key reason identified by a number of our participants as to why they perceived that the manner in which the case was handled in Australia had failed to offer justice in either a procedural or subjective sense. This view is evident in the comments of Gabe's family and civil attorney, Bob Austin, who claimed, "they got it in their mind, the Australian police … they got it in their mind that he was guilty, and they did everything [based on that]". Austin further argued:

> If you read his [Gabe's] statements, they didn't vary one tenth of one per cent on anything. He volunteered to go back and give a second statement. Does a guilty person do that? ... He was trying to cooperate and get the facts out to them, and they didn't really let the facts get in the way of their determination that he was guilty.

A similar perception was held by Gabe's US defence attorney, Brett Bloomston, who explained that:

> The way the Queensland police handled the investigation had given us trouble all along … Anything that was favourable towards Gabe was buried … The Queensland police were convinced … that Gabe's story did not ring true … One of the faults that we also had with the police investigation is that … they reached out to a few [witnesses] and fed them just bits and pieces of information, just to elicit what they wanted from them … an answer that helped their case.

This view was also reflected in the closing statement presented by Gabe's Australian defence counsel, Steve Zillman, at the Queensland coronial inquest into the cause and circumstances of Tina's death, where Zillman claimed that "one is left with an uneasy feeling in this case that the police have, at some point, determined that Gabe was guilty of murder and have endeavoured to construct a case to that end, rather than to simply gather the evidence".[8]

---

[7] Thomas, above n 1.

[8] Transcript of Proceedings, *Inquest into the death of Christina Mae Watson* (19 June 2008) 14 (Steven Zillman QC).

One of the primary factors informing this view of a biased police investigation evolved out of the testing of Gabe's dive computer, which, unbeknownst to the police at the time, led to an erroneous test result. Without knowledge of its inaccuracy, the test result pointed to an implausibility in the version of events that Gabe had given to the police, which was seen to provide him with an opportunity to murder Tina without any eyewitnesses. On this basis, it has been argued that the erroneous test result was responsible for shifting police perceptions, and subsequently the investigation, from a focus on an accidental death to an assumption of a premeditated homicide. Therefore, by relying upon this result, not only would the investigation be considered erroneous, but it would also be perceived as procedurally and substantively unjust.

A dive computer is used to measure the profile of a dive and to display relevant safety information throughout the dive. To achieve this, a dive computer provides dynamic and constant information based on accurate calculations of dive table readings, so it continuously monitors the time against the depth (the dive log information/profile) and calculates the level of absorption of gases that might be entering a diver's body while they are underwater.[9] This means that rather than the diver having to rely on pre-calculations of information about their dive, including how long they can safely remain at a particular depth or whether they need to make any decompression stops during their ascent (to avoid decompression sickness), the diver can instead check this information on their digital watch display.[10] Gabe's dive computer was made up of two components: the wrist module, which is the main component and is worn on the wrist; and the transmitter, which attaches to the tank. However, in testing Gabe's dive computer, the police only examined one component—the wrist module. The second component, the transmitter, was never tested, and in fact was never collected by the police as evidence. As a consequence, the tests produced an erroneous finding which suggested that Gabe had lied in his two police statements.

Gabe made two relevant comments to the police that led to the testing of his dive computer. The first involved the justification that he had provided for resurfacing with Tina shortly after their first dive attempt, and the second involved his ascent rate when trying to get help for Tina during

---

[9] Anders Jacobson, "How Does a Dive Computer Work" on *Anders Jacobson's Blog* (25 January 2005) <http://www.jacobsen.no/anders/blog/archives/2005/01/25/how_does_a_dive_computer_work.html>.

[10] John Bantin, "Dive Computers on Test: Which Do You Trust?' on *DiverNet* (8 May 2012) <http://www.divernet.com/Diving_Gear/group_tests/158650/dive_computers_on_test.html>.

their second and fatal dive on the morning of 22 October 2003. The contentious test result related solely to the first claim by Gabe, that his dive computer beeped to indicate that his battery was incorrectly inserted, and so he and Tina resurfaced from their first dive to fix the problem. As Gabe explained in his first statement to the police on 22 October 2003:

> We started to go down [on the dive] and my computer was beeping, cause the ah batteries were in backwards so ... we came back up, got in the boat and then headed in the little boat back to the big boat [*Spoilsport*] ... Then probably ten minutes later or something like that um, I had the battery changed out and all that and then we got in the ah little boat [and] went back out [to dive].[11]

Because Gabe and Tina returned to the *Spoilsport* to fix the battery, their dive to the *SS Yongala* wreck was delayed. As a consequence, there was a significant time delay, and therefore distance, between when Gabe and Tina went underwater for their second dive, and when the majority of divers from the *Spoilsport* descended. This could arguably have provided Gabe with the opportunity to murder Tina with less likelihood of detection by the other divers.

To examine this theory, and the viability of Gabe's claim that the computer does indeed beep when the battery is incorrectly inserted, several tests were conducted on the wrist module component of Gabe's dive computer in November 2004 and February 2005. These tests were conducted by Adam White, the Customer Service Manager at Oceanic Australia, the company who manufactured Gabe's dive computer, and by Dr David Griffiths, a (now retired) registered specialist medical practitioner. White was responsible for testing both Gabe's and Tina's dive computers, which included pressure and time testing, and a general examination of their accuracy. As part of a discussion of several tests he conducted, White observed in his 2007 statement to the police that:

> I can say that if the battery of the Oceanic–Data Trans dive computer [Gabe's computer] was in back to front, that the unit would not operate. The Oceanic–Data Trans dive computer would not display or record any information. The Oceanic–Data Trans dive computer would not give off any warning signals of any sort.[12]

Griffiths reached a similar finding when he performed a pressure test on Gabe's dive computer to assess whether an incorrectly inserted battery

---

[11] Gabe Watson, witness statement, 22 October 2003.

[12] Adam White, witness statement, 9 September 2007.

would result in an alarm sounding. This test involved immersing the dive computer in a bucket of salt water within a hyperbaric chamber and slowly pressurising the chamber. As a result of this test, Griffiths determined that "the dive computer does not in fact beep when underwater at a depth between surface and five metres when its battery is reversed, contrary to the report that Gabe made in his [police] statement of October 22nd 2003".[13]

On this basis, the police believed that Gabe had lied about experiencing problems with his dive computer, creating a situation that gave him the opportunity to separate himself and Tina from the rest of the dive group. This became an important finding in the police investigation, and its discovery marked a moment when it appeared that there was a clear fabrication in Gabe's story that did not fit with the likely occurrence of an accidental death.

The perceived importance placed by the police on this evidence was presented in H. Thomas's article, which appeared in *The Australian* newspaper on 11 December 2010. Drawing from selected excerpts (see below) of media interviews provided by Campbell and Gehringer,[14] H. Thomas highlighted the reliance he perceived the police had placed on this piece of, what turned out to be, erroneous evidence:

> Campbell: Red flags went up everywhere when it appeared he [Gabe] was telling straight-out lies. These weren't just inconsistencies; they were absolute lies, like when he said his dive computer beeped and he had to return to the dive boat, the *Spoilsport*, and discovered the battery was in backwards. We tested the dive computer and found that to be an absolute impossibility. The machine did not work at all when the battery was back to front, let alone make beeping sounds. It was those sorts of clear untruths that led us to begin believing there was much more to Tina's death than what he had said ...
>
> Gehringer: We initially started with his dive computer, and his version in relation to it, giving out an audible alarm when he first descended with Tina. We carried out tests on the dive

[13] Transcript of Proceedings, *Inquest into the death of Christina Mae Watson* (23 November 2007) 492 (David Griffiths).

[14] ABC Television Network, "Unfathomable: Part One", *Australian Story*, 2 August 2010 (Detective Senior Sergeant Gary Campbell and Detective Senior Constable Kevin Gehringer) <http://www.abc.net.au/austory/content/2007/s2971395.htm>; Andy Toulson, "Gabe Watson Deserved Murder Trial", *Townsville Bulletin* (Queensland), 29 May 2010.

computer in the hyperbaric chamber both with the batteries in correctly, and with them in incorrectly, and what we found is that with the battery in back to front, the computer merely doesn't work. It's unable to put out an audible alarm.

Campbell: His actions in relation to the dive computer were a straight-out lie and that then raised the question with us, what was he trying to hide?[15]

In addition to selecting these interview passages, H. Thomas quoted Rohan Armstrong, one of the members of Gabe's Australian defence team, to further advance his argument pertaining to the importance placed on the battery evidence by the Queensland Police Service (QPS) investigators, claiming that "the dive computer evidence was one of the most important planks of the police investigation".[16] In drawing on these sources, H. Thomas questioned the legitimacy of the entire police investigation, suggesting that the police had made a "fundamental mistake … [which] had a compounding and collateral impact [on the investigation]".[17]

The "mistake" to which H. Thomas referred as a basis for challenging the justness of the entire police investigation was that, had both components of Gabe's dive computer been tested simultaneously, the police would have established that "in its complete form of display module and transmitter, [the computer] does perform the way Watson had described".[18] That is, the wrist module component of the dive computer will emit an audible alarm when the transmitter component of the computer's battery is inserted incorrectly. This outcome was acknowledged by Adam White upon cross-examination at the coronial inquest into the cause and circumstances of Tina's death in Queensland on 23 November 2007:

Zillman: Right. So, I just want to confirm those matters. You can conceive of a situation where a diver, having the computer system that was spoken about in two components, that is the transmitter and data module?

White: Mmm-hmm.

---

[15] Detective Sergeant Gary Campbell and Detective Senior Constable Kevin Gehringer, cited in Thomas, above n 1.

[16] Rohan Armstrong cited in Thomas, above n 1.

[17] Thomas, above n 1.

[18] Ibid.

Zillman:	Inserting the battery into the [wrist] module correctly but inserting the battery into the transmitting [sic] incorrectly?
White:	Yes.
Zillman:	You can conceive of that?
White:	Yep. Mmm-hmm.
Zillman:	That person gets into the water, descends to a depth of four or five or six feet or whatever … There's not going to be any proper signal coming from the transmitter?
White:	No.
Zillman:	An alarm will beep?
White:	Yes.
Zillman:	And flash. But the dive will be conceivably recorded?
White:	Yes.[19]

In light of the perceived significance of the test, it has been argued that the police, informed by an erroneous piece of evidence, developed tunnel vision, which then led the investigation to focus solely upon Gabe as a murder suspect. On this basis, the investigation was arguably unjust, or at least a perception of injustice engulfed it; as journalist and co-author of *Honeymoon Dive*, Jennifer Cooke, claimed, "if they were wrong about that [the dive computer], were there other issues that needed more probing? ... This was a pivotal issue that police felt proved that Gabe Watson was lying, and that helped colour the whole investigation".[20] Bloomston raised a similar concern in his opening address to the jury in Gabe's capital murder trial in Alabama, when he claimed, "the police didn't test the whole computer, they built the case based on a confused lie … They had a man and they created a crime".[21] He repeated this concern in our discussions with him, noting that:

---

[19] Transcript of Proceedings, *Inquest into the death of Christina Mae Watson* (23 November 2007) 588 (Adam White, Steven Zillman QC).
[20] Jennifer Cooke, cited in Thomas, above n 1.
[21] Brett Bloomston, court observations, 14 February 2012.

> We were aware that the dive computer had two parts and two components, and we were in possession of the transmitter from the time that Gabe came back to the US [in 2010]. The fact that it was tested and they did not test both components together or even consider that they work in tandem, started off the investigation on the wrong foot.

However, if further excerpts of Gehringer's and Campbell's media interviews are examined, it is evident that the police point to a number of factors, in addition to the dive computer battery tests, that shaped their perceptions and investigation into Tina's death, leading them towards an assumption of likely homicide. Indeed, even in considering the excerpts used by H. Thomas, Campbell can be seen to identify the absence of the audible alarm as just one example of multiple inaccuracies in Gabe's versions of what occurred underwater on 22 October 2003:

> Campbell: Red flags went up everywhere when it appeared he was telling straight-out lies.... These weren't just inconsistencies—*they* were absolute *lies*, like when he said his dive computer beeped and he had to return to the dive boat the *Spoilsport*, and discovered the battery was in backwards.... It was *those sort of clear untruths that led us to begin believing* there was much more to Tina's death than what he had said. We had a *hell of a lot of suspicions about his actions* under the water that day.[22]

Similarly, in examining additional passages of the police interviews with the Australian ABC network's *Australian Story* program, which aired in two parts in August 2010, it is clear that Gehringer and Campbell acknowledge a number of inconsistencies within Gabe's statements, beyond that related to the inaudible alarm, which when considered in their totality, pointed towards Gabe as a potential murder suspect:

> Gehringer: Gabe's statement that Tina was sinking quicker than he could keep up to her, obviously we sought the opinion of a number of expert divers, and all of them stated that Gabe could have reached Tina very easily, in fact, just with a couple of kicks of his fins. We also did research into his rescue qualifications and what we found is that he had been trained in bringing unconscious divers to the surface. So we realised that Gabe had manifestly downplayed his qualifications in relation to his rescue certification.

---

[22] Emphasis added, Detective Sergeant Gary Campbell, cited in Toulson, above n 14.

Campbell: We also came into possession of a photograph taken by another diver, a Mr Stempler. And he's taking a photograph of his wife. In the background you can see Wade Singleton diving in the direction of Tina lying on the ocean floor. Yeah, it's one of them photographs I think that's one in a million. We had a specific location on the ocean floor where Tina was photographed. The significance of that is that it contradicted what Gabe told us about where he had left Tina. Tina's body should have been found on the wreck or adjacent to it. Not 16 meters away from the wreck at a 90 degree angle to the currents.

Gehringer: He also mentioned in his statement that after he left Tina he encountered two divers and he was quite direct and quite firm in that he substantially shook these divers, pointed in the direction that he'd last seen Tina, trying to raise the alarm.

Campbell: We contacted every crew and passenger on both vessels that were moored at that location on the day of the death.

Gehringer: And there was nobody that had a single male diver approach them on the diver descent line and try and raise an alarm with them. One of the really big things that we focused on was Gabe's version where he said he rocketed to the surface to seek help for Tina.

Campbell: When we compared it to the [test] results ... we found that Gabe had only descended to 15 metres and it took him between two and three minutes to reach the surface to raise a call for help. Speaking to various people in the dive industry umm, that was classed by some as literally pedestrian under the given circumstances. We compared that dive profile of Gabe's to the dive profile of Wade Singleton. Wade Singleton had gone to twice the depth and from the point that he has picked up Tina on the ocean floor and gone to the surface, he has covered twice the distance in nearly half the time. In addition to that, he was carrying Tina, who was not assisting in her own ascent.

Gehringer: When we first embarked on this investigation, my initial thoughts were that this was just a tragic drowning. We spent a couple of years investigating, and as much as we followed the evidence, we couldn't corroborate Gabe's version.

Campbell: We kept coming up with all these lies from Gabe and our suspicions were growing substantially to the point that we believed that Gabe Watson had murdered Tina Thomas on their honeymoon at the shipwreck *SS Yongala*.[23]

In contrast to H. Thomas's claims, these interview excerpts illustrate the extent to which the Queensland police attempted, but were unable to corroborate Gabe's version of events. Importantly, these attempts extended well beyond the evidence surrounding the audible sounds of the dive computer battery—a fact that was supported by our discussions with the lead police investigators, including Gehringer, who explained that the importance attributed to the dive computer testing of the battery and its lack of an audible sound was "that it was just one piece of evidence in a sea of evidence".

Beyond the Dive Computer: Pre-determined Guilt

Further to the erroneous dive computer testing being considered a key flaw in the police investigation, the involvement of the Helena Police Department—one of the local police departments for Tina's family, as opposed to the local police department from the municipality within the state of Alabama in which Tina and Gabe had lived—has been criticised as contributing to an already negatively perceived, unjust homicide investigation. Gabe's father, David Watson, has suggested that the QPS investigators were negatively influenced by the involvement in the investigation of Lieutenant Brad Flynn and the Helena Police Department, whom he argued had no jurisdiction over the case, and only got involved at the request of Tina's father, Tommy Thomas. In critiquing what he saw as an unjust and biased perception of Gabe's guilt held by the US police, David explained:

> Mr Thomas went to the Chief of Police [and] the Chief of Police suggested, we'll offer our help. So I don't think the Australians came to Helena, Alabama looking for help. Why wouldn't they have come to Birmingham—the biggest city in the state? … How would you pick Helena out of a phone book? Why would you pick it out of a phone book? … Tina was not a resident of Helena, she was not a native of Helena, nor was Gabe. The only people that make the connection to Helena are Mr and Mrs Thomas.

---

[23] ABC Television Network, above n 14.

This issue was also raised in our discussions with Bloomston, who similarly argued that the "Helena Police Department had absolutely no jurisdiction over this case. Tina and Gabe did not live in Helena. At the time of her death, she was a resident of a different municipality, a different city, in a different county". Like David, Bloomston attributed the Helena Police Department's involvement to the influence of Tina's father:

> We understand that Tommy Thomas went to the Helena PD [Police Department] and said, I'm not getting any help from these Queensland police officers, it has been a drag. The investigation has dragged out. Can you do anything? And they basically proclaimed themselves as agents for them [the Thomas family] … But there was no connection [between Tina, Gabe and the Helena Police Department], never any connection, other than the Thomas family calling their local friends in law enforcement.

The inference from these statements is that Tommy's belief in Gabe's premeditated involvement in Tina's death somehow negatively impacted the police investigation, although neither David nor Bloomston provided specific details as to how Tommy's involvement achieved this.

While acknowledging that the Helena Police Department Chief, Doug Jones, suggested that their involvement in the Australian police investigation would assist in "getting some quick information for her [Tina's] father who lives in the city", Flynn claimed that his primary role in the investigation was to assist the QPS, and that he was instructed by his chief to "help them out wherever you can and we'll probably be done with it". Indeed, while secondary victims often play an important role in police investigations, it is unlikely that the Thomas family's perceptions of Gabe's guilt would have significantly influenced the investigation to the extent of colouring the police's perceptions or hindering the professionalism of their approach to the investigation. Despite this, the depth of the distain for Flynn's involvement in the investigation was demonstrated by Bloomston's comments regarding their decision to subpoena him as a defence witness, which prevented Flynn from being able to observe any of the Alabama trial. As Bloomston explained:

> So Brad Flynn was all over the Australian media, disappointed with this and that ... He boasted that he would have Gabe in his backyard, that he would take him home to Alabama for justice, and frankly, it gives me great personal satisfaction to see—we subpoenaed him, we were potentially going to call him in our defence, obviously as a hostile witness, but he was unable to sit in on the trial, because he was excluded from the trial, as any other witness would be under our rules. And I just hated that he wasn't able to see it.

Responding to questions over Helena's jurisdiction in the case, Flynn indicated during our discussion with him that the Helena Police Department "has dual jurisdiction in Jefferson and Shelby Counties", noting that "Shelby County is where Helena is, but our city limits extend into Jefferson County which is where Birmingham is. So I have dual jurisdiction and sometimes we prosecute cases in Jefferson County". In further explaining his role in the investigation, what was evidently of central importance to Flynn was that his involvement was motivated by a commitment to seeking justice, not to borders or jurisdiction. He claimed, "we owed it to justice to pursue everything that we could do. I mean it's—just because the incident or the crime didn't occur within the city, doesn't mean that we're not going to help. It's just not the way we operate … and I'm very thankful for that".

Perhaps of most significance in the context of this discussion is that Flynn also acknowledged that when he initially became involved in the investigation in December 2004, Gabe had not yet been identified as a murder suspect. He explained:

> I started speaking with Kevin [Gehringer] ... and they were beginning to lay some of the groundwork out for me and explain to me what their concerns were, that essentially we want to believe that this is an accident, that there's a logical explanation for what happened to her, but at this time we cannot sign off on that. And [I said] I can understand that, I've been in similar situations, so it's fine.

This comment from Flynn is significant because it indicates, from a procedural justice standpoint, that regardless of whether the Helena Police Department was also assisting Tommy by providing him with information on the progress of the investigation, Gabe's culpability in Tina's death was not predetermined at this stage of the investigation. This comment also supports our wider discussions with the lead police investigators, which revealed that the moment at which each of the investigators independently became confident that they were no longer dealing with an accidental death occurred several years into the investigation. Indeed, the police investigators' perceptions of Gabe's intentional involvement in Tina's death were informed by an array of evidentiary sources, including Gabe's own statement and actions, the statements provided by other witnesses, and various scientific tests undertaken throughout the course of their investigation—a process which Gehringer described as "fitting together the complex pieces of a puzzle". This view was shared by Tina's father, Tommy, who claimed that:

> Him [Gabe] and his attorneys want to blame the dive computers, and his really weak story about the dive computers for the investigation, but the whole reason he got investigated is because he couldn't tell the same story twice, and every time somebody challenged something he told them, the next time he told it, he'd tell it a different way and try to leave that part out or change that part.

Thus, in contrast to the concerns raised by Gabe's family, his US and Australian defence teams and journalist, H. Thomas, our discussions with Gehringer and Flynn suggest that their suspicions of Gabe's involvement in Tina's death arose well after the Helena Police Department began assisting the QPS, and well after the dive computer test results were compiled.

Moments of Clarity

In discussing the stage of the investigation at which he came to believe that Tina's death was not an accident, Gehringer described a lengthy and difficult process that involved him questioning and requestioning the evidence, and often putting himself in Gabe's position. Gehringer recalled that while "there was all these little pieces [of evidence] … there was still no one big dominating smoking gun or smoking barrel or what have you". It was not until late 2006, almost three years into the investigation, and approximately two years subsequent to the involvement of Flynn and the Helena Police Department, that Gehringer believed a murder charge could and should be brought against Gabe. He explained:

> When I look back at the investigations I've done in the past, Gabe has probably gotten my sympathy or empathy more than anybody else, of giving him the benefit of the doubt for such a long time … I was the most sceptical to think that he was a murderer because I was seeing everything that was coming in … but I was probably still giving Gabe a benefit of the doubt up to a particular point, where I was always questioning myself as to, well, maybe he did just panic ... People do irrational things when they're panicked. As simple as it seems ... she's sinking to the bottom and all he had to do was kick his fins down a couple of kicks and grab her and bring her to the top, you know? If you're panicked, if you're genuinely panicked, then I would sort of—I was always lending myself to giving him that benefit of the doubt, but then within my own mind, I just kept thinking it over and over again, and then I'd ask myself the question, well if that's the case, why was he telling me during his versions [statements] that he'd fought and it was—the words he used was, I can't believe how clear it was in my mind that I was thinking of all these other things I could do, like I could inflate her BCD [buoyancy control device], I could take her back to

> the [access] line. You know, it's such a literal thought process. To be able to go through a thought process of, hold on, when I go spear fishing I have a clip; that clip's still on my BCD. If I can get her to the [access] line I can take that clip off and then I can tether her to the [access] line and then I can go to the surface.
>
> So I'm thinking to myself, you know you can't have your cake and eat it too. If you're genuinely panicked and you're scooting to the surface, how can you have the rational thought to then go through four different procedures that you could possibly do, yet you decided not to do? And then of course, again, how can you have your cake and eat it too, if you are genuinely panicked, you're not going to be worried about ascending no faster than your smallest bubble. You're only at 45 feet and you've only been in the water for a couple of minutes. It's impossible for you to get the bends. You're not going to get the bends at 45 feet as a maximum depth when you've only been in the water for a couple of minutes …
>
> [So] I'm still questioning myself a couple of years down the track as to, is he just a coward? Or did he just panic? So I always in my mind was trying to give him—or I was giving him the benefit of the doubt, but then questions would keep arising … It wasn't until the dive re-enactment [conducted by the QPS in September 2006] which was very mathematically correct and distances were exact. And that was probably the point for me … [I thought] he's definitely—he's murdered her. Because in my mind, there is absolutely—and from everything that Gabe told me—there is no reason for him to have taken Tina out 15–16 metres away from the *Yongala*… So to me, that was where I finally couldn't give Gabe the benefit of the doubt any more ... I'm sure he killed her.

As evident in this excerpt from our discussions with Gehringer, coming to believe that Gabe was a murder suspect was not an easy determination, nor was it a decision that appears to have been unduly influenced by any single piece of evidence. Instead, it was the result of a drawn-out and complex assessment of many elements of the evidence obtained during the investigation, which led Gehringer to what appeared to be a difficult determination that Gabe deliberately and with premeditation caused Tina's death.

Mirroring Gehringer's reflections, Detective Senior Sergeant Gary Campbell also identified a range of evidence collected across multiple years of the police investigation, which led him to re-evaluate his perceptions of the case from a non-suspicious death to a homicide investigation. In his testimony at Gabe's capital murder trial in Alabama, Campbell stated that over the course of the investigation particular factors "heightened his suspicions of Gabe's involvement".[24] Specifically, Campbell identified the discovery of a possible insurance motive, Gabe's slower than anticipated ascent rates, and the photograph depicting the location of Tina's body, which was substantially different from where Gabe had said they were diving in his police statements, as influencing his determination of Gabe's involvement in Tina's death. The "eyewitness statement of Stutz was [also] significant"[25] as a determining factor for Campbell; as Gehringer similarly explained, "Stutz's statement … that was really, for Gary … that was a big red flag … He [Gary] came to me with this statement and said, look at this. He's seen something. This just isn't right". The most influential elements of Stutz's statement related to his observations of Tina and Gabe in an embrace underwater, before Gabe ascended and Tina sank towards the bottom of the ocean. This embrace was later commonly referred to within the media as "the bear hug".[26] Other than Gabe, Stutz was the only person who could provide direct evidence as to what occurred between Gabe and Tina on 22 October 2003, and the differences in their statements were substantial. As Stutz explained in his 2007 statement to the police:

> When I saw diver one [Tina] my belief was that she was in distress. This was conveyed to me by her movements initially. Her arm and leg movements were disorganised and this is what caught my peripheral vision. I believe that my training as an Accident and Emergency Doctor enabled me to recognise that she was in distress. I did a lot of diving when I was younger and this coupled with my training as a physician left me in no doubt ... When I first saw diver two [Gabe] he was about ten feet away from diver one [Tina] and approaching her from her left. Diver two [Gabe] moved on top of diver one [Tina] and was basically a mirror image of her body position. Diver two [Gabe] was facing towards the ocean floor and diver one [Tina] was still facing towards the ocean surface ... The arms of diver two [Gabe] were circling the torso of diver one [Tina] under her armpits. I am not in a position to say what the hands of diver two [Gabe] were doing behind her back ... The two divers seemed to be in this embrace for about 30 seconds at the maximum; however, most likely it was less and may be even as little as ten seconds ... I do not recall anything about their

---

[24] Gary Campbell, court observations, 21 February 2012.

[25] Ibid.

[26] See, for example, Peter Michael and Stefanie Balogh, "Gabe Watson Faces Murder Change over Wife's Scuba Death", *The Courier Mail* (Queensland), 21 June 2008; Will Storr, "New Investigation into Honeymoon Death of Tina Watson", *The Sunday Mail* (Queensland), 28 August 2010; Tuck Thompson, "Legal Stoush over Gabe Watson Honeymoon Scuba Trial", *The Courier Mail* (Queensland), 20 December 2011.

dive suits or dive gear that caught my attention. I do not recall while the two divers were under my observation any hand signals between the two of them.[27]

Stutz also noted in his 2007 police statement that at no point did he see either of the divers' masks or regulators become dislodged or come loose.[28] This statement differed significantly from the version of events that Gabe had described to the police and to his fellow divers. Accordingly, it provided a very strong basis from which the investigators sought to question the validity of Gabe's claims as to what happened underwater between him and Tina immediately before she died.

In responding to what he perceived as an increasingly strong and growing body of evidence, Campbell revisited and analysed Gabe's police statements, and subsequently identified a number of inconsistencies and contradictions in the information Gabe had provided to the police and in the accounts he had provided to others. Campbell also identified inconsistencies between Gabe's statements and those provided by other dive witnesses, all of which pointed him towards the view that Tina's death was not accidental. As Campbell testified at the Alabama trial, "we did not create a crime to fit this man … It was not based on emotion. We took the investigation where the evidence led us".[29]

Coroner David Glasgow, who oversaw the coronial inquest examining the cause and circumstances surrounding the death of Tina Thomas, similarly perceived that the police were convinced by the evidence before determining that Gabe intentionally caused Tina's death. He explained:

> Zillman [Gabe's defence lawyer at the coronial inquest in Queensland] used to say, in his submissions [to the inquest] … that the police started with the intention of getting him [Gabe] … that they came to that conclusion and looked for the evidence ... I think that's untrue ... I'm sure it was the other way around. They looked at all the evidence, then came to the conclusion, and I think as much as police officers can be objective, they were … I think they formed a fairly quick impression that he was a bloody coward … I remember him [Gary] saying, I think the Americans are convinced he's done it. I'm still yet to be convinced. That was the difference, and I think you'll find that's his [Gary's] attitude, and I don't think Steve [Zillman] accepted that. And it wasn't in his interests to accept it … It's only after they [the police] sat down to consolidate things [that] their suspicions started to look at, what if he is not a bullshit artist? [What] if there's something more sinister there?

---

[27] Dr Stanley Stutz, witness statement, 18 April 2007.

[28] Ibid.

[29] Gary Campbell, court observations, 21 February 2012.

For US police investigator Lieutenant Brad Flynn, there were also multiple factors that influenced his belief in Gabe's premeditated and intentional involvement in Tina's death. In a similar vein to Gehringer, Flynn claimed that "originally I said this is just a horrible accident. There's no way—I mean who kills somebody underwater? … When I came on board … we weren't really considering Gabe as a suspect". However, one of the key influential pieces of evidence that Flynn identified arose during his discussion with Gabe and Tina's accredited diving instructor, Tom Jackson, on 5 June 2005. As Flynn explained, in his early communications with Gehringer and Campbell it was "readily apparent that Gabe was dismissing his rescue qualifications and what he was trained to do". However, when he spoke with Gabe's diving instructor, Flynn was informed of what skills were included in the open water, rescue and advanced scuba diving accreditation levels that Gabe had attained. Flynn recalled that:

> He [Jackson] explained to me in detail what each level of certification [was] that Gabe had attained [and] what was required to attain that certification … He provided me with the printed materials that Gabe had, and in that—you look at these materials and I mean, in every book it covers how to handle a panicked diver, distressed diver situation, things like that. And you look at that and I'm like, the guy [Gabe] had the skills. Why? And you tend to think back of—well, [some] people react differently under stressful conditions than other people, and I see that out here. I see that at work all the time. And that in and of itself is not a big red flag to me, but when you started adding that along with the other things … that's what started really as the core for me that something wasn't right. There may be something to this after all … I realised that, well, we've eliminated any doubt that this guy was a novice, and we've eliminated any doubt that he did not have the training to perform a rescue, or at least bring her to the surface.

In our discussions with Flynn, he identified another pivotal moment which occurred later that same year in November, when he filmed Gabe using bolt cutters to remove the flowers that Tina's parents had placed on her grave. Flynn explained:

> I remember talking to both of them [Gary and Kevin] and saying it's the damndest thing, flowers keep coming up missing. All of Gabe's family's flowers tend to stay there and I was like, why in the world would anybody do this? Why? It just doesn't—I'd never heard of … something so bizarre … So I set up camp for almost three days waiting for somebody to show up and of course the whole world knows what I got [video footage of Gabe removing the flowers from the gravesite] … At the time I didn't know how

> that would be helpful for the case, but that, right there, gave me a glimpse into what was inside his [Gabe's] head. He hated Tina and that family to disrespect her time and time and time and time again.

It is unlikely that this video evidence of Gabe removing the flowers would have been admissible as evidence in an Australian-run trial, because it was not directly related to the circumstances surrounding Tina's death or to Gabe's alleged involvement in it. Similarly, under Rule 403 of both the *Alabama Rules of Evidence* and the *Federal Rules of Evidence* (US), which govern court proceedings in Alabama, the video was deemed inadmissible in Gabe's capital murder trial in Alabama, on the basis that it was too prejudicial and may direct the jury towards a negative view of Gabe, thereby colouring their ability to look beyond this evidence in determining his guilt or innocence. Given the differing rules that govern the coronial inquest process in Queensland—discussed in Chapter Two—this video was admitted as evidence and shown during the coronial inquest in order to depict a negative, harmful pattern in Gabe's behaviour which could demonstrate that he was the type of person capable of criminal misconduct and harm. In line with the purpose of showing the video at the inquest, for Flynn, Gabe's actions provided an insight into his character, revealing him to be someone with a "cold", "calculating" personality, capable of offending and committing very harmful and insensitive conduct. As Flynn acknowledged, at this stage he had begun to "kind of dismiss the whole accident thing, thinking there's another explanation here, but what is it?" He claimed that "at that phase of the investigation, it wasn't really to the point where we could say yes he did it, because it was still early. But you're beginning to get this opinion [that] … maybe this guy is capable of doing something".

Like his Australian counterparts, Flynn was also heavily persuaded by Stutz's eyewitness statements, one of which he obtained from Stutz on 16 January 2006. As Flynn explained:

> I went and interviewed Dr Stutz … I remember after I turned the camera off and I was leaving his apartment, I turned around to shake his hand and thank him for talking to me, and he says, I know what I saw. And he says, nobody's going to change my mind. And that kind of stuck with me and I relayed that to Gary [Campbell] the next day, and I said, you may have something here … He's not wavering on what he saw.

While Stutz's police statements and later testimony at the capital murder trial are explored in more detail in Chapter Seven, it was this moment, in conjunction with the evidence that Flynn had collected personally and that which he had been given access as part of the QPS investigation, which he identified as a key turning point. As he described:

> It was at that point that I just [thought] game on, you know? ... I'm going to do everything I can to ... get it in court. I'm not a judge and a jury, I don't take my job like that ... [but] I'm making this my life's mission to get this in court, because guilty [verdict] or not, the [Thomas] family is going to get their day... It's my opinion, it's my professional opinion as a police officer, Kevin's [Gehringer] and Gary's [Campbell], that Gabe should be taken into court and it's up to a jury to make their mind up ... And that was the time that I said, this is it.

As pointed to in Flynn's reflections, a significant number of factors and pieces of evidence influenced his perception of Gabe as a potential murder suspect. Importantly, following this determination, a key issue for Flynn was his desire to have the matter heard and determined by a jury, in a court of law. As discussed more extensively in Chapters Three, Four and Ten, for Flynn, among other participants, a jury trial in Queensland was where the investigation needed to be finalised, in order for justice to be attained.

Procedurally Just?

In examining whether the police investigation can be considered "just" from a procedural justice perspective, the outcome of the investigation cannot be the sole determining factor. Consideration must also be given to whether or not the processes that led to a murder charge being laid are perceived as just. While individual concerns have been raised regarding potentially undue influences on the police and their investigation, it is important to note that even amid the criticisms of the dive computer testing and the "blinded" focus of the police, it has not been suggested that the police intentionally tested only the wrist module component of Gabe's dive computer. As H. Thomas acknowledged, "there is no suggestion that the police deliberately failed to test it [the transmitter]".[30] Instead, it is believed that only the wrist module was seized and tested because during the course of providing his statements to the police, Gabe could be seen pointing to or holding his wrist where a watch would sit, when talking about a "dive computer", and when discussing the transmitter component of the computer, he refers to this as the "transponder". As Gehringer explained:

---

[30] Thomas, above n 1.

> Gabe's—you know the word he'd always use was computer. His body language always led me to believe he was talking about the computer that he'd worn on his wrist. He'd spoken, in the times that he had given me those versions, he'd spoken about his transmitter or his transponder which denoted that that was the part that was on his tank. So to me, I'd never even thought that there could possibly be any confusion about whether he was talking about his transmitter or the receiver. To me, it [the wrist module] was always, that's what he'd been talking about.

Furthermore, a transmitter component of a dive computer is often sold as an optional extra and is not required for the wrist module component of the computer to work. The transmitter component only provides guidance on how much gas (oxygen) is left in the diver's tank, enabling the diver to access this information by checking the digital display on their wrist. Accordingly, the transmitter is not required in order for the wrist module component to perform its primary function of informing the diver about their dive profile. Indeed, even the dive computer used by Gabe on the fatal dive "can be used without a transmitter".[31] In light of this fact, as well as the supporting video footage of Gabe giving his second police statement, which showed him often pointing towards his wrist when discussing the dive computer, and Gehringer's subsequent comments about Gabe's physical and verbal descriptions of the computer, it was reasonable for the police to believe that Gabe's reference to the dive computer battery, and the dive computer in general, referred only to the wrist module, rather than both components.

It is also important to note that while significant attention has been drawn to the one erroneous finding of the dive computer testing, several accurate and significant pieces of evidence pertaining to Gabe's diving logs and profile were also obtained from the dive computer tests, which did not require anything other than the wrist module component be tested. As White explained in his testimony during the Alabama capital murder trial, the important elements of the testing—those related to Gabe's diver logs and profile—"did not require the transmitter component be tested, it only required the wrist module component be tested".[32] Similarly, Coroner Glasgow explained to us that "[the police] did the tests. The tests were done … [What H. Thomas says], that's wrong and he should read the bloody [coronial inquest] transcript and I thought of writing to him, but you never win with journalists … You never win".

[31] Transcript of Proceedings, *Inquest into the death of Christina Mae Watson* (23 November 2007) 559 (Adam White).

[32] Adam White, court observations, 20 February 2012.

The relevant tests that were conducted by White on the wrist module component of Gabe's dive computer provided pertinent information about the fatal dive, including in relation to Gabe's and Tina's diving logs. As part of this testing, White determined that Gabe's dive lasted for a duration of seven minutes, at a maximum depth of 54 feet (16 metres), while Tina's dive proceeded to a depth of 89 feet (27.1 metres) and lasted for a duration of ten minutes. Importantly, White was able to provide a graph representing the approximate overall dive profile, based only on the wrist module component of Gabe's dive computer, which showed changes in Gabe's dive profile in ten-foot increments, including an approximation of his ascent rate. This finding accordingly became an important piece of evidence in the police investigation.

Griffiths was also able to identify relevant information on Gabe's ascent by testing only the wrist module component of the dive computer. The information collected from Griffiths's tests suggested that Gabe's ascent to the surface involved him covering approximately 15 metres in somewhere between two and three minutes, which Griffiths described as a "faster than usual … ascent rate, such as would occur if he followed an inclined anchor rope to the surface, but not a panicking rapid ascent directly to the surface".[33] This data was then contrasted with the ascent rates of Tina and Wade Singleton—the diver who brought Tina to the surface—which involved covering approximately 27 metres in around 90 seconds. Thus, these tests demonstrated that in rising to the surface, Singleton was able to cover almost double the distance, in significantly less time—somewhere between 30 and 90 seconds faster than Gabe. This finding supported the testimony given at the capital murder trial in Alabama by one of Gabe and Tina's fellow divers on the *Spoilsport*, Kenneth (Ken) Snyder, who described the rate of Gabe's ascent as equivalent to "a pedestrian stroll".[34] Using the findings from these tests, the police were able to highlight inconsistencies in Gabe's statements pertaining to the pace of his ascent, in particular, his claim that he "just rocketed to the top and I just swam up to the top and that was one of the things I thought about later … you know, I'm amazed that I didn't end up with the bends or something … I just turned and kicked and went straight up to the top".[35]

Consequently, while the failure to test the battery component on the transmitter was erroneous, it was not deliberate. As the author of *Crucial Errors in Murder Investigations*, Ted Duhs, purports in his analysis of the

---

[33] David Griffiths, witness statement, 18 February 2005.
[34] Kenneth Snyder, court observations, 16 February 2012.
[35] Gabe Watson, witness statement, 27 October 2003.

case, it was an "error by the investigating police, but not a crucial error".[36] Importantly, this was not an error intentionally made by a group of police investigators who had predetermined guilt upon a single suspect. Indeed, as our analysis revealed, it was several years before all three of the lead police investigators became convinced that they were dealing with an intimate homicide case, and these individual determinations were based on a significant body of evidence that was collected over that time. From a procedural justice perspective, it can thus be argued that the processes leading to the outcome of the police investigation were primarily just.

[36] Ted Duhs, *Crucial Errors in Murder Investigations* (Bond University Press, 2012) 24.

CHAPTER TWO

DELAYING JUSTICE? THE PROLONGED POLICE INVESTIGATION

> Every time we turned around things had been delayed. Going through the police investigation we had had all kinds of delays. Going through the coronial inquest we had had all kinds of delays ... We were trying to move it along, trying to move it along, and then you know ... there were more delays.
>
> —Tina's father, Tommy Thomas

Almost five years after Tina Thomas died, an arrest warrant was issued for Gabe on a charge of murder. The prolonged transnational police investigation that led to his arrest encountered several obstacles arising from a problematic climate of inefficiency, an absence of available funding, and at least in the initial stages of the investigation, a seemingly unsupportive senior management within the Queensland Police Service (QPS). Despite the geographical and political complexities inherent to the investigation, the police were finally able to present their evidence before a coronial inquest hearing in Queensland in 2007. In Queensland, when a "reportable" death occurs,[1] a coroner, working within the relevant state coroner's office, is tasked with determining the identity of the deceased and the circumstances surrounding their death. To achieve this, the police provide the coroner with an initial report outlining the circumstances surrounding the death. If after reviewing this report the coroner requires the police to collect further information or evidence, the police investigation into the person's death becomes a coronial investigation.

---

[1] A reportable death includes where:

> The identity of the person is unknown; the death was violent or unnatural, such as accidents, falls, suicides or drug overdoses; the death happened in suspicious circumstances; a "cause of death" certificate has not been issued and is not likely to be issued; the death was a health care related death; the death occurred in care; the death occurred in custody; or the death occurred as a result of police operations.

See, Queensland Courts, *Coroners Court* (2012) <http://www.courts.qld.gov.au/courts/coroners-court>.

Once the coroner is satisfied with the investigation, s/he determines whether or not to hold an inquest. As Gehringer described in the context of the *Watson* case:

> For our report for the coroner, we wanted to make sure we had as much detail as we could … In Queensland, if you have a sudden death, you've got to do that initial *Form 1* report which gives a brief outline of what police have found, and then you have the abridged statements from your witnesses last to have seen the person. Then it goes to the coroner and then the coroner will either say okay, I'm satisfied with the information I've got and deem it a non-suspicious, accidental death, or the coroner then decides, well, we need an inquest.

Inquests are generally only held in cases where the coroner determines that it is in the public interest to do so. There are four primary categories that fall within the coronial definition of "public interest". The first is when a death has occurred in custody, while the person is under state care, or as a result of police operations. The second is where the state coroner or Attorney-General orders that an inquest be held. The third arises when there is doubt about the cause and circumstances of a death, as was the case with Tina's death. And finally, an inquest is held where it may assist in preventing future deaths. Accordingly, the primary purpose of an inquest is to determine the identity of the deceased, the cause and circumstances of their death, and any further information required to register that death.

In Tina's case, as her death occurred prior to the enactment of the "new" *Coroners Act 2003* (Qld), which applies to all deaths that have occurred since 1 December 2003, the coronial process was run according to the "old" *Coroners Act 1958* (Qld). Significantly, under s 24(1D) of the "old" Act, in addition to determining the cause and circumstances of the death, the purpose of an inquest included to establish details of "the persons (if any) to be charged with murder". On this basis, if the coroner determined that there was sufficient evidence to commit a person to stand trial on a charge of murder, then under s 41(1) of the *Coroners Act 1958* (Qld), they may "order that person to be committed to trial for the offence before some court of competent jurisdiction" and issue a warrant for their arrest. In making his determination regarding Tina's death, Coroner David Glasgow had to operate within these legislative parameters. Thus, on 20 June 2008, at the conclusion of the inquest into Tina's death, Coroner Glasgow was required to outline in his findings, his determination of how Tina had died, and importantly, whether anyone should be charged with her murder.

The Queensland Police Investigation: Low in Support and Resources

In advancing the case to the point of a coronial inquest, *Operation Charlie Oswald* encountered a number of obstacles that prevented the police from being able to complete their investigations within a shorter timeframe. Indeed, throughout its almost five-year duration, a lack of resources was a prominent issue that prolonged and at times hindered the police investigation. As Gabe's father, David Watson, pointed out, "with the economy like it is, all cities are hurting for revenue. So you're [Queensland] going to send one of your guys to Australia and all over the eastern United States ('US'), from Florida to Rhode Island ... That's not cheap". The impact of limited resources is specifically evident in the police being prevented from using new technologies and approaches to investigate Tina's death. For example, at one point in the early stages of the investigation, Detective Senior Constable Kevin Gehringer suggested that the QPS compile a 3D model of the *Yongala* dive site, which could be uploaded onto a computer and used to re-enact the versions of events that Gabe had provided. This technology, while expensive, had been used in prior police investigations in Queensland, and would have provided an important and conclusive overview of the dive site, allowing the police to ascertain the plausibility of Gabe's account of events. As Gehringer explained:

> I said to Gary [Campbell], why don't we look at trying to do that [a 3D model], but do it underwater? Because that's what we need to do. We need to retrace Gabe's version as far as exactly what has happened underwater. And because he'd been so—he'd given us so much detail in those two versions [statements] about what had happened underwater. So we spoke with our forensic people, the photographic forensic people down in Brisbane, and as it turned out, again, it's resource based. We just didn't have the resources … to take that camera underwater and do those 360 still shots to then stitch it together to give us a scene and then to try and look at some sort of re-enactment.

The frustrations, such as those described by Gehringer, appear to have been ongoing challenges for the police investigators in this case, and are illustrative of the negative influence of a struggling financial climate in hindering criminal investigations, regardless of the severity of the alleged crime. This problem was one that we discovered to be a common theme that permeated each stage of this case's progression throughout the Queensland and Alabama legal systems.

In addition to the costs of the investigation impacting on the case's progression, delays also arose due to the general nature of policing in Australia, in that police typically work on multiple cases at any one time. As Gehringer explained:

> It wasn't as if Gary and I were given this job and told, go and look after this job ... We still had to deal with–we weren't given any extra time or we weren't told that other teams would take on our workload. So if something came in over the counter, anything, a rape, a fraud, a death, we were still dealing with all of that on top of this particular job.

Gehringer further explained that during the course of the investigation, both he and Detective Senior Sergeant Gary Campbell sought some relief from their other policing duties to enable them to concentrate on this case, "because, as you know, time is of the essence [in an investigation] ... the longer it takes the harder it [gets]". However, at an early stage of the investigation, it became apparent that there was a lack of support for the case from within the QPS senior management, which continued to impact the investigation and ultimately was a strong contributing factor in its protracted duration.

The absence of internal support was particularly evident in relation to Gehringer and/or Campbell seeking permission to travel to the US in 2005 to undertake further necessary investigations. As Gehringer claimed, "we had the frustration of not being able to get approval to come over here [Alabama] to make further enquiries". Gehringer noted that this was particularly "frustrating" because Campbell was continually writing reports outlining the importance of a trip to progress the investigation, and the difficulties that they were encountering in having to rely solely on Lieutenant Brad Flynn, from the Helena Police Department, to make all US-based enquiries on their behalf. As Gehringer explained, "Gary highlighted in the reports that it was necessary for us to go over and speak further to witnesses that had initially given statements on the night, just to start clarifying different issues. And we had a hard time trying to get our hierarchy to believe that". This absence of internal support from senior management in the QPS was also acknowledged by Flynn, who claimed that Gehringer and Campbell "started communicating to me that some of their supervisors weren't really in the mindset to believe that this was anything that they needed to be investing their officers and their time and their money into".

In considering why this internal support was lacking, Gehringer expressed some confusion, commenting, "Why? I don't know". However, from his accounts of facing this lack of support, it appeared that limitations in resources may well have informed the absence of support and the frustrating decisions that were being made. He explained:

> The people that had to make the decisions–I don't know whether they didn't understand what evidence we had or the information we had. We'd prepared a PowerPoint presentation to show to the then Assistant Commissioner [Bob Atkinson] and there had been a meeting scheduled for Gary and I to go and present this to him and to say, this is what we've got, and as a result of that, we need to make these enquiries. The morning of that scheduled meeting, we got a phone call to say he's got another appointment now … To my understanding, it was a fairly minor other appointment that he had to go to and we just got shut down and there was never another meeting rescheduled. So I don't know whether they just didn't understand it or it was just in the too-hard basket because … they were looking down the track as to what resource implications it might have.

This absence of support for the police investigation was also identified by Coroner David Glasgow as hindering the progress of the coronial investigation and inquest. Glasgow explained that he first became aware of the lack of support and resources being allocated to the police investigation while trying to obtain information beyond the initial report he had received from the QPS in late 2004, in order to determine whether an inquest into the cause and circumstances of Tina's death was required.

After meeting with Campbell in 2005 to discuss the progress of the police investigation, Glasgow explained that he "wrote a letter of support to the officer in charge of [the] police [at] Townsville, which went down south [to Brisbane]. The letter got nowhere". Gehringer also noted the disregard for Glasgow's letter, stating that "we had a unique situation where we even had the coroner writing letters to our hierarchy saying, I'm the coroner, [the] police are my investigators. I need them to go to America and make these enquiries". Gehringer suggested that even at this stage there "still seemed to be this apparent lack of any urgency attached to getting Gary and I over [to the US]". Indeed, Gehringer explained that shortly after Glasgow had sent his letter to the QPS senior management, the *Operation Charlie Oswald* file was sent to the Brisbane Homicide Squad for review, at which point a report came back to the Townsville CIB which dismissed Campbell's requests to conduct investigations overseas, because "it was felt external agencies could do what was required".

Disappointed with the lack of response he had received from the QPS hierarchy, Glasgow sent a letter to the Queensland State Coroner, Michael Barnes, requesting his support for the police to proceed with their investigation, including conducting elements of the investigation in the US. Glasgow sent the letter to Barnes, in addition to the report that he had already sent that explained (as required by s 15 of the *Coroners Act 1958* (Qld)) why a decision on whether to hold an inquest into Tina's death had not yet been made, despite over 12 months having passed since 22 October 2003. Glasgow recounted:

> I wrote a letter to him [Barnes] and I said that Gehringer and Campbell, or [just] Campbell would fly down [to Brisbane] at his own expense and have a discussion with him [Barnes], and I wanted him to have a look at it to see whether the matter should be investigated … I said … maybe our office would split the cost, we pay half, they [the QPS] can pay half. I was just looking for some solution.

Glasgow also explained that he sent the letter because the state coroner was in a position to make a submission to the hierarchy of the QPS to specifically request that they fund Campbell's visit to the US to continue the investigation. As Glasgow maintained, "if they [the QPS] were going to end up charging him [Gabe], they had to go and get the evidence themselves, because they had to be in the position to give direct evidence … So I sent the letter off and I heard nothing".

At this point, Barnes, who had received Campbell's file, closed the coronial investigation into Tina's death. No information or reason was provided to Glasgow for Barnes's decision to do this. Thus, it can only be assumed that the decision was made according to the law stipulated in s 17(1) of the *Coroners Act 1958* (Qld), which allows for an investigation to be closed and the "holding of an inquest [deemed] unnecessary" when "the death was due to natural causes and did not occur in such place or in such circumstances as to require the holding of an inquest; or that no good purpose will be served by the holding of an inquest".

As discussed throughout this book, the *Watson* case has been plagued by criticisms of the decisions made by single authoritative agents of the legal system, which have hindered the opportunity for justice to be attained. Had Coroner Glasgow not responded to the state coroner's authoritative decision to close the coronial investigation, it may well have provided another example of one person controlling the outcome of a process that is designed to provide justice and closure. In place of this result, however, Glasgow's insistence to have the coronial investigation reopened can be seen, from all perspectives, as a moment when justice was given an opportunity to be achieved. This is primarily because at this stage there was no finality surrounding Tina's death. However, unbeknownst to Glasgow or anyone else at the time, due to the future decisions of individuals in authority; namely the prosecutor in charge of the case in Queensland, Assistant Director of Public Prosecutions Brendan Campbell SC, and the judge who oversaw the Alabama trial, Judge Tommy Nail—limited closure or clarity would ultimately be attained in relation to the death of Tina Thomas. At this point in 2005, however, had Glasgow accepted Barnes's decision to close the file, this may very well have been the end of the *Watson* case; but Glasgow did not accept this decision. As he explained:

> I said, he can't do that with my files. So I rang up Gary and I said, I don't know what he's [Michael Barnes] done Gary, but have you gone down there? [Gary said] no, I got a letter from him to say there was no decision, [that it] was still with Michael Barnes, nothing else. So I rang up the [State Coroner's] office and said, where's my file? They said he's [Barnes] closed it. I said he can't do that, I haven't written the bloody thing off because you've got some final things to do. I want it back. So I think I wrote a stinking letter … an email in which I used the phrase, pissed off.

When Glasgow was asked why the decision to close the investigation was made by the state coroner, the problematic impact of limited resources emerged again. As noted by Glasgow, "we were starved. There was no money". In addition to financial restrictions halting the police and coronial investigations, Gehringer identified "the then Assistant Commissioner [Bob Atkinson]" as being "the blocking point as far as us needing to do what we had to do". Indeed, by late 2006, the lack of progress in the police and coronial investigations into Tina's death had become not only a source of frustration for those involved, but also a focus of the media. In an article appearing in the *Townsville Bulletin* on 16 September 2006, Tina's mother and father, Cindy and Tommy Thomas, were quoted as having "lashed out at Australian police authorities for the lack of action in finding answers to their daughter's tragic death".[2] Specifically, this article identified internal blockages within the QPS as a key issue hindering the case, stating that "QPS's refusal to send Townsville detectives over to the US to finalise investigations was the main cause of [the] delay".[3] The article further stated that Tommy had "challenged the office of Queensland Police Commissioner Bob Atkinson to remedy the situation by approving the trip, so that the final report could be placed before the coroner by next month for an inquest as promised".[4] A similar article, entitled "Dad attacks police

---

[2] *Townsville Bulletin*, "Seeking Answers: Frustrated Parents Tom and Cindy Thomas", *Townsville Bulletin* (Queensland), 16 September 2006.
[3] Ibid.
[4] Ibid.

inaction on tragic anniversary–I know how my daughter died",[5] appeared a little over one month later on the third anniversary of Tina's death on 22 October 2006 in Brisbane's *Sunday Mail*. This article also drew attention to the "Townsville detectives … repeatedly be[ing] denied permission to travel to the US to interview witnesses".[6]

Media publicity, particularly that generated by the Thomas family, placed additional pressure on the QPS senior management to respond to the mounting criticisms of Coroner Glasgow, Detective Senior Sergeant Gary Campbell and Detective Senior Constable Kevin Gehringer, by taking some course of action in relation to the prolonged police investigation and delayed coronial process, which had by this time been ongoing for over three years. At this point, it appeared that Gehringer's initial perception that the Assistant Commissioner Bob Atkinson was blocking the investigation might have been accurate. As Glasgow identified, "the Assistant Commissioner ... was a whole blockage going through ... suddenly that Assistant Commissioner was moved and ended up taking up a desk job in Brisbane". In his place, Paul Wilson was appointed as the Assistant Commissioner in Townsville, and he requested a meeting with Gehringer and Campbell. Reflecting on this meeting, Gehringer identified the appointment of Wilson as a key turning point in the police investigation. As he recalled:

> I remember the day that Gary and I went there ... to give him a briefing on what we had and it was on that very same day that he shook my hand and Gary's hand and assured us that the QPS was going to do everything, whatever resources were available would be given to us, and that it would be progressed, and that the justice process would be followed. And it started happening as quick as that. As quick as Paul Wilson had seen us, things were in motion, things got rolling, [airline] tickets are all of a sudden being booked ... Without guys from the hierarchy, the people that you need in the high places, to give you the resources and the approvals to get things done ... from a justice aspect, things can't happen.

Flynn similarly noted the supportive response of Paul Wilson, whom he claimed, even at this early stage, recognised that Gehringer and Campbell were "onto something". Flynn explained:

> He sent Gary [Campbell] over here ... [He] had the faith in us to say, I trust your judgement, I trust your opinion, it's worth spending money ...

---

[5] David Murray, "Dad Attacks Police Inaction on Tragic Anniversary: I Know How My Daughter Died", *Sunday Mail* (Queensland), 22 October 2006.
[6] Ibid.

> Thankfully [once] Commissioner Wilson came in ... he said, hey, there's just too much of this [evidence]. You can't just dismiss it.

Primarily as a result of the new Assistant Commissioner's support, Campbell was finally able to conduct inquiries in the US in April 2007. While this was perceived as a positive step forward in the police investigation, Gehringer still expressed his frustration at the delays involved in this process, explaining that because of "resources and hierarchy … we lost a good year and a half". However, in spite of the delays, Flynn described this moment in early 2007 as when "the wheels of justice began turning in Queensland"—"wheels" that ultimately resulted in a 24-day coronial inquest examining the cause and circumstances of Tina's death being run over seven months. Between November 2007 and June 2008, 64 oral and written witness statements were presented by individuals from eight countries in the coronial inquest. In describing this process, Tommy explained:

> It was thorough. A four-week coronial inquest where the witnesses have to testify, the evidence has to be presented, the exhibits are all thrown out there for everybody to see and look through and talk about, and basically it's a trial before a trial. As far as the thoroughness part of it, the coronial inquest's thorough.

Not unexpectedly, given the thoroughness of the process and the struggling financial climate that existed in Queensland, the resource concerns and delays that were experienced during the police investigation were also present throughout the coronial inquest. Indeed, and as argued in several of the following chapters, resource concerns pertaining to expenditure and delays seemed to increase in prominence as the case progressed further into Queensland's criminal justice process, and later within the Alabama justice system. In relation to the coronial inquest, resource concerns emerged from the logistics of running the hearing. As Glasgow acknowledged, "we knew it was going to be hugely expensive ... because we were having to pay—Queensland was having to pay—for all these witnesses to fly in and to accommodate them and to feed them". This was a requirement under s 57 of the *Coroners Act 1958*(Qld), whereby all witnesses at a coronial inquest must have their attendance, travelling and any travelling-related expenses funded by the state. In total, Glasgow estimated that the inquest cost the Queensland Government at least "several hundred thousand dollars".

Further to financial costs, Gehringer also explained that there were ongoing resource problems arising from the practicalities of running the inquest. He claimed:

> We had witnesses from all over the world. Obviously our court systems operate during the day time, and at that time, it's night time in different places of the world. We had people that whilst they had [some] understanding and could speak the English language, for a court process we had to have certain interpreters and they had to be to the standard that are accepted in the court ... And then we had, of course, witnesses that lived on the other side of the world and couldn't travel or didn't want to travel, whether it was for work reasons or personal reasons. So we had to try and organise if we could get video link-ups for those sorts of people, and then if they lived in a little place that didn't have video link facilities, it was a case of trying to find places that they could travel to, to then get those video link-ups happening ... So then began the logistical nightmare of gathering and speaking to all of these witnesses to try and get them in this period of time.

Glasgow similarly maintained that:

> Because we had so many people from so many different places around the world, we had to actually do a timetable on who we were going to do and when we would do them, in what sequence, at what timeframes and where they were, all that sort of strategy [was involved]".

These issues are further demonstrated by the fact that the inquest was set to run for 24 days, but due to logistical and practical considerations it took seven months for all of the evidence to be heard. Such logistical issues are increasingly being faced by criminal justice agencies, whether in the context of running an inquest or a trial, where the offence, offender and/or the legal response spans multiple jurisdictions.

Despite the resource and practical issues contributing to an already prolonged police and coronial investigation, at the conclusion of the inquest on 20 June 2008, operating under the "old" legislative provisions, Glasgow determined that there was "evidence of sufficient reliability ... that a properly instructed jury could make a finding of guilt against David Gabriel Watson on a charge of murder".[7] Thus, using his powers under ss 104 and 108(1) of the *Justices Act 1886* (Qld) and s 41(1) of the *Coroners Act 1958* (Qld), Glasgow formally charged Gabe with murder, which included issuing a warrant for his arrest and committing him to stand trial on this charge before the Queensland Supreme Court.

Interestingly, the requirement on Glasgow to, in effect, determine guilt significantly differs from the requirements applied to all deaths that have occurred post 1 December 2003 and are subject to a coronial investigation

---

[7] Transcript of Proceedings, *Inquest into the death of Christina Mae Watson* (20 June 2008) 64 (Coroner David Glasgow).

and/or inquest. Under the "new" *Coroners Act 2003* (Qld), a coroner is strictly prevented from making any statement in either their written or spoken findings as to whether a person may be guilty of an offence.[8] Therefore, had Tina's death occurred just 39 days later, Coroner Glasgow would not have been able to attribute any blame to Gabe or commit him to stand trial for murder. This adds an interesting element to the *Watson* case, as one is left wondering what might have been had Glasgow's statement that "a properly instructed jury, could make a finding of guilt against David Gabriel Watson on a charge of murder"[9] not been included in his findings, and consequently not been released into the public realm. Would the Queensland Office of the Department of Public Prosecutions (ODPP) have pursued any charges against Gabe? Would Tina's family have been as convinced of Gabe's guilt? Would the State of Alabama have pursued a capital murder trial? Would justice have been obtained?

Questioning the Coronial Inquest

In reflecting on the processes and outcome of the coronial inquest, some concerns regarding the just nature of the inquest and the legitimacy of Coroner Glasgow were raised by members of Gabe's US defence team and the Watson family. As David critiqued, "we were confident with the inquest, when the inquest started, that the truth was going to come out. We found out real quick that that wasn't going to happen". In particular, questions were asked of the motivations underpinning Glasgow's early involvement in writing letters concerning the police investigation, and his subsequent decision to indict Gabe for murder.

The concerns raised by members of the Watson family and Gabe's US defence team were predominantly based on the fact that Glasgow's early involvement and alleged relationship with the Thomas family demonstrated his lack of independence and impartiality, thus hindering his ability to fairly oversee the inquest and thereby enabling the inquest to produce a just result. As David suggested, "the coroner was unduly influenced. He wrote a letter to his superior, and he said to his superior, be aware that the parents of the deceased could cause significant political embarrassment". The undue influence described by David related specifically to Coroner Glasgow's perceived close relationship with Tina's family. As David further claimed, "the coroner could have shut this thing down [the inquest], but he had become so schmoozey with the Thomas family. He

---

[8] *Coroners Act 2003* (Qld) ss 45(5) and 46(63).

[9] Ibid.

knew they were going to pitch a fit if it [the inquest] didn't happen". Similar concerns were also expressed by Gabe's family and civil attorney, Bob Austin, and Gabe's US defence attorney Brett Bloomston. Austin claimed that "the coroner established a rapport with the Thomas family, or so it appeared from what the attorneys over there [Queensland] said". Similarly, Bloomston maintained, "we heard rumours that he had tea every day with the Thomas family". While claims of Glasgow's bias in overseeing the *Watson* inquest have not been pursued in a legal or public context, they illustrate how in situations where the processes are perceived as leading to unjust decisions, the legitimacy of the outcome itself becomes questionable. Within this context, critiques levied at Coroner Glasgow's impartiality create an avenue of doubt for Gabe's supporters as to the viability and justness of both the coronial process and its outcome, which included Gabe being indicted for murder.

While media publicity surrounding the delayed police investigation and its impact on the Thomas family did appear to expedite the progress of the investigation, it is not clear what role, if any, the Thomas family played in influencing Glasgow's decision to proceed to an inquest, or to write to his superiors to seek support for the police investigation. In our discussions, Glasgow acknowledged that there were some "economic" and "political" pressures—in relation to potential damage caused to US tourism in Townsville—to resource the police investigation and that he did point out in his letter to State Coroner Barnes "the political necessity of something being done" about delays in the investigation into Tina's death. However, in his role as coroner, it was appropriate, and thus procedurally just, for Glasgow to have been involved in the police investigation in this manner. This is because, as the coroner assigned to the case, he held a number of powers of investigation under s 50 of the *Coroners Act 1958* (Qld), which included having the police effectively operate as his investigators. In addition, Glasgow was required by the legislation current at the time to justify why a decision on whether to run an inquest had not been reached within 12 months of Tina's death. Thus, it is in this context that his seeking at an early stage to accelerate the investigation can be legitimately explained and understood. As Glasgow noted, "when it is a coronial matter ... the police officers ... I use the phrase my investigators [to describe them]".

Further to the concerns over Glasgow's early involvement in the case, Gabe's family and US defence team also criticised some of the evidence that Glasgow allowed as part of the inquest. This also led to questions around Glasgow's legitimacy and experience, and the justness of the coronial process itself. As Austin claimed, "the only thing they had [as evidence] was the double hearsay about Tommy saying that she [Tina] said whatever [about life insurance]. They had no factual evidence ... The coroner was a legal lightweight as far as I'm concerned". Bloomston also raised concerns about the weight that Glasgow appeared to attach to various pieces of evidence, claiming that the coroner appeared to be unduly influenced by evidence that would be inadmissible at trial. While acknowledging the thoroughness of the coronial inquest at Gabe's bond hearing in Alabama, and describing it as offering "an intensive review of the evidence",[10] Bloomston still questioned the legitimacy of the process in our discussion:

> If you look at the coronial inquest ... hearsay is admissible, and a lot of ridiculous character evidence came in. Stuff about Tina going to see a boy in Atlanta a couple of weeks before she got engaged; that's not relevant to what happened underwater ... Dr [Carl] Edmonds ... we knew he was the foremost expert on dive medicine in Australia ... His opinion [was] that this [death] was an accident ... He was referenced a number of times in the coronial inquest as the expert and his book was cited, but it was ignored. The evidence that the [defence] counsel elicited from that book seemed to be ignored by the coroner.

In light of these concerns, Bloomston put forward a motion in a pre-trial hearing in the US that Glasgow be prevented from testifying at Gabe's capital murder trial in Alabama, on the basis that he had no personal knowledge of the facts and would be basing his opinion on other people's hearsay. As he later noted in our discussion, this motion was also motivated by his opinion of Glasgow: "the coroner in this case, I don't know what his previous reputation is in Queensland ... [but] I was questioning his integrity [in the motion]".

The concerns held by the US participants regarding the evidence permitted in the coronial inquest in Queensland potentially indicate a lack of understanding of the process and the intricacies involved within it. Such confusion is to be expected given the differences that exist between the two jurisdictions of Queensland and Alabama, particularly in terms of indicting offenders, trying offenders and the legislation governing criminal justice procedure. This is evident in relation to the US participants' allegations of the unjust nature of the coronial inquest on the basis of the hearsay evidence permitted in the hearing. In this regard, section 34(1) of the *Coroners Act 1958* (Qld) stipulates that:

---

[10] Brett Bloomston, bond hearing, 14 December 2010, 18.

> The coroner may admit any evidence that the coroner thinks fit, whether or not the same is admissible in any other court, provided that no evidence shall be admitted by the coroner for the purposes of the inquest unless in the coroner's opinion the evidence is necessary for the purpose of establishing or assisting to establish any of the matters within the scope of such inquest.

Thus, under the legislation, hearsay evidence can be admitted for consideration in the inquest process. This rule was also identified by Glasgow, who explained that "it's an inquiry, it's not a trial and it's subject to all sorts of restrictions because it's an inquiry. And it also has some benefits, because you can allow evidence in, which would be hearsay somewhere else". On this basis, Glasgow was not acting unjustly or without integrity when permitting perceived hearsay evidence into the coronial inquest, even if such evidence would not have been admissible in a Queensland or Alabama trial.

Another misapprehension of the coronial inquest can also be seen as emerging from the different process used in Alabama to determine an indictment—that of the grand jury—which as discussed in Chapter Six is based solely on a presentation by the prosecution, with little scrutiny or challenge of the evidence presented. As noted by Tommy, "people over here [Alabama] have compared the coronial inquest to a grand jury. There is no fricking [sic] comparison. They are completely different ... They don't compare". This misperception was evident from the comments made by representatives from the prosecution and defence teams at Gabe's bond hearing in Alabama on 14 December 2010, during which Bloomston described the coronial inquest as being "the equivalent of a grand jury proceeding",[11] while Tina Coker, representing the Alabama Office of the Attorney-General, described the coronial inquest as being "much like a grand jury".[12] As a consequence, the criticisms pertaining to the inquest and Coroner Glasgow may primarily be the result of a misunderstanding or lack of appreciation of the parameters of the Queensland coronial inquest, rather than being legitimate criticisms of whether the processes used in the inquest facilitated a just outcome.

In response to the criticisms levied at the coronial inquest, Gehringer maintained that:

> At the end of the day, the inquest was held, everyone gave their evidence, and there were four barristers. You had your barrister representing Mike Ball Dive Expeditions [the dive company that ran the seven-day

---

[11] Ibid, 6.

[12] Tina Coker, bond hearing, 14 December 2010, 16.

> expedition]; your barrister representing Gabe; the barrister representing Tina and Tommy; and the barrister assisting the coroner.

Importantly, as illustrated by Gehringer's comments, any issues around the legitimacy of the process or Glasgow's conduct would likely have been addressed by the relevant legal counsel during or at the conclusion of the inquest in 2008. Furthermore, as Glasgow explained:

> There was a great interest to see this thing right to the finish and I was very happy that that happened because nothing was left untapped. For instance, in our office, to actually have an untapped, unrestricted international ID phone sitting around the place, you'd have to almost have the Premier sign off on that, but it was done. We wore the costs of it because it was needed.

In addition to Glasgow's desire for the inquest to proceed in a thorough and just manner—regardless of the costs involved—making him a suitable person to oversee the inquest, his prior experience in running coronial inquests for diving deaths also demonstrated his suitability. Glasgow noted that in his ten years spent working as a coroner he "always looked after any deaths at sea in Townsville ... and I did a number of inquiries over the years of people who'd died accidentally or just disappeared at sea, and there are a number of complex issues involved". Thus, in drawing from his experience in determining the cause of diving-related deaths, and based on the testimony and evidence collected, Gehringer explained that "in the end ... the coroner was satisfied that there was a prima facie case [for murder]". As such, at the conclusion of the inquest, the *Watson* case was moved to the next phase of the Queensland criminal justice system, at which point the Queensland ODPP took responsibility of the case, subsequently gaining control over the justness of the processes and ultimately the outcome of Queensland's legal response to the death of Tina Thomas.

Charging Gabe with Murder: More Delays

In Queensland, when a person who is charged with an indictable (serious) offence has been committed for trial, the ODPP must present the indictment to the relevant court no later than six months after the date on which the person was committed for trial.[13] Internally, this timeframe is restricted to no later than four months after the date on which a person is committed to trial.[14] Consequently, operating under its internal guidelines,

---

[13] *Criminal Code 1899* (Qld) s 590(1).

[14] *Director's Policy* (Qld) s 10.

the Queensland ODPP was required to make a decision on whether to proceed with any charges against Gabe by 20 October 2008. Operating under external legislative provisions, the ODPP had until 20 December 2008 to make this decision. As Gehringer explained, the ODPP used a significant portion of this time, which had the unfortunate consequence of creating even more delays in the *Watson* case:

> From a justice side of things, again, the frustrating part came from—well, we had that honeymoon phase then where we thought everything was on track and everything was going good, because Glasgow had issued the arrest warrant. We'd gotten in the process for the extradition, [we were] starting to get the wheels in motion and all the paperwork that's associated with getting that into place ... So I myself made an initial contact to [the] ODPP to say, have you got everything? Do you need anything more? Do you need to see physical exhibits? And Gary and I found it a little bit strange because we weren't getting a lot of feedback from them. They'd acknowledged that they'd received the email but they'd say, yep, everything's okay, leave it with us. It wasn't until four months or so [later] that they then started to say, hey, we need this, we need that. So I spent a lot of time on the phone with Brad [Flynn] in that period. And I remember us discussing, why are they doing this? It's already in the brief [of evidence]. This has already been covered. But anyway, just to appease the necessary departments ... we went and got all this additional addendum statements, made all these additional enquiries, passed that all on to the ODPP ... And I remember having a conversation with this particular prosecutor saying, with all due respect, have you read the transcripts of the [coronial] inquest? To which I got a reply of, with all due respect, yes we have. Now go and get what I've asked you to. So I took that as a sit back in your chair and do as you're told—which I did ... And I just didn't question them any more from then. I just did everything that they asked. Even though I thought a lot of it was duplication, we just did it.

This delay in the ODPP's decision to proceed with the murder charge against Gabe provided the first indication that the case might not advance to a jury trial. As David claimed, the delay occurred because "they [the ODPP] were allotted to find something that they could charge him with ... If they felt so strongly, why didn't they just confirm the indictment and proceed? ... I think they were at a real loss [as] to what to do". This view was also supported by Gehringer, who explained that during the ODPP deliberations, a contact he had made within the office told him that:

> The people that were reviewing the brief of evidence, [their] camps were split. There was one camp that was saying, yes, we're looking at a manslaughter [charge] and there was another camp saying no, it's more than manslaughter, there's enough to take it to trial for murder.

Proceeding well over the deadline stipulated in its internal guidelines, and using close to the six-month legislative limit, the Queensland ODPP presented an indictment before the Brisbane Supreme Court on 28 November 2008, charging Gabe Watson with the murder of Tina Thomas. This moment was described by Gehringer as the "highest point" of the police investigation:

> I got a phone call from this fellow to say a decision's been made: we're going to indict him for murder. And my first question to him was, have you rung and told Tommy? To which he said he had. So that was the phone call that I just thought, we're there. It's happening. We've fought the battle ... That was all I ever wanted to do, personally from my own perspective, that's all I wanted to do. I just wanted to get it before a jury to let them see all the evidence and then just let the jury decide. And if the jury acquitted him, I was happy with that. If the jury found him guilty, I was happy with that. I just wanted to fight the fight ... We wanted to rather fight and lose than not fight at all ... So to me that was, that's probably been the highest point throughout the nine years, that phone call from [the] ODPP.

Flynn similarly expressed an emotionally charged and elated response to the news of Gabe's indictment for murder in Queensland, explaining that:

> I wanted the satisfaction of walking into a courtroom in Australia and sitting there and seeing justice take its course. That's what I wanted. So it was right after we got the call, the ODPP, they told us that they were going to take the case, because you have to understand, there was a six-month period there, it felt like it was six years, because we had moved [*clicks fingers*] so quick and gotten everything together and we got the indictment, and so much momentum like we had never had before.

But then, as Flynn described, "it just stopped. Everything just stopped. And it was the, don't call us, we'll call you ... We hit a big wall ... a big wall [called] the Queensland ODPP". This wall would perhaps prove to be the biggest obstacle preventing the attainment of procedural, subjective or substantive justice, of any of the obstacles and questions of justness that plagued the *Watson* case throughout its nearly nine-year duration.

CHAPTER THREE

"DEALING" WITH GABE

> I think more trials should be tried. That's where the problem is in Australia. The breakdown in your country is not the coronial, it's not the [defence] barristers, it's not the judges; it's the deals.
>
> \- Tina's mother, Cindy Thomas

On 5 June 2009, almost seven months after the Queensland Office of the Department of Public Prosecutions (ODPP) indicted him for murder, Gabe Watson pleaded guilty to manslaughter by criminal negligence in the Brisbane Supreme Court. Under s 303 of the *Criminal Code 1899* (Qld), manslaughter is defined as a person who "unlawfully kills another under such circumstances as not to constitute murder". To be charged with manslaughter by criminal negligence, the death must be caused by conduct that involves a negligent act, or an omission that breaches a duty outlined in the *Criminal Code 1899* (Qld). In other words, the accused person must have had a legal duty to act in a certain way, and in breaching that duty they caused the death of another person. The prosecution must also be able to prove that in breaching their duty, it was reasonably foreseeable to the accused person that death or serious harm might occur. The basis for this offence, as established in *R v Nydham*, is that the death occurred:

> Consciously and voluntarily, without any intention of causing death or grievous bodily harm, but in circumstances which involved such a great falling short of the standard of care which a reasonable person would have exercised and which involved such a high risk, that the death or grievous bodily harm would follow, that the doing of the act merited criminal punishment.[1]

In the *Watson* case, this negligence was evident in the act of Gabe breaching his statutory duties as Tina's "dive buddy". As stated in s 290 of the *Criminal Code 1899* (Qld):

---

[1] [1977] VR 430, 445.

> When a person undertakes to do any act, the omission to do which is or may be dangerous to human life or health, it is the person's duty to do that act: and the person is held to have caused any consequences which result to the life or health of any person by reason of any omission to perform that duty.

As outlined in the *Diver Manual* of the Professional Association of Diving Instructors, a diver owes a duty of care to their "dive buddy", such that they are held responsible for their partner's dive and safety. In relation to Tina's death, Gabe's guilty plea to this category of manslaughter meant that he breached his dive buddy duty by not maintaining at all times a distance between himself and Tina that could be closed within a couple of seconds, and given the existence of an emergency situation, Gabe also failed to assist Tina in removing her from any danger. Additionally, Gabe failed in his duty to never leave his dive buddy alone.

The requirement to prove that Gabe could reasonably have known the risk of harm to Tina when he negligently left her was fulfilled by his own admission in the second statement he gave to the police on 27 October 2003, whereby not only did he acknowledge being aware of the potential dangers of leaving Tina, but he also listed the various ways in which he could have attempted to save her, noting "how clear ... the thoughts were going through my head".[2] Consequently, as Gabe himself later identified in an interview in 2012 with the US ABC network's *20/20* program:

> It was failing to render aid, [a] breach of duty of care. Under their [Queensland] law, that's what I was guilty of. How could I not go in there and plead guilty to that when that's what I did? There was no way I could have been found not guilty [of the manslaughter charge].[3]

Although Gabe was originally charged with murder, he was able to plead guilty to manslaughter by criminal negligence as a result of a plea bargain agreement reached between himself and the Queensland ODPP. This agreement involved his murder charge being withdrawn and the preparation of a very favourable agreed summary of facts outlining the alleged circumstances surrounding Tina's death, from which the judge then sentenced Gabe. Some of our participants also noted that the deal

---

[2] Gabe Watson, witness statement, 27 October 2003.

[3] Gabe Watson, cited in Carol Robinson, "Interview: Gabe Watson Looks to Leave Shadow of his Wife's Honeymoon Death and His Murder Trial", on *Birmingham News* (Alabama) (3 March 2012) <http://blog.al.com/spotnews/2012 /03/interview_gabe_watson_looks_to.html>.

included a recommendation from the prosecution that any prison sentence imposed on Gabe be fully suspended after 18 months.

In Queensland, when a plea deal is made involving the withdrawal or amendment of a homicide-related charge, in addition to being supported by the crown prosecutor running the case, approval must also be obtained from the Director of the ODPP. In the only public statement ever made to explain their decision to enter into the plea agreement with Gabe, ODPP Director Anthony Moynihan SC described how the decision was made "after a careful and thorough examination of the admissible evidence ... [it] was not taken lightly".[4] Director Moynihan went on to state that "given the complex circumstantial nature of the case, Mr Watson's admission that he breached his duty to render assistance to his wife ultimately meant there was no reasonable prospect of proving, beyond a reasonable doubt, that he was guilty of murder".[5] Our analysis in the following two chapters, however, challenges several of the propositions outlined in this one and only statement offered by the ODPP, justifying the deal that was made with Gabe.

Plea Bargaining: What, When and Why?

After an individual has been charged and indicted for an offence(s) in Queensland, the prosecutors working within the ODPP maintain the discretionary powers to decide how best to proceed with the case. Guided by internal policy, a prosecutor must evaluate whether the sufficiency, quality and persuasive strength of the available evidence can justify a prosecution, and whether proceeding to trial or looking towards a settlement of the case is in the public's best interests.[6] Like justice itself, defining public interest is a difficult task. Within the Queensland ODPP's *Director's Policy*, competing definitions of public interest are provided: one focusing on the benefits of the trial and the other on the benefits of attaining a guilty plea. Under s 4, the policy states:

> The more serious the offence, the more likely that the public interest will require a prosecution. Indeed, the proper decision in most cases will be to proceed with the prosecution if there is sufficient evidence. Mitigating factors can then be put to the court at sentence.

---

[4] Director Anthony Moynihan, cited in Cosima Marriner, "DPP Defends Decision to Drop Bride Murder Charge", *Sydney Morning Herald* (New South Wales), 10 June 2009.

[5] Ibid.

[6] *Director's Policy* (Qld) s 4.

Somewhat in contrast to the above, s 16 of the policy dictates that "the public interest is in the conviction of the guilty. The most efficient conviction is a plea of guilty ... Early negotiations (within this guideline) are therefore encouraged". Prosecutors thus "face difficult challenges in reconciling their obligations to respect various rights with their obligations to pursue the public interest".[7] As noted by a former Attorney-General in the United Kingdom (UK), "there is no greater nonsense talked about ... than that suggestion that in all cases … the [prosecutor] ought to decide to prosecute merely because he [sic] thinks there is what the lawyers call a case".[8]

Accordingly, and as seen in the *Watson* case, rather than proceeding to trial, the prosecution can engage in the process of plea bargaining to resolve a case. Plea bargaining essentially refers to the discussions and agreements reached between the prosecutor(s) and defence lawyer(s) regarding an accused person's likely plea, and the possibility of negotiating the charge(s), case facts and/or the prosecution's sentencing submission. Depending on the jurisdiction, plea bargaining is also referred to as plea negotiations, charge bargaining and plea agreements.

There are multiple forms of plea bargaining; for example, the prosecutor may reduce the seriousness of the charge(s), or withdraw one or more charges in exchange for a guilty plea. As seen in *Watson*, this can involve reducing murder to manslaughter. Plea bargaining can also involve negotiating the agreed statement of facts based upon which the accused will be sentenced by the court, which can then have a significant effect on the sentence imposed. Regardless of its form, the primary aim of plea bargaining is to arrive at a mutually acceptable deal between the prosecutor and the defence, to which the accused pleads guilty. At the very minimum, plea bargaining is used to identify any issues not in dispute, thus reducing the length of subsequent hearings and limiting the likelihood of later delays—for example, through trial adjournments.

Across western criminal jurisdictions, increases in the number of matters commencing each year has unsurprisingly led to prosecutors facing heavier workloads, often without the necessary resources to pursue every case through to a contested trial. As a consequence, plea bargaining has taken on a more prominent and more significant role in the delivery of modern justice. However, in Queensland, like most comparable criminal justice systems, no external administrative data is kept which outlines

[7] Kent Roach, "The Attorney General and the Charter Revisited" (2000) 50 *Dalhousie Law Journal* 1, 28.

[8] Sir John Simon, cited in *House of Commons Debates*, Vol 88, Col 2105 (1 December 1925) 189.

when or why plea bargaining occurs, or how often discussions result in guilty pleas. It is therefore difficult to accurately determine how often plea bargaining is used to resolve a case. While no official data is kept, much research considers plea bargaining to be a frequently used process around the world; as Rebecca Krauss observes in the US context, "today, plea bargaining and prosecutorial discretion determine the outcome of the vast majority of criminal cases".[9] Similarly, in the Australian context, research from the past two decades firmly supports the contention that plea bargaining is used regularly across all court levels and for all types of offences.[10]

The regular occurrence of plea bargaining is further demonstrated by the internal guidance given to prosecutors within their respective offices, as well as externally by the courts and in legislative guidance, which encourages them to consider the possibility of engaging in plea bargaining in order to reduce the number of contested issues that proceed to trial. This is evidenced by an excerpt from s 16 of the Queensland *Director's Policy*, which states that as a response to the need for greater efficiency, "early negotiations" are to be "encouraged." As a result, prosecutors have become what Professor Stephanos Bibas refers to as "the key gatekeepers who ration criminal justice".[11]

Within Queensland specifically, the majority of criminal cases are resolved by pleas of guilty rather than running a jury trial. As the Honourable Martin Moynihan stated in his 2008 evaluation of the Queensland criminal and civil justice systems, "although the criminal trial is seen as the end point for the criminal justice system, in fact, in the order of 90 per cent of all criminal cases in all jurisdictions are resolved without

---

[9] Rebecca Krauss, "The Theory of Prosecutorial Discretion in Federal Law: Origins and Developments" (2009) 6 *Seton Hall Circuit Review* 1, 9.

[10] Asher Flynn, "Non-Transparent Justice and the Plea Bargaining Process in Victoria", in Marie Segrave (ed.), *Australian and New Zealand Critical Criminology Conference Proceedings 2009* (Australian and New Zealand Critical Criminology Network, 2009) 88; Asher Flynn, "Bargaining with Justice: Victims, Plea Bargaining and the *Victims' Charter Act 2006* (Vic)" (2012, forthcoming) *Monash University Law Review;* Arie Freiberg and Robert Seifman, "Plea Bargaining in Victoria: The Role of Counsel" (2001) 25 *Criminal Law Journal* 64; Rowena Johns, "Victims and Plea Bargaining: Victims of Crime—Plea Bargains, Compensation, Victim Impact Statements and Support Services Briefing Paper" (Briefing paper, Parliament of New South Wales, 2002) <http://www.parliament.nsw.gov.au/prod/parlment/publications.nsf/0/578C6F10C6D98565CA256ECF00083B4D>.

[11] Stephanos Bibas, "The Need for Prosecutorial Discretion" (2010) 19 *Temple Political and Civil Rights Law Review* 369.

a trial".[12] This claim is supported by statistics from Queensland's superior courts (including the court in which the *Watson* case was resolved), which show that in the 2006–07 financial year, 83 per cent (4,387 cases) of matters committed for trial were resolved by a guilty plea, with similar figures in 2007–08 (81.5 per cent, or 4,261 cases) and in 2008–09 (78 per cent, or 4,262 cases).[13] Significantly, during the period in which Gabe pleaded guilty, 73 per cent (3,938 cases) of matters finalised in Queensland's superior courts were the result of a guilty plea, leaving only 27 per cent of cases proceeding to a contested trial.[14] One of the primary explanations for this large number of guilty pleas is the increased use of plea bargaining, based on the assumption that plea bargains provide an incentive to accused persons to plead guilty. In their UK-based analysis, Professors John Baldwin and Mike McConville found that of the 122 accused persons who pleaded guilty, almost three-quarters claimed to have been motivated to do so after plea bargaining.[15] This finding is supported by Professor Mary Vogel, who claims that "negotiated guilty pleas now [account] for the majority of guilty pleas in America".[16]

In addition to offering a quick means of resolving a matter, another reason for the perceived increase in the use of plea bargaining is the potential benefits it offers to those directly involved in a case, particularly the accused, who receives some form of concession in exchange for their guilty plea, such as reducing the nature or number of charges proceeded with, and/or the sentence imposed. Victims may also benefit from plea bargaining, as the matter is determined quickly and without the ordeal of having to attend court or testify. Furthermore, an acknowledgement of guilt by the accused may facilitate the victim's emotional recovery.[17] Perhaps the main perceived benefit of plea bargaining for victims, and in turn the public, is that it offers a guaranteed conviction, which means that, to varying extents, the accused is held accountable for their criminal

---

[12] Honourable Martin Moynihan AO QC, *Review of the Civil and Criminal Justice System in Queensland* (Queensland Government, 2008) 58.

[13] Ibid, 32; Queensland Supreme Court, "Annual Report", *Supreme Court Website* (2009) <http://www.courts.qld.gov.au/_data/assets/pdf_file/0004/84775/sc-ar-2008-09.pdf> 22.

[14] Queensland Supreme Court, above n 13, 26.

[15] John Baldwin and Mike McConville, *Negotiated Justice: Pressures to Plead Guilty* (Martin Robertson, 1977) 224.

[16] Mary Vogel, "The Social Origins of Plea Bargaining: An Approach to the Empirical Study of Discretionary Leniency" (2008) 35 *Journal of Law and Society* 201, 202 .

[17] Lynn M Mather, *Plea Bargaining or Trial: The Process of Criminal Case Disposition* (Lexington Books, 1979).

actions. This view underpins the internal policy governing prosecutorial conduct at the Queensland ODPP,[18] and the findings of Professors Mike McConville and John Baldwin's UK analysis, that "it is in the public interest that those who are indeed guilty should admit their guilt".[19]

While plea bargaining potentially offers some benefits, because it falls under the discretionary powers of the prosecution, victims and the public more broadly are solely reliant upon those who engage in the process to ensure that any deals made uphold the same judicial principles—namely, consistency, accessibility, equality and fairness—that apply to the more transparent process of a contested trial. As a consequence, some doubts exist as to the legitimacy of plea bargaining as a method of case resolution, because plea deals can alter the seriousness of the conviction and sentence imposed on an accused, while removing the opportunity for the victim to testify or for the jury, representing the voice and moral standards of the community, to determine guilt. Plea bargaining also removes the requirement on the prosecution to prove its case to the required criminal standard. Instead, the key issue at play is factual guilt, "in the sense that the accused probably committed the criminal act".[20] On this basis, while the occurrence of Gabe's plea deal is not in itself unusual, there are several aspects inherent to the deal, including when and why this agreement was reached, and what impacts it had on perceptions of justice, which make the resolution of the case in Queensland in 2009 by a plea bargain particularly noteworthy.

Motivations Underpinning the *Watson* Deal: Money, Resources and Delay

Questions surrounding the legitimacy of plea bargaining largely arise in relation to the process of making a deal. That is, given its inherently private nature, when a deal is accepted, it is often unclear why this option was favoured above running a traditional jury trial, particularly given that justice systems are premised on being open and transparent to the public. When an accused person pleads guilty and the case resolves without the need for a contested trial, court backlogs, workloads and expenditure are reduced, and court clearance rates increase. Thus, in addition to having to

---

[18] *Director's Policy* (Qld) s 16.

[19] Mike McConville and John Baldwin, *Courts, Prosecution and Conviction* (Oxford University Press, 1981) 66.

[20] Kent Roach, "Four Models of the Criminal Process" (1999) 89 *Journal of Criminal Law and Criminology* 678.

uphold "public interests",[21] prosecutors face mounting pressures to obtain convictions in a timely manner, including using plea bargaining to acquire early guilty pleas, in order to obtain these associated benefits.[22] The consequences of this have been increased workload pressures among prosecutors and an (empirically perceived) rise in the use of plea bargaining aimed at facilitating and encouraging accused persons to make early pleading decisions. As Professor Mike McConville claims, plea bargaining is "defended as an essential weapon in … the quest for cost-effective criminal justice systems".[23] Indeed, the findings of a 2002 review into plea bargaining in the state of New South Wales (Australia) found that the process can offer annual savings in excess of $AUD15 million.[24] In Queensland, the importance of making decisions on prosecutions in light of efficiency considerations is outlined within s 4 of the *Director's Policy* (Qld), which states that "the scarce resources available for prosecution should be used to pursue, with appropriate vigour, cases worthy of prosecution and not wasted pursuing inappropriate cases".

Given the efficiency benefits that plea deals can offer, concerns exist as to whether this may unduly motivate a prosecutor's decision to engage in plea bargaining. As a prosecutor in an Australian study of plea bargaining explained:

> There is always pressure—too many cases, not enough resources, budgetary cuts from above. It sort of all comes down to, can we get through all these cases? And every now and again someone complains about the [court] backlog. There will always be that pressure, as well as the fact that if we can get a nice plea bargain, rather than run a ... trial, there is incentive just from a work viewpoint.[25]

A defence lawyer in the same study similarly acknowledged the resource pressures facing prosecutors to use plea bargaining at almost any cost, claiming that "there are advantages to the prosecution accepting

---

[21] *Director's Policy* (Qld) s 16.
[22] Ibid, s 4.
[23] Mike McConville, "Development of Empirical Research Techniques and Theory", in Mike McConville and Wing Hong Chui (eds), *Research Methods For Law* (Edinburgh University Press, 2007) 211.
[24] Gordon Samuels, *Samuels' Review of the New South Wales Director of Public Prosecutions' Policy and Guidelines For Charge Bargaining and Tendering Of Agreed Facts* (New South Wales Parliament, 2002).
[25] Asher Flynn, "'Fortunately We in Victoria Are Not in That UK Situation': Victorian and United Kingdom Legal Perspectives on Plea Bargaining Reform" (2011) 16 *Deakin Law Review* 361, 383.

something less than they should, because basically it cuts down their workload. So if you have prosecutors who are overworked, they may settle for something, just to clear their books".[26]

Court delays and inefficiency are significant problems that regularly confront prosecutors and criminal justice systems. They negatively affect every aspect of proceedings, and have harmful impacts on all parties in a case. Of most significance in the context of the *Watson* case, delays also negatively impact the quality of justice that is available. As a former Director of the Victorian Office of Public Prosecutions explained:

> How often have we stopped to consider what delay in justice really means in human terms? What delay means to victims, to witnesses, to accused persons, to police investigators, to judges, to the community? Can any of us who have not been either a victim of crime or accused of committing a crime conceive of the stress associated with waiting for a matter to be concluded? Lives are interrupted and put on hold. Family life is disrupted. Jobs are sacrificed. Freedom is curtailed. And when the matter finally meanders its way into court, the quality of the evidence led is adversely affected. Who benefits from this? No one—and it is certainly not justice.[27]

During the period in which the *Watson* case (2003–09) was handled and resolved in Queensland, the extent of court delays and the lack of available resources within the Queensland Supreme Courts and the ODPP were immense, and were compounded by the fact that the Queensland ODPP received lower levels of funding than its state counterparts.[28] In Australia, there are three primary indicators used to assess the effectiveness and efficiency levels of the courts: the backlog indicator, the clearance indicator and the final costs indicator. In relation to the backlog indicator, for Supreme Courts, an efficient court requires that no more than ten per cent of cases be pending completion for more than 12 months, and that no cases be pending for more than 24 months.[29] Yet in the Queensland Supreme Courts, the most recent data available prior to Gabe's plea deal

---

[26] Ibid.

[27] Jeremy Rapke QC, "25th Anniversary Speech Delivered by the Director of Public Prosecutions" (Speech delivered at *Victorian Office of Public Prosecutions 25th Anniversary Presentation,* Victoria, Australia, 27 October 2008) <http://www.opp.vic.gov.au/wps/wcm/connect/Office+Of+Public+Prosecutions/resources/file/eb493844164f1f3/25th_Anniversary_Speech_delivered_by_DPP-2727Oct08.pdf> 4-5.

[28] Tony Koch, "Queensland DPP Overworked and Underpaid", *The Australian* (Australia), 17 May 2008.

[29] Steering Committee, Australian Federal Government, *Report on Government Services* (2009) <http://www.pc.gov.au/gsp/rogs/2009> 27.

revealed that at June 2008, 18.8 per cent of cases remained pending for over 12 months and 7.8 per cent were pending for more than two years.[30] Significantly, at this time, Queensland's Supreme Courts had the highest number of cases pending for longer than two years nationally, by almost two per cent. At 30 June 2009, Queensland's Supreme Courts retained the highest pending caseload of all Australian superior courts, with 430 cases pending—12.6 per cent of these for over 12 months and 4.4 per cent for over two years.[31] Thus, at the time when Gabe's murder trial was to be heard the court that was listed to hear it was failing to adhere to the national standard measures of efficiency and effectiveness in relation to pending caseloads.

The second indicator of an efficient and effective court is the clearance indicator.[32] A result of 100 per cent or above indicates an efficient and effective court. Between June 2008 and June 2009, the Queensland Supreme Court's clearance rate dropped from 103 per cent to 99.6 per cent, while there was only a 2.5 per cent (38 cases) increase in the number of cases initiated.[33] As a result, the court that was listed to hear Gabe's murder trial reported the third-lowest clearance rate nationally—falling well below the 165.5 per cent clearance rate of the nation's leader—and was failing to meet the second national standard measure of court efficiency.[34]

The final indicator of court efficiency and effectiveness is the cost per finalisation indicator.[35] In the 2008–09 period, Queensland had the lowest

---

[30] Ibid.

[31] Steering Committee, Australian Federal Government, *Report on Government Services* (2010) <http://www.pc.gov.au/gsp/rogs/2010> 28.

[32] The clearance indicator is measured by dividing the number of finalisations in the reporting period by the number of lodgements. The result is then multiplied by 100 to provide a percentage. A result of 100 per cent indicates that the court finalised as many cases as were lodged; a result of greater than 100 per cent indicates that the court finalised more cases than were lodged; while a result of less than 100 per cent indicates that the court finalised fewer cases than were lodged, and thus that the pending caseload will have increased. See, Steering Committee, above n 29, 37.

[33] Queensland Supreme Court, above n 13, 28

[34] Steering Committee, above n 29, 38.

[35] This indicator measures the court's achievement against the objective of providing court administration services in an efficient manner. Cost is taken as the total net recurrent annual expenditure (excluding payroll tax), which includes income that is derived from court fees and other revenue, but excludes revenue from fines. The cost per finalisation indicator is measured by dividing the total net

cost per finalisation of all Australian states and territories, having approximately $8,000 less to spend on each case than its other state counterparts.[36] What this data reveals is that at the time when a decision was being made on how to proceed with the *Watson* case and what would best serve the interests of the Queensland community, the Queensland Supreme Court was failing to meet the basic national standards on all three of the effective and efficient court indicators. This therefore highlights the complex climate prevalent at the time, which may well have motivated the prosecution's decision to avoid running what would have been an expensive, and resource-intensive, transnational murder trial.

The pressures on the Queensland prosecutors to respond to this level of inefficiency were augmented by the limited resources available to them directly, evident in the Queensland ODPP reporting a $264,751 deficit in the 2008–09 financial year—the year in which the *Watson* case was settled. Furthermore, a confidential report released in May 2008 described the precarious financial situation at the ODPP, labelling it as under-resourced and the prosecutors as "overworked and underpaid".[37] The report (Davey Report) was conducted by Paul Davey, at the request of then Queensland Attorney-General Kerry Shine. It revealed that the ODPP received less than one-third of the annual funding of Legal Aid Queensland, and that on average, individual prosecutors handled 79 matters annually, as opposed to the average of 27 handled by their other state counterparts. In addition, the report estimated that each Queensland matter received resources equivalent to approximately $5,500, in contrast to the much higher national average of $16,000 spent per matter.

This lack of resources, particularly in comparison to other states, may also go some way towards explaining why the Queensland ODPP has a history of withdrawing the highest number of prosecutions in Australia. In the 2006–07 financial year, a comparison of withdrawn cases across the superior courts of four Australian state jurisdictions—Western Australia, New South Wales, Victoria and Queensland—showed that Queensland had the highest number of matters withdrawn, at 17.3 per cent (1,010 cases), compared with 6.5 per cent (204 cases) in New South Wales, 3.9 per cent (89 cases) in Victoria, and 15.8 per cent (286) in Western

---

recurrent expenditure within each court for the financial year by the total number of finalisations for the same period. See Steering Committee, above n 29, 41.

[36] Steering Committee, above n 29, 42.

[37] Koch, above n 28.

Australia.[38] Similarly, between June 2007 and June 2008, the prosecution withdrew all charges in 18 per cent (1,108) of all cases (a total of 6,070) in Queensland's superior courts, with 41 per cent of these cases pending for over two years before the decision to withdraw was made.[39]

The Davey Report recommended that to address the ODPP resource issues, at least 49 new prosecutors were needed in Queensland, and that the ODPP required an additional $5.9 million funding each year from 2010 to 2012, with approximately $23.6 million being spent on the ODPP over four years. In making this recommendation, the Davey Report highlighted the existing strains on Queensland prosecutors to prepare and resource cases, and the potential pressures they consequently faced to promptly resolve matters, possibly to the extent that resource limitations might be prioritised above the interests of justice. As the Honourable Martin Moynihan stated in his evaluation of the Queensland criminal and civil justice systems in the year prior to Gabe's deal being made, "put shortly, there is a trade-off between ... a [guilty plea] resolution ... and saving [the] cost of a trial".[40]

Given that the *Watson* plea deal was made within this resource-starved climate, concerns emerge as to whether Gabe's plea deal was made to save resources or to provide a just outcome that accurately reflected his level of culpability in causing Tina's death. This is particularly concerning given the underfunding of the ODPP and the likely costs that the *Watson* trial would have incurred, as indicated by the expenses of running the 24-day coronial inquest. As Glasgow explained:

> Whilst my inquiry might have cost several hundred thousand dollars, theirs [the trial] would have been a million or more because they'd have to bring the people ... When we go to a trial, the evidence that is produced has got to be first-hand ... So all those people have got to be brought to Australia ... Consider the cost of that?

In light of Glasgow's comments and the resource-stricken climate, questions arise around whether Gabe's plea deal can be considered procedurally or substantively just, in terms of both the process through which it was attained and its outcome.

The concern that Gabe's plea deal was motivated by a lack of resources as opposed to being a reflection of what had occurred was a

---

[38] Australian Bureau of Statistics, *Criminal Courts 2007–08* (2009) <ausstats.abs.gov.au/ausstats/subscriber.nsf/0/2EBE862732FDD915CA257567001 6BDE7/$File/45130_2007-08.pdf> 21.

[39] Ibid, 31.

[40] Moynihan, above n 12, 58.

prominent view expressed by many of the participants in our research. As Glasgow explained:

> I think the DPP was delighted when the offer came up because it saved them probably a couple of million dollars and it goes back to underfunding. I think the DPP, you can read his report, is underfunded ... [And] here's a man who will cop 18 months in jail or 12 months in jail for something he's done. There's still a possibility or a probability we won't convict him. We'll spend $1.5 million or whatever it is on a trial ... but it seems logical that that's the way it was done.

The potential for motivations based on concerns around efficiency to have informed the ODPP's decision to engage in plea bargaining, as opposed to running a time-consuming, expensive murder trial, was similarly identified by the police and the Thomas family. As Tina's father, Tommy Thomas, explained:

> My primary belief that the plea deal happened, was that it was all about money. You know, I knew that an extradition process, especially if it wound up being a lengthy one that he was fighting, it could have been very expensive. I knew that a criminal trial over there [Queensland] … was going to be very expensive, especially when you consider that most of the witnesses were from the US, and other parts of the world, Korea and whatever, and they might have brought them all ... So you're looking at a potential for a million dollar or a two million dollar criminal trial. And my belief was that they cut a plea deal with him. No extradition process to worry about, no trial to worry about, we've saved a couple of million dollars, we can use that for something else ... You can be as outraged as you want to. If we save two million bucks, we save two million bucks.

In a similar vein, Detective Senior Constable Kevin Gehringer believed that the ODPP's decision was influenced by the need to "save money":

> The only thing I can get back to is, well, it would have been easier to take a manslaughter plea because you don't have to go through [a trial] and I knew, I'd set up the [coronial] inquest so I knew the logistics and had an idea of the costs of everything that goes on to do it, and obviously doing that for a trial is going to be even more because they wouldn't probably accept the video link-ups. They would have wanted everyone there in person.

A similar view was expressed by Lieutenant Brad Flynn, who believed that the deal with Gabe was made for reasons of "ease and cost".

Of the comments expressed by our participants, perhaps the most disturbing was that of Coroner Glasgow, who suggested that even at the point of indicting Gabe for murder in June 2008, he believed that the ODPP would be unlikely to take the case to trial due to a lack of available resources. He explained:

> I was pretty sure they'd get it knocked out of the DPP office because of costs ... that's something that really is an indictment on the sort of thing we're talking about, of underfunding of the DPP ... Even once it went through the [coronial] process and then all the filing with the DPP, I thought that probably the DPP wouldn't prosecute him ... because of costs.

The fact that the coroner involved in the case believed resources to be a key reason for the matter not proceeding to trial highlights the extent of the resource constraints facing the ODPP when the *Watson* deal was made. Further to this, it raises significant questions around the capacity of the ODPP to provide justice not only in the *Watson* case, but also in other cases finalised during this period. Accordingly, Glasgow's comments raise the possibility that at the time when the *Watson* deal was made, the department responsible for upholding public interests and prosecuting individuals for committing criminal acts was making decisions in a resource-starved, efficiency-driven and pressurised environment, where the sparing of resources was prioritised without consideration for the need to ensure procedural justice.

One of the interesting issues that was raised by several US participants in our discussions related to the additional funding that the Queensland ODPP was given by the state government in the period following the coronial inquest, to counter some of the ODPP's resource problems. Indeed, several participants believed that this funding was specifically provided by the government to enable the ODPP to try, among others, the *Watson* case. As Tommy explained:

> What pissed me off about it [the deal] was that it happened right after a time … when the Queensland Government had come out ... and gave the DPP a much larger budget because of two cases and they named both the cases: one of them was [Jayant] *Patel*, and the other one was ours. So I thought, well they've got the money to prosecute this case.

Flynn was also aware of the existence of this additional funding, stating that "in that year prior, the DPP had been appropriated X amount of more money specifically to prosecute this case. It was there". As correctly identified by Tommy and Flynn, in July 2008, just two months after the Davey Report was released and while the ODPP was in the process of deciding how to proceed with Gabe's indictment, then Premier of Queensland Anna Bligh announced that the ODPP was to receive an extra

$8 million (23 per cent) funding to "allow the ODPP to employ the additional resources it needs to meet this growing demand [of cases]".[41] As Bligh noted:

> There are a couple of high profile and complex cases that are above and beyond the normal workload of the DPP ... [and] the new DPP has identified the need for a one-off allocation in this financial year to ensure that those cases are managed as effectively as they can without compromising the other work of the DPP.[42]

The "high profile and complex cases" to which (then) Premier Bligh referred were cited in various media reports as including three specific cases. The first was known as the "Doctor Death" case. This involved a former surgeon from the Bundaberg Base Hospital in Northern Queensland, Jayant Patel, who was charged with three counts of manslaughter and one count of grievous bodily harm. Patel's trial began in March 2010 and ran for 58 days. He was found guilty of all charges. In August 2012, however, the Australian High Court overturned Patel's conviction on the grounds that the trial constituted a miscarriage of justice. This decision was made primarily because the Queensland ODPP erred in its presentation of the case against Patel, whereby it changed its approach to the prosecution 43 days into the 58-day trial, ultimately rendering a large portion of the evidence that had been submitted for jury consideration either irrelevant or inadmissible.[43] On 30 August 2012, ODPP Director Anthony Moynihan SC announced that in order to uphold "public interests",[44] the ODPP would re-try Patel on the manslaughter and grievous bodily harm charges, but that the charges would be tried separately, meaning up to four trials could be held—the first was scheduled for February 2013.

The second of the high profile and complex cases involved corruption charges against former Queensland Government minister Gordon Nuttall. Interestingly, in this matter the Queensland ODPP proceeded with not one, but two trials. The first trial began on 29 June 2009, at which Nuttall was

---

[41] Former Premier Anna Bligh, cited in Malcolm Weatherup, "Government Delivers Unexpected Budget Adjustment for Office", *Townsville Bulletin* (Queensland), 22 July 2008.

[42] (Former) Premier Anna Bligh, cited in Gabrielle Dunlevy, "Queensland's ODPP Gets $8 Million Boost", *Sydney Morning Herald* (New South Wales), 21 July 2008.

[43] *Patel v The Queen* [2012] HCA 29 24 August 2012 at 256.

[44] Director Anthony Moynihan, cited in Cameron Atfield and Amy Remekis, "Patel Case Returns to Court", *Brisbane Times* (Queensland), 31 August 2012.

found guilty of 36 counts of corruption. The second trial commenced in October 2010, and after 16 days, Nuttall was found guilty of five counts of perjury and five counts of corruption.

The third of the high profile and complex cases was the murder trial of Gabe Watson. Thus, as Tina's mother, Cindy Thomas, claimed, "even the state gave them the money for the trial ... Where's that money gone now? ... What did they do with that money?" Without confirmation from the ODPP, it is not clear how this funding was spent, yet we can assume it was prioritised for those cases that might have been viewed as "more important" from the Queensland ODPP's perspective. Thus, while we can only presume that the money was spent running a 58-day flawed prosecution attempt against Patel, and two trials against Nuttall, it is clear that the money was not spent running the murder trial of Gabe Watson.

Beyond resource and efficiency concerns, another confusing aspect of the ODPP's decision to accept a manslaughter plea in this case involves the actions of the crown prosecutor running the case in Queensland, Assistant Director of Public Prosecutions Brendan Campbell SC, which appear to significantly contradict ODPP Director Anthony Moynihan's public statement that the case was "circumstantial" and that "there was no reasonable prospect of proving, beyond a reasonable doubt, that he [Gabe] was guilty of murder".[45] In November 2008, when Gabe was indicted for murder, Brendan Campbell phoned Tommy to advise him of the decision to proceed with a murder charge, and in doing so, stressed to him that the case would proceed to trial. As Tommy reflected:

> Brendan Campbell with the ODPP called me up and [was] telling me that they had indicted Gabe for murder—this was in November [2008] after he'd been charged [by the Coroner] in June—and I had asked him that night if there was anything that would get in the way of us now seeing him tried before a jury, and as we know now, he lied to me and said no, you're going to get your day in court and you'll see a trial before a jury. My understanding was when we got off the phone in November and he had told me that he had indicted Gabe, that there would be a trial.

Less than two months after this phone call, on 27 January 2009, well before any deals or discussion had allegedly occurred between Gabe and the ODPP, Detective Senior Sergeant Gary Campbell and Detective Senior Constable Kevin Gehringer were asked to attend a video conference with several people from the ODPP and Queensland Police Service (QPS), including Brendan Campbell, ODPP Director Anthony Moynihan and the QPS Deputy Commissioner, Ian Stewart. Gehringer explained that it was

[45] Director Anthony Moynihan, cited in Marriner, above n 4.

at this meeting that he first heard of the possibility of a plea deal involving a manslaughter charge. While the timing of this meeting will be examined in more detail in the next chapter, from a behavioural standpoint, what is interesting is that around the same time—that is, late January 2009—Brendan Campbell contacted Alabama Assistant Attorney-General, Don Valeska (the lead prosecutor in the 2012 capital murder trial), to advise him of the strength of the Queensland prosecution's murder case against Gabe. As Valeska described:

> I wasn't very complimentary of the ODPP prosecutors and there are several reasons … [One] is that they called me, unsolicited and said we've got a strong case. We're going to go forward with this and we're going to win. So I said, great ... They're telling me that we have a strong murder case and we're going to win it and I'm saying, makes sense to me ... Of course you're going to take them at their word … [but] it's very puzzling. Why would they come and tell me that? ... Don't tell [me] that there'll be no plea bargain, when obviously they knew there was, because they're the ones that had to be involved or start it.

It is unclear what Brendan Campbell's intentions were in highlighting the strength of the case against Gabe and the likelihood of it proceeding to trial to both Tommy and Valeska, particularly given that when he spoke to Valeska, a plea bargain involving manslaughter had already been identified as a potential alternative. Such actions either indicate a complete disregard for Tommy and Valeska, or that at this stage Brendan Campbell did in fact believe that there was a sufficient basis to proceed to trial. Either way, this behaviour does not fit with the decision to accept a guilty plea to manslaughter on the basis that the evidence was not strong enough to support a murder conviction at trial. As Flynn astutely stated:

> The phone call out of the blue [to Valeska] from Brendan Campbell, just to let Don know that they had a really strong case … That just stuck in my brain, because again it just doesn't wash. If Brendan Campbell's calling Don Valeska just for an FYI [for your information] call, to say hey, we've got a really strong case. How do we go from that to such a hasty manslaughter plea?

Manslaughter: The Alternative Verdict

Another confusing aspect of the decision to accept Gabe's guilty plea to manslaughter relates to the statutory alternatives that operate when a jury trial is run. In Queensland, at the conclusion of a murder trial, the jury can return the alternative verdict of manslaughter, even if the accused was not specifically charged with the offence of manslaughter at the outset. This option is governed by s 576 of the *Criminal Code 1899*(Qld), which states that "upon an indictment against a person containing a count of the crime of murder, the person may be convicted on that count or the crime of manslaughter, if that crime is established by the evidence". Thus, a manslaughter verdict is always an alternative outcome for a jury at a murder trial. This was a significant issue identified by Gehringer, who explained that he had raised this option with the ODPP at the January 2009 meeting, when the possibility of a manslaughter plea deal was first revealed to him. He explained:

> What was frustrating for me is that in our court system, manslaughter is a natural alternative, and that was one of the things I raised with [Director] Moynihan in that video link-up and I said ... we've indicted him for murder. Why can't we run with that? Because if at the end of the day, at the end of the trial, if the jury isn't satisfied that there's [a] sufficient [basis] for murder, there's a natural alternative for them to come back with a verdict of manslaughter. There doesn't have to be another indictment presented, it's just a natural alternative. And I can't phrase it the way Moynihan did, because he used prosecutor speak, but he was somehow trying to tell me that you can't go into it with that intention. You can't go into trial with the intention that you think you can win it, but if we don't, well it's all good because we've got manslaughter as a back-up. It was essentially, we have to go in there knowing 100 per cent that we're going to win it. And then if it's a case of knowing that we can't win it 100 per cent, well then there's that alternative for manslaughter [by plea bargain]. And I couldn't understand it, but obviously I've got the Deputy Commissioner, [Director] Moynihan and you know there was at least six or seven of them on that video link-up, and like I said, the only people at this end were Gary and I. But that was just, I've never been able to understand that reasoning, because it just didn't make sense to me why.

In a similar vein, Valeska, Flynn and Gehringer questioned why the Queensland prosecutors would "bother" going through the almost six-month indictment process, to then accept a deal that would amount to Gabe being criminally negligent and receiving only a 12–18 month prison term. As Valeska commented:

> Why would the Australian prosecutors be satisfied with a year? It's like, if that's all you wanted, why didn't you just drop it? Or why not just go for it? I mean, you really can't do much worse than a year. Just try the case. If the jury in Australia says not guilty, I'd say well, we tried it; but to pick a year. What's the point? If you thought that little of it, maybe you should have dismissed the case to start with. If they were just going to take a year, why not just drop it, or why not just try it to the jury ... There are a lot of

cases, especially in America, that need to be tried to a jury whichever way it goes. We thought that would be the case in Australia when they had the case, it was like, what possible reason wouldn't you do it, because you're going to get a defendant to answer in front of the jury ... And therefore, our view was why didn't they just do it?

Flynn also expressed his confusion over this aspect of the decision:

Well if it's not that winnable, why did it take you six months to figure that out? I mean your job is to—that should have been the least difficult decision you had to make in looking at the brief, looking at everything that we've done, looking at everything that happened in the inquest, to go yep, either it will fly or it won't fly. That's your only decision and you made the decision to go with it. And now, a few months later, you're back-tracking on that decision ... It doesn't make sense.

A similar point was made by Gehringer, who questioned why the ODPP spent so long assessing the case, and proceeding with a murder charge, to then accept a plea to negligent manslaughter:

It just didn't make sense that they'd spent six months to decide whether they wanted to indict him. They didn't give me a few requisitions to do, they gave me a shitload of requisitions to do … And I just, why? Why go to all that trouble? Why look at it so much, scrutinise it so minutely to say yes and to then ... well maybe there's a window there that manslaughter might somehow come into the equation … It went from we've got a strong case for murder, to all of a sudden there's a manslaughter [plea].

From the ODPP's perspective, one of the potential reasons for not proceeding with a murder trial, despite the natural alternative manslaughter option and taking almost six months to decide whether to proceed with a murder charge originally, may have been that after a thorough review of the case, it was perceived that it undermined the golden thread rule established in *Woolmington v DPP*.[46] In the *Woolmington* case, the House of Lords established the burden of proof and the importance of the prosecution only proceeding in cases where it can prove the case beyond reasonable doubt. As Viscount Sankey stated:

Throughout the web of the English Criminal Law, one golden thread is always to be seen, that it is the duty of the prosecution to prove the prisoner's guilt ... If, at the end of and on the whole of the case, there is a reasonable doubt created by the evidence given by either the prosecution or the prisoner ... the prosecution has not made out the case and the prisoner

[46] [1935] AC 462.

> is entitled to an acquittal. No matter what the charge or where the trial, the principle that the prosecution must prove the guilt of the prisoner is part of the common law of England and no attempt to whittle it down can be entertained.[47]

In our discussion, Glasgow identified the golden thread argument as a possible justification for the ODPP's decision:

> There's an authority in Queensland on circumstantial evidence at a trial and they use the phrase the golden thread. Basically what happens, if you're going to convict someone on a circumstantial trial, you link together every piece of evidence and you know how gold can stretch as long as it is, it also can break very easily, so they call it a golden thread. If there's a break anywhere, you give the benefit of the doubt to the defendant. That's the simplistic way of explaining it ... So basically, everything on circumstantial falls for the defendant. If he can pull anything apart and clearly I think the phrase is, if there is an alternative explanation which has credibility, you give him [sic] the benefit of the doubt.

In light of the golden thread authority and Gabe's acquittal in Alabama, it could be proposed that Brendan Campbell and the ODPP's decision to enter into a plea deal was justified on the basis of the evidence not being sufficient. As Glasgow maintained, "at least they [Queensland] got him for something". This suggestion was implicit in the comments made by (then) Queensland Premier Anna Bligh shortly after Judge Tommy Nail's acquittal decision in February 2012, when she claimed:

> Here in Queensland we made every effort to ensure that justice was done ... A court and a judge there [Alabama] have made a decision and it is not something over which we have influence ... The person was found guilty in Queensland of manslaughter and put in jail ... We made every effort to make sure that justice was done [here].[48]

However, as will be discussed in Chapter Nine, in explaining his decision to acquit, Judge Tommy Nail identified the lack of proof of a definitive financial motivation by the prosecution as a prominent issue informing his decision, stating that "any evidence to support a financial motivation is sorely lacking".[49] This motivation, as will be discussed in Chapter Six, was not something that the prosecutors would have had to

---

[47] Ibid, at 482.

[48] (Former) Premier Anna Bligh, cited in *The Australian*, "Queensland Did Its Best to Ensure Justice was Done over Gabe Watson, Said Bligh", *The Australian* (Australia), 24 February 2012.

[49] Judge Tommy Nail, court observations, 23 February 2012.

prove in order for Gabe to have been found guilty of murder in Queensland. The financial motivation was only required in Alabama, because in order to have legal jurisdiction to try the case, they had to prove that Gabe had planned the crime in their state. Additionally, even in his acquittal statement, Judge Nail raised some concerns surrounding Gabe's actions in the water, noting that he was "not sure what happened in the waters down there".[50] As will be explored in Chapters Five and Seven, financial constraints limited the number of Australian witnesses who could be flown to Alabama to testify in the trial, which in turn impacted on the strength of the evidence presented and what could be deemed admissible in relation to the fatal dive and establishing what happened underwater. Most, if not all, of these participants would have been able to testify in Australia. In light of such, the acquittal in Alabama does not prove that the Queensland ODPP made the right decision; if anything, it fuels questions as to what could have been, had a murder trial been run in Queensland in 2009.

The *Watson* Deal: The Impacts on Gabe

Moving beyond questions surrounding the motivations underpinning the plea deal, the nature of the outcome of the case also raised questions of justice – procedurally and substantively. Indeed, one of the recurring comments to emerge in our discussions with those involved in the *Watson* case, and which also featured in much social and media commentary, related to Gabe's continual claims of innocence. Specifically, questions have been asked as to why Gabe would have pleaded guilty to manslaughter by criminal negligence in Australia, if he was indeed innocent and had no criminal involvement in Tina's death. As Cindy claimed:

> If they're innocent, they're not going to make a deal ... I mean innocent people do not plead guilty to any deal or anything if they're totally 100 per cent innocent. And innocent people also want it to go to a jury; they want the jury to have all of the evidence, because they want to be found innocent, so they can walk out of that courtroom an innocent person. He did not walk out of that [Australian] courtroom innocent.

A similar view was expressed by Flynn, who asked:

> If Gabe was as steadfastly innocent as he proclaimed himself to be, why in the world do you accept a plea bargain? If that case was that weak, why don't you show up and plead your case ... Okay, you've got a case against

[50] Ibid.

> me? Prove it. That's what I would have done, because if I was innocent, I'm not taking a plea deal to anything ... If I stand behind everything that I've done, every statement that I've given, you bring it and you take your best shot at me. Now that's just me, but if you want to believe Gabe's attorneys and believe that he's as innocent as he says he is, why don't you show up and fight a case that the [Queensland] ODPP is admitting, well it's not strong, we can't get a conviction?

Implicit in Flynn's and Cindy's comments is a traditional view often held that an innocent person will never plead guilty to an offence and that they will always contest their innocence by going to trial. This view is evident in the comments of a prosecutor quoted in an Australian analysis of the pressures accused persons face to plead guilty, who claimed, "an innocent accused is never going to plead guilty. I think the pressure probably is on them and that is there to get them to plead ... but if you are an accused and you are totally innocent, you are never going to plead whether you get a [sentence] discount or not".[51] As alluded to in this prosecutor's comments, however, the traditional perspective that an innocent person will always proceed to trial can be challenged in light of the concessions that are offered to an accused in plea bargaining, which in addition to the financial and emotional pressures inherent to a trial may compel even an innocent accused to plead guilty. As Professors Mike McConville and Chester Mirsky maintain, the plea bargaining process "transforms criminal justice from one which seeks to determine whether the state has reliably sustained its burden of proof to another which seeks to determine whether the defendant, irrespective of guilt or innocence, is able to resist the pressure to plead guilty".[52] In highlighting the potential dangers of this process, legal analyst Duncan Watson (no relation to Gabe) further argues that "the danger is that [plea bargaining] ... will lead to excessive or otherwise improper pressure being applied to the defendant, resulting in an unacceptable risk of the innocent pleading guilty".[53]

In Gabe's situation, there are two significant reasons why he can continue to maintain his innocence in relation to Tina's death despite having pleaded guilty to a form of manslaughter in Queensland. The first relates to the definition of the offence to which he pleaded guilty and the contents of the agreed summary of facts presented to the court as part of

---

[51] Asher Flynn, above n 25, 369.
[52] Mike McConville and Chester L Mirsky, *Jury Trials and Plea Bargaining: A True History* (Hart Publishing, 2005) vi.
[53] Duncan Watson, "The Attorney General's Guidelines on Plea Bargaining in Serious Fraud: Obtaining Guilty Pleas Fairly?" (2010) 74(1) *Journal of Criminal Law* 77, 79.

the plea bargain, which served to significantly reduce his level of criminal culpability. The second is due to the financial, emotional and practical pressures that he faced, which may have unduly influenced his decision to plead guilty, particularly in light of the mandatory penalty of life imprisonment applied to those found guilty of murder in Queensland.[54]

Pressures arise from a multitude of factors when an accused engages in plea bargaining. Pressure is generated from the charging concessions that are made to facilitate a plea deal, particularly if it involves a significant change, as was the case with Gabe who had a murder charge withdrawn in exchange for his guilty plea to manslaughter by criminal negligence. The general financial burdens imposed by a trial also create pressure on an accused. This factor was identified by Gabe's US defence attorney, Brett Bloomston, as a significant factor in Gabe's pleading decision in Queensland, given the anticipated length of the trial process, and the amount of money he had already spent procuring legal representation at the coronial inquest. As Bloomston explained, "I found him his lawyers in Australia, and those guys charged him almost a half a million dollars US, [just] for a coronial inquest". Glasgow also identified the financial costs of the coronial inquest as being significant for Gabe, claiming that:

> When [Steve] Zillman turned up I knew things were serious. You don't get a senior counsel at a coronial inquest which is going to go for a month. The thousands of pages of material that were there and all that he had to read, so if you worked out approximately, he's got to spend two or three weeks reading the stuff ... He spent all the days of the inquest, I can't remember now how many there were, his fee has got to be four or five grand a day, then he had to do the submissions in the end ... There's hundreds of thousands of Australian dollars involved in that.

In light of the cost of his legal representation at the coronial inquest, and the anticipated financial costs of the Queensland trial—which would have included having to cover legal representation throughout any period of delay—electing to challenge the murder charge in court may have appeared particularly onerous to Gabe, when contrasted with the potential benefits of pleading guilty to the manslaughter offence, as offered by the ODPP.

Further to financial pressures, pleading-related pressures can also arise from delays, of which there have been many throughout the legal handling of the *Watson* case. When the criminal justice process is prolonged, the trauma and stress of a trial is often exacerbated for all involved, including an accused. As the (former) Chief Magistrate in the state of Victoria

---

[54] *Criminal Code 1899* (Qld), s 305.

(Australia), Ian Gray, proclaimed, "delays produce a lack of confidence and produce frustration. The greatest eroder in the confidence of courts is delays, not perceived inadequate sentencing, but waiting, waiting, waiting".[55] The capacity for delay, or the threat of delay, to put pressure on an accused to plead guilty is further demonstrated by the comments of a defence lawyer quoted in an analysis of the operation of plea bargaining in the state of Victoria (Australia), who claimed that:

> There is a pressure created from the situation of delay. It is not individuals placing pressure on defendants to plead guilty, it is the pressure of the system of delay and everyone wanting to get through it that puts pressure on them to plead, especially if they are being held [in remand].[56]

The possibility that this form of pressure influenced Gabe's 2009 pleading decision was implicit in comments made by his family and civil attorney, Bob Austin, who claimed:

> Had he [Gabe] gone to trial, we don't know how long it would have taken for him to go to trial, so he could have been over there two or three years, and still possibly have to serve a sentence of some sort ... Based on what the prosecution presented ... [he went] for a guilty plea.

This pressure was also identified by Gabe in his interview with the Australian Nine Network's *60 Minutes* program, subsequent to his acquittal in Alabama, during which he stated that "to fight the whole thing [in Queensland], I could have been held on remand for two, three, four, five years. [Then there was] the amount of money that it would have cost for a trial".[57] This explanation offers just a glimpse into the thought processes that an accused faces in weighing the benefits of a plea bargain against the risks of a contested trial, and contributes to an understanding of why Gabe may have pleaded guilty, while simultaneously maintaining his innocence.

The pressures confronting Gabe may also have been exacerbated given that he was facing a prolonged criminal trial in a foreign country. Indeed, the negative impact of the delays experienced by Gabe were acknowledged in the judicial remarks of the Queensland Justices involved in his initial and appeal sentencing hearings. As Justice Lyons remarked in

---

[55] Chief Magistrate (Victoria) Ian Gray, "Shades of Gray" (2012) 86 *Law Institute Journal* 18.

[56] Asher Flynn, "Victoria's Legal Aid Funding Structure: Hindering the Ideals Inherent to the Pre-Trial Process" (2010) 34 *Criminal Law Journal* 48, 61.

[57] Nine Network Australia, "Deep Trouble" on *60 Minutes* (23 March 2012) (Gabe Watson) <http://sixtyminutes.ninemsn.com.au/stories/8440110/deep-trouble>.

June 2009, when sentencing Gabe to four and a half years imprisonment, fully suspended after 12 months:

> I have referred to the delay in the prosecution of the case against you. It is plainly considerable delay ... You have carried the burden of these events for a substantial period ... I accept that for you, in Australia, time in prison will be harder than it will be for people who serve a sentence of imprisonment in their own country.[58]

Similarly, in the appeal hearing, in which the suspension period of Gabe's sentence was increased to 18 months, two of the three Justices acknowledged that the delays in the case had negatively impacted upon Gabe, with Justice Chesterman stating, "there was considerable delay in charging the respondent and bringing the case to trial. The delay appears unnecessary… [and] caused the respondent considerable anxiety".[59]

Pressures to engage in plea bargaining can also be increased by the sentence discount applied in exchange for a guilty plea, which can significantly impact on the length and type of sentence imposed. As Professor John Willis notes, "even for an innocent defendant, the guilty plea with an expectation of [sentence] leniency can be an attractive, soft option".[60] Although the sentence discount itself does not technically form part of a plea bargain agreement in Australia, it is used as a tool in negotiations to substantiate the benefit of a guilty plea for an accused. Under s 13 of the *Penalties and Sentences Act 1992* (Qld), the court "must take the guilty plea into account; and (b) may reduce the sentence that it would have imposed had the offender not pleaded guilty". In determining the amount of discount to be applied, s 13(2) of the Act states that the court must apply a reduction with regard to "the time at which the offender (a) pleaded guilty; or (b) informed the relevant law enforcement agency of his or her intention to plead guilty".

A reduction in one's sentence can create a significant incentive, and place subsequent pressure on an accused to plead guilty, particularly when it is combined with concessions on the charges and the agreed summary of case facts. As a defence lawyer in an Australian study of plea bargaining claimed:

---

[58] *R v Watson* [2009] QSC 438 (Lyons J) 3.
[59] *R v Watson; ex parte A-G (Qld)* [2009] QCA 279 at 106-107.
[60] John Willis, "Sentencing Discount for Guilty Pleas" (1985) 18 *Australian and New Zealand Journal of Criminology* 131, 141.

> The defendant obviously has more to lose than the Crown, particularly if it may involve a jail term. There is of course a natural pressure because if you go on with the trial and lose, there are bigger consequences. If you don't settle you may get an acquittal, but it is unknown. It is a gamble either way and unpredictable. So there is pressure on them to plead.[61]

The extent to which the pressures created by the sentence discount impacted on Gabe's pleading decision were alluded to in discussions with his father, and his family and civil attorney. As Austin claimed, "his Australian attorneys and I said, if you take this plea, it'll get it over with, you'll be there for X number of months, whether it be 12 or 18 or whatever". Similarly, David explained that "we had several calls back from Roland and Steve Zillman [Gabe's Australian lawyers] and Steve told us that we should expect between 12 and 18 months ... but [had he gone to trial] it could have gone to anything". As implicit within these comments, not only was Gabe potentially facing ongoing financial pressures, and the threat of being held on remand for an unknown period of delay, but his family and legal team were also strongly advising him to take the deal, and enter a guilty plea to manslaughter. As Austin recalled explaining to Gabe, "I said ... get it over, get it behind you [and] come on back".

From Gabe's perspective, concerns pertaining to the "justness" of the plea bargain also arise in relation to the title and nature of the charge to which he pleaded guilty. While the requirements of the offence could certainly be applied to Gabe's conduct in leaving Tina underwater during the fatal dive, the use of the term "manslaughter" was identified by Bloomston as problematic because of the meaning applied to manslaughter in the US which generally carries a more serious level of culpability than that stipulated in Gabe's plea deal. As Bloomston claimed, "if you read that very obscure negligent manslaughter statute that they used, it's applicable; it wasn't a stretch for Gabe to accept responsibility under that, [but] I hate that it's called manslaughter". The use of the term "manslaughter" may also explain some of the confusion that persists around Gabe maintaining his innocence, despite having pleaded guilty to the offence. As Bloomston noted:

> Alabama has a misdemeanour charge called criminally negligent homicide, and criminally negligent homicide, at least the lawyers recognise that's a misdemeanour. If you're operating a boat recklessly, and your passenger falls out and dies, you didn't intend [for] it [to happen] ... It's negligent, at least we know what the mens rea [guilty mind] is of a case like that ...

[61] Asher Flynn, above n 25, 378.

> Over here [Alabama], manslaughter is a felony, it's reckless, it's a reckless mens rea, and my understanding of what he pleaded to was a negligent state of mind ... which is different ... But when you hear manslaughter, he pleaded [guilty] to manslaughter in Australia, it sounds real bad.

David also questioned the validity of the manslaughter charge itself, claiming:

> I don't think we had any concern at all that it would become a criminal matter ... [and then] they decided to charge him with this cockamamie law that had been on the books 110 years and had never been used ... So it was a shock because we knew then, and we know now, he didn't do anything criminal.

In similarly doubting the justness of the charge, Austin questioned whether similar charges would have been applied if the situation between Gabe and Tina were reversed:

> If he had gotten in trouble and she [Tina] had gone to the surface, would they have charged her under the same Act? Because it doesn't say, well, unless you're unequally trained or you've got more experience than the other. It doesn't say that. It says that you owe a duty, and it doesn't differentiate, so what would have happened? We'll never know of course, but there is no such equivalent law in the US. If Dave and I go rock climbing and he falls down a cliff and I don't risk my life to go after him to save him, I'm not going to be charged with a crime ... In Australia, they knew they didn't have the proof to convict him of murder ... They found a weak statute that's—well, okay, we have a pretty good idea of—we can prove this.

As demonstrated by the above comments, the legitimacy and justness of the plea deal was somewhat questionable from a defence perspective, in terms of its reflection of Gabe's perceived level of criminal culpability, given that the charge to which he ultimately pleaded guilty, while technically falling under the manslaughter umbrella, is considered one of the lowest-level homicide-related offences. Furthermore, while Gabe was able to avoid the costs and duration of a criminal trial in Queensland, and in turn the possibility of being convicted of murder, the plea deal could be viewed as unjust given the financial, emotional and practical pressures confronting a US citizen facing a protracted trial in Australia. Further to the pressures and limitations the plea deal may have created for Gabe, the significantly resource-stricken climate in which the ODPP made its decision to resolve the case through plea bargaining raises serious questions about the justness of the outcome in Queensland and importantly, the processes used to attain that outcome.

CHAPTER FOUR

"BARGAINING" WITH THE THOMAS FAMILY

> Our initial hope was to get justice for Tina in Australia where the crime was committed. The only way to do that would have been for Watson to stand trial before a jury and face the evidence, witnesses, and exhibits formulated through a most thorough police investigation by the Queensland Police Service. Evidence that was thoroughly tested in the coronial inquest resulting in a murder charge by senior Coroner David Glasgow—evidence which underwent a thorough review by the DPP resulting in an indictment for murder—but evidence that was never presented in court before a jury. I feel that the DPP not only betrayed Tina and our family, but also betrayed the Australian and American public by not prosecuting Tina's case before a jury as it should have.[1]
>
> —Tina's father, Tommy Thomas

Further to its potentially negative impacts on an accused person, plea bargaining can also have a harmful impact on the victim(s) and their families. When charges are reduced or withdrawn, this can also reduce the status of a victim and their experience of victimisation, because the conviction recorded as part of the plea bargain will be unlikely to reflect the full extent of an accused person's culpability and the crime(s) committed. This can be seen in the *Watson* case, where Tina became a victim of manslaughter rather than a victim of murder. On this basis, plea deals can be perceived as failing to provide justice to victims. The perception of failed justice for victims reflects some of the concerns surrounding the very nature of plea bargaining. As identified by the US President's Commission on Law Enforcement and the Administration of Justice, "few practices in the system of criminal justice create a greater sense of unease and suspicion than the negotiated plea of guilty".[2] This is primarily because plea bargaining is a highly contentious process that

---

[1] Tommy Thomas, cited in Marissa Calligeros, "Killer's Return to US in Doubt", *Brisbane Times* (Queensland), 21 September 2009.

[2] United States President's Commission on Law Enforcement and the Administration of Justice, *Taskforce Report on the Courts* (National Institute of Justice, 1967), 9.

"smacks of wheeling and dealing";[3] thus it is often regarded with scepticism by those outside the legal community.

Prosecuting agencies have historically been criticised for the lack of information they provide to victims when a plea bargain agreement is reached, and for the perceived lack of consideration they give to victims in the decision to accept a bargained guilty plea. This failure to address the needs of victims has consistently been identified as a major limitation of the plea bargaining process because it means victims are "not paid the fundamental courtesy … of being informed of significant events and occurrences in the prosecution".[4] In this respect, plea bargaining has also been criticised for providing victims with "no opportunity for input … [which] is a source of frustration and anger for many victims".[5] In line with a procedural justice framework, it has been recognised that in many cases involving plea bargaining "victims not only felt frustrated and alienated from the justice system but, importantly, that this dissatisfaction focused on the process rather than the outcome of their cases".[6]

In order to address these types of concerns and better incorporate victims' rights into legislation, the *Victims of Crime Assistance Act 2009* (Qld), in addition to outlining the financial compensation available to victims, provides guidance on the principles that govern the actions of the Queensland Police Service (QPS) and prosecuting agencies when responding to victims of crime. This includes detailing the required conduct and the manner in which this conduct should be carried out during the prosecution process. Similar requirements are also outlined in the internal guidelines governing prosecutorial conduct at the Queensland Office of the Department of Public Prosecutions (ODPP).[7] Importantly, both this external legislation and internal guidelines were in place at the time that Gabe's plea deal was made.

One of the primary purposes of the *Victims of Crime Assistance Act 2009* (Qld) is to "declare fundamental principles of justice to underlie the

---

[3] Peter Solomon, *Criminal Justice Policy: From Research to Reform* (Butterworths, 1983) 44.

[4] Judith Dixon, "Rights of Victims" (Speech delivered at the Prosecuting Justice Conference, Melbourne, Australia, 18–19 April 1996) <http://www.aic.gov.au/events/aicupcomingevents/1996/~/media/conferences/prosecuting/dixon.ashx>.

[5] Heather Strang, *Repair or Revenge: Victims and Restorative Justice* (Clarendon Press, 2002) 10.

[6] Ibid, 12.

[7] *Director's Policy* (Qld).

treatment of victims by certain entities dealing with them",[8] and to "inform victims of the principles they can expect will underlie the treatment of them by prescribed persons".[9] A prescribed person is an individual who is acting in the capacity of a government entity, such as a prosecutor or a member of the police. Under s 8 of the *Victims of Crime Assistance Act 2009*(Qld) (and s 24 of the *Director's Policy* (Qld)), one of the "fundamental principles" identified is that a prosecutor, as a prescribed person, has a legal obligation when dealing with a victim to "treat the victim with courtesy, compassion, respect and dignity; and (b) take into account, and be responsive to, the particular needs of the victim". Further to treating the victim with respect, s 18 of the Act requires that a prosecutor (prescribed person) "must not, in dealing with the victim, engage in conduct that is inconsistent with the principles".

In relation to plea bargaining, s 12(c) of the *Victims of Crime Assistance Act 2009* (Qld) alludes to the process by describing "a decision to substantially change a charge, or not continue with a charge or accept a plea of guilty to a lesser charge". It then identifies a prosecutor's obligations to the victim when engaging in this process, stating:

> So far as is reasonably practicable, a prosecuting agency is to, if asked by a victim, give the victim the following information about the crime committed against the victim … (c) notice of a decision to substantially change a charge, or not to continue with a charge, or accept a plea of guilty to a lesser charge.[10]

While this is the only legislative requirement in Queensland that somewhat pertains to prosecutorial conduct in plea bargaining, s 16 of the ODPP's internal *Director's Policy* outlines the required conduct of prosecutors when engaging in plea bargaining—which is referred to as "charge negotiations". In relation to victims, this policy requires that:

> In all cases, before any decision is made, the views of the investigating officer and the victim or the victim's relatives, should be sought. Those views must be considered but may not be determinative. It is the public, rather than an individual interest, which must be served.[11]

There is no question that the crown prosecutor in charge of the *Watson* case in Queensland, Assistant ODPP Director Brendan Campbell SC,

---

[8] *Victims of Crime Assistance Act 2009* (Qld) s 1(a).
[9] Ibid, s 6.
[10] *Director's Policy* (Qld) s 12(c).
[11] Ibid, s 16.

sought the views of the Thomas family and the Queensland police officers before Gabe pleaded guilty to manslaughter. However, and most importantly, it is not clear whether this consultation occurred prior to a final decision on the plea deal being made, and whether Brendan Campbell's conduct in consulting with the Thomas family fully reflected his legislated or internal ODPP obligations to victims.

Based on the accounts provided to us by Tina's mother and father, Cindy and Tommy Thomas; Alabama Assistant Attorney-General and lead prosecutor in the capital murder trial in Alabama, Don Valeska; Lieutenant Brad Flynn; and Detective Senior Constable Kevin Gehringer, it appears that Brendan Campbell not only failed to treat Tina's family—the secondary victims of her death—with "courtesy, compassion, respect and dignity",[12] but he also strayed from his legislative obligations by providing them with deliberately inaccurate information. As Tommy explained:

> There's no telling how many lies this guy [Campbell] actually told me. I have learned through this entire process that lawyers will lie, and it's not just criminal defence lawyers, it's all of them! ... And evidently it's okay for them to lie ... Now I'll be honest with you, if they're representing the accused, I can understand them lying because they've got to, but I do not understand people that are in positions like Brendan Campbell was in, with the ODPP, I don't understand somebody in that position lying to the victim's family when they're supposed to be there for the victim.

Tommy's reflection here illustrates not only his own disappointment with the Queensland legal system's response to Tina's death, but also the absence of involvement and trust that was afforded by the ODPP to the secondary victims in this case. As a result, further questions emerge in relation to the achievability of justice in the Queensland ODPP's handling of the *Watson* case, given that the process by which the guilty plea was attained generated significant dissatisfaction and disillusionment for the secondary victims involved. Importantly, the perceived failure of Brendan Campbell to adhere to both his external and internal obligations is another example of the inability of the legal response to Tina's death in Queensland to achieve justice, procedurally and subjectively.

---

[12] *Victims of Crime Assistance Act 2009* (Qld) s 8.

The *Watson* Deal: The Impact on Tina and the Thomas Family

One of the significant concerns arising for victims from the use of plea bargaining relates to the deals made on the facts of the case, which then turn into the agreed summary of facts presented to the court. An agreed summary of facts provides an overview of the offence(s) and the circumstances surrounding the commission of the offence(s), which has been determined and agreed upon by the prosecution and the defence. This summary of facts is then used by the court, in conjunction with the relevant prosecution and defence written and verbal sentencing submissions and arguments, as the basis for sentencing an accused.

When a plea deal is reached, in addition to amending the charges it almost always involves a negotiation on the agreed summary of facts. This is because when charges are altered, the facts presented to the court must reflect these alterations. As a result, factual elements of the crime may be removed, or the severity of aspects of the crime may be understated. For example, if an accused recklessly assaulted a victim and stole their mobile phone, yet a plea bargain was entered into in which the accused pleaded guilty to the reckless assault only, the agreed summary of facts presented to the judge would not include any details of the mobile phone theft; it would only detail the circumstances and information surrounding the charge of reckless assault. As a consequence, a reduced level of culpability is assigned to the accused person's conduct.

The implications of amending the agreed summary of facts extend beyond affecting a victim's status and the level of culpability assigned to the accused, to also limiting how much of a person's victim impact statement can legally be considered by the judge when imposing a sentence. Under s 9(2)(c) of the *Penalties and Sentences Act 1992*(Qld), when sentencing an offender, the court must have regard to "the nature of the offence and how serious the offence was, including— (i) any physical, mental or emotional harm done to a victim, including harm mentioned in information relating to the victim". To assist the judge in obtaining this information prior to imposing a sentence, a victim impact statement is read to or by the judge which details the effects of the crime for the victim(s), including any physical and emotional harm, property loss or damage, and other impacts, such as ongoing suffering. In cases where the primary victim has died as a result of the offence, such as in the *Watson* case, these statements are prepared by the secondary victims, who typically include the deceased victim's family and closest friends.

The victim impact statement is a significant yet highly contentious victim-focused reform, and its (in)effectiveness in addressing victims' needs has been the focus of much debate.[13] While not immune to criticism, victim impact statements provide an avenue for victims' voices and needs to be heard in sentencing by offering an opportunity for victims to play a greater role than simply that of a prosecution witness. Accordingly, these statements have become an important part of the sentencing process, both in terms of ensuring proportionality in sentencing and in facilitating some consideration of victims. However, when a case is resolved by a plea bargain and the case facts are subsequently altered, the judge can only consider the impact of the crime on the victim for those matters with which the accused is convicted. If the facts surrounding certain elements of the crime are altered or minimised to allow a lesser charge, the full victim impact statement cannot be disclosed to the judge.

This situation was highly prominent in the *Watson* case as a result of the changes made to the agreed summary of facts to reflect the negligent manslaughter offence in place of the original charge of murder. The prosecution was provided with four victim impact statements: from Tommy Thomas (Tina's father), Cindy Thomas (Tina's mother), Alanda Thomas (Tina's sister) and Amanda Phillips (Tina's best friend). However, in sentencing Gabe, the judge was only able to consider selected parts of each statement. In fact, 14 of the 31 pages of the transcript from Gabe's initial sentencing hearing in June 2009 were dedicated to discussing which elements of the victim impact statements needed to be disregarded by the judge. Sitting in the courtroom, the secondary victims of Tina's death were subjected to the following discussion, as a direct result of the plea deal that was made:

B.Campbell: Your Honour, can I highlight those points that your Honour shouldn't be concerned about? Sorry, that the Crown says you shouldn't place weight upon? ... Can I take your Honour to the first page, the fourth paragraph?

[13] See, Bree Cook, Fiona David and Anna Grant, *Victims' Needs, Victims' Rights: Policies and Programs for Victims of Crime in Australia* (Research and Public Policy Series No 19, Australian Institute of Criminology, 1999); Jo Goodey, *Victims and Victimology: Research, Policy and Practice* (Pearson Longman, 2005); Leslie Sebba, *Third Parties: Victims and the Criminal Justice System* (Ohio State University Press, 1996); Strang, above n 5; Martin Wright, "The Rights and Needs of Victims in the Criminal Justice Process", in Hendrik Kaptein and Marijke Malsch (eds), *Crime, Victims and Justice: Essays on Principles and Practice* (Ashgate, 2004) 141.

Justice L: Just a moment, please. It commences, "my little girl ..."

B.Campbell: Yes, "my little girl"... There are ... a number of references to murder.

Justice L: Yes, in view of the Crown's position I should ignore that?

B.Campbell: Yes. Your Honour, the authors are firmly convinced that the accused murdered the deceased. That is reflected in the statements ... Your Honour is not being asked to sentence on that basis. Your Honour is to sentence on the basis that the accused unlawfully killed the deceased ... And more than that, her [Cindy's] views about that are not relevant to your Honour's consideration of the appropriate sentence for unlawful killing.

Justice L: So I should disregard the balance of that paragraph?

B.Campbell: Yes ... In relation to Alanda's statement ... the references to murder in the third and fourth paragraph should be dealt with in the same way [disregarded]. And the last sentence of the last paragraph on page 8, should also be dealt with in the same way ... In the statement of Amanda Phillips, in the last paragraph of the second page, her views—it's really, the first sentence of that, her views about that are conjecture ... The first paragraph is essentially conjecture.[14]

The type of discussion evident in this excerpt reveals a disregard for the secondary victims' experiences, which can result in them feeling unheard and effectively silenced by the courts. Additionally, the above excerpt illustrates the significant disparities that existed between the offence that the secondary victims perceived occurred and the offence that was outlined in the summary of facts presented to the judge.

The "watered-down set of agreed facts", as Gehringer described them, was also a key point of contention for the police because, beyond not recognising the experiences of victimisation felt by members of the Thomas family, the summary failed to fully reflect the crime and the extent of Gabe's culpability, even in light of the reduced charge. Gehringer claimed, for example, that the agreed summary of facts and the prosecution's submission did not pay significant heed to the importance of the statement given by the only eyewitness to directly observe Tina and Gabe underwater: Stanley Stutz. The police considered Stutz's observations

[14] Justice Lyons and Brendan Campbell, sentencing hearing, 5 June 2009.

to be highly significant in demonstrating inconsistencies in Gabe's versions of Tina's death. The importance of Stutz's statement was similarly identified in the coronial inquest findings, in which Coroner David Glasgow described Stutz as "a significant observer of the events under the sea at the time of Tina's death",[15] and referred to his statement as being "an honest and reliable account".[16] Yet limited attention was given to this direct evidence in the agreed summary of facts upon which the judge was bound to sentence Gabe.

The agreed summary of facts, and the prosecution's verbal submission, also did not describe in any detail the many inconsistencies the police identified in Gabe's alternate versions of events, or provide an adequate account of the factual inaccuracies in Gabe's stories. Instead, only one inconsistency in Gabe's various accounts of what occurred on 22 October 2003 received significant attention in the agreed summary and the prosecution's verbal submission to the court. As Tommy described, "the only thing that Gabe admits lying to in the agreed statement of facts was going to the anchor rope, and the only reason he admitted to lying about that is because there was nobody on the anchor rope that saw him". As indicated in Tommy's comment, the only inconsistency identified in the facts presented by the prosecution related to Gabe's claims that he approached two divers on the access line to get help for Tina, before reaching the surface. However, as demonstrated in the excerpt below, while this inaccuracy is acknowledged by Brendan Campbell, no significant level of criticism or concern is attributed to it:

> The prisoner [Gabe] stated that he swam back over to the anchor rope and started going up. At around about 20 feet he saw other people hanging onto the rope. He tapped them to gain their attention and pointed in the direction of the deceased; however, he had no way of telling them what he needed. The Crown allegation is that the prisoner did not approach anyone on the line. His point of surfacing was inconsistent with being on or close to that access line.[17]

While we cannot present Brendan Campbell's direct response as to why the decision to exclude seemingly pivotal and relevant information was made, Tommy recalled that "when it was all over, I asked Brendan why they didn't get him [Gabe] to admit to more of the lies that he told". Tommy explained that Brendan Campbell had told him that "if we would

---

[15] Transcript of Proceedings, *Inquest into the death of Christina Mae Watson* (20 June 2008) 57 (Coroner David Glasgow).

[16] Ibid.

[17] Brendan Campbell, sentencing hearing, 5 June 2009.

have got him [Gabe] to admit to anything else, the judge would have probably thrown it out and it would have had to go to criminal trial", to which Tommy replied, "well that's exactly what I want".

Tommy's comments provide a strong indication of the problems that exist in omitting important points from the agreed summary of facts, but perhaps more poignantly, they highlight the extent to which the facts in this case were manipulated to fit a certain level of conduct that reflected the negotiated plea of manslaughter by criminal negligence. Fitting the facts to the plea was important because in Australia, case law dictates that a judge can reject a guilty plea being entered, and require the matter to proceed to trial on a more serious charge, if the facts bestowed upon the court do not match the culpability of the charge presented.[18]

The concerns raised by our participants regarding the content of the prosecution's sentencing submission and the agreed summary of facts extend beyond them not fully reflecting Gabe's level of culpability or the circumstances surrounding Tina's death, to also include criticisms of the significant role that the summary played in informing the sentences imposed on Gabe. As Tommy explained:

> I'm sitting there listening to that judge [Justice Lyons] talk. And I'm just getting madder and madder and madder but ... it wasn't the judge's fault. He only had the information given to him. It was the stuff that he got from the agreed statement of facts, from Brendan Campbell and [Steve] Zillman, and the information that they got from [Brendan] Campbell and the ODPP, which caused him to say what he said. There was no evidence on this case whatsoever to show anything other than what was in the agreed statement of facts. And I'm sitting there going, the judge wasn't at fault. It wasn't his fault, he's looking at the information he's [been] given by Brendan Campbell and the ODPP. So that's the sole problem there. That was it.

Beyond the numerical value of the sentences imposed, which were most likely significantly informed by the agreed summary of facts available to the Justices, the comments made by the four members of the Queensland judiciary in sentencing Gabe illustrate another key point in this case where there is a strong perception that the system failed to deliver justice, both procedurally and subjectively. To some extent, this can be understood in light of historical trends, as Australian courts have traditionally treated men involved in the death of their female intimate partners with a degree of leniency and sympathy that has not been afforded

[18] *R v Maxwell* (1995) 184 CLR 501.

to those who have killed, or been involved in the death of, a stranger.[19] As author and domestic violence and child abuse advocate Lundy Bancroft suggests, the courts have viewed these men as a "special class" of criminal whose crimes can be understood, and in many cases legitimised, as an aberration of their otherwise good character.[20] This perception was evidently applied in the *Watson* case, where the comments made regarding Gabe's "good" character by the Justices who determined his initial and appeal sentences promoted a favourable construction of Gabe and advocated a reduced level of his culpability in Tina's death.

The favourable construction of Gabe's character in the initial sentence imposed in Queensland in June 2009 was evident in Justice Lyons's description of him as a man "of good character … a person who is known to help others".[21] In the same paragraph, Justice Lyons further described Gabe as a man who "loved" his wife and was "devastated by her loss".[22] A similar construction of Gabe was also evident in the judicial remarks pertaining to his appeal sentence. While the Queensland Supreme Court of Appeal ultimately found in favour of the prosecution, and increased the length of time that Gabe was required to serve in prison by six months, in doing so, the three Justices still reinforced a positive view of Gabe. This is clearly demonstrated in the remarks made by Justice Chesterman, who described Gabe as "a man of good character, well regarded by his community and given to selfless acts of charity … [who was] devastated by the loss of his wife whom he loved".[23] This favourable profile of Gabe is also evident in the comments made by Justice Muir, who dissented from the majority opinion, opposing the appeal. In expressing his view, Justice Muir stated that "[Gabe] had no intention of harming his wife. He did help her initially. His reprehensible decision to swim for assistance was made in a hostile environment when he was under stress".[24] Justice Muir's sympathetic construction of Gabe's character ultimately resulted in the

[19] See Myrna Dawson, "Rethinking the Boundaries of Intimacy at the End of the Century: The Role of the Victim–Defendant Relationship in Criminal Justice Decision Making Over Time" (2004) 38 *Law and Society Review* 105; Elizabeth Rappaport, "Capital Murder and the Domestic Discount: A Study of Capital Domestic Murder in the Post-Furman Era" (1996) 49 *Southern Methodist University Law Review* 1507.

[20] Lundy Bancroft, *Why Does He Do That? Inside the Minds of Angry and Controlling Men* (Berkley Trade, 2002).

[21] *R v Watson* [2009] QSC 438 (Lyons J) 2.

[22] Ibid.

[23] *R v Watson; ex parte A-G (QLD)* [2009] QCA 279 (Chesterman J) 106.

[24] Ibid (Muir J) 57.

minimisation of his level of culpability and responsibility for Tina's death, beyond the already reduced manslaughter charge and highly favourable agreed summary of facts.

Another way in which the "good" character of Gabe was reflected in the sentences imposed is demonstrated in the disregard that the initial and appeal Justices gave to several sentencing principles. In Queensland, when sentencing an accused a judge must consider five sentencing principles: punishment, rehabilitation, deterrence, denouncement and protection.[25] These principles underlie all criminal sentences; however, the judge can use their discretion to decide whether one or more of the principles should be prioritised above the others in determining an appropriate sentence in each individual case. In both the initial and appeal sentences imposed on Gabe, the principles of punishment, rehabilitation and deterrence were effectively disregarded due largely to the favourable assessment of Gabe's character. As Justice Lyons stated, "there is, naturally, no suggestion of a risk of reoffending".[26] Later in the appeal judgement, Justice Chesterman went even further to stress that punishment, deterrence and rehabilitation were "not necessary", given that the accused was unlikely to offend again. As Justice Chesterman commented:

> The respondent is not in need of rehabilitation as that term is understood in the criminal jurisdiction of the courts. Punishment is not necessary as a deterrent, either to the respondent or anyone else. The offence is unlikely to be repeated. Nor is retribution important.[27]

While it is common practice for some principles to be prioritised over others in light of the individual circumstances of a criminal case, the disregard for deterrence, rehabilitation and punishment serves to further perpetuate perceptions of the "good" character of Gabe, and consequently may be seen to unjustly downplay the seriousness of Tina's death, and Gabe's role within it.

This favourable construction of Gabe's character was also evident in the comments of the Justices regarding the factual inconsistencies in Gabe's differing versions of Tina's death. It is noted that these comments were largely influenced by the agreed summary of facts tendered to the court as a result of the plea bargain, yet they go so far as to justify the changes in his version of events. While Justice Lyons explained in his sentencing remarks that there may have been "some inconsistencies and

[25] *Penalties and Sentencing Act 1992* (QLD) s 9(1).
[26] *R v Watson* [2009] QSC 438 (Lyons J) 2.
[27] *R v Watson; ex parte A-G* (QLD) [2009] QCA 279 (Chesterman J) 98.

some attempts to put blame on other people",[28] which does "not speak particularly well" of Gabe,[29] he moved beyond paying minimal credence to these inconsistencies to using them as a basis to create a sympathetic construction of Gabe's character, explaining that any inconsistencies were "no doubt" reflective of how "deeply upset" he was by the death of his wife.[30]

The sympathetic representation of Gabe's character, and what appears to be an attempt to explain and excuse the inconsistencies in his various accounts of Tina's death, was also present in the remarks made by the appeal Justices, whereby Justice Chesterman described Gabe's multiple accounts as the result of his "evident and understandable distress at his wife's death".[31] For this reason, Justice Chesterman noted that he did not "attach the same significance to the inconsistencies as did the prosecutor".[32] Consequently, in both Gabe's initial and appeal sentences, the level of culpability attached to his conduct was reduced to an even lower level than the "watered-down version" of facts provided by Brendan Campbell.[33] On this basis, it is clear how the sentences imposed in Queensland can be subjectively viewed as unjust outcomes, in that they failed to adequately consider the possible implications arising from Gabe's various versions of events. Additionally, given the construction of Gabe as a man of good character, his actions were further excused on the basis that a "good person" would not intentionally hurt or kill their wife, or indeed deliberately lie about the circumstances surrounding her death.

The only opportunity that existed for an alternate version of Gabe's character to be put forward for consideration in the sentencing process was through the victim impact statements of the secondary victims. However, because much of the content of these statements had to be disregarded as it fell outside the version of facts made as part of the plea bargain agreement, the markedly different image of Gabe that was presented by the secondary victims was not reflected in the Justices' sentencing remarks. In fact, the extent to which the secondary victims' depictions of Gabe's character were ignored and even challenged is demonstrated in the comments of Justice Chesterman in his appeal judgement, where in acknowledging that the construction of Gabe offered by Justice Lyons is "challenged in the

---

[28] *R v Watson* [2009] QSC 438 (Lyons J) 3.
[29] Ibid.
[30] Ibid.
[31] *R v Watson; ex parte A-G (QLD)* [2009] QCA 279 (Chesterman J) 89.
[32] Ibid.
[33] Detective Senior Constable Kevin Gehringer.

victim impact statements provided by her family and friends",[34] Justice Chesterman referred to the secondary victims as "bitter" and exhibiting "hostility towards the respondent"[35]—a hostility that he noted was based on the incorrect assumption that Gabe intentionally killed Tina. Through these comments, Chesterman silenced the voices of the secondary victims, disregarding their comments as being "colour[ed]" by this incorrect belief.[36] Through this determination, the voices of Tina's family were effectively ignored and Gabe's construction as a grieving husband and a "man of good character" was further promoted. As Tommy stated outside the Brisbane Supreme Court in response to the initial sentence imposed in June 2009, "it's [a] total injustice, it's ludicrous what we have seen. This is in no way, shape or form even beginning to get justice for our daughter".[37]

Given that the voices of the victim and secondary victims had already been silenced by the acceptance of a plea deal, which meant that no evidence was revealed, tried or tested in a Queensland court of law, this second form of silencing can be seen as a significant point at which justice was subjectively seen as not being attained through the Queensland handling of the *Watson* case. As Tina's sister, Alanda, publicly declared immediately following the first sentencing hearing, "I'm shocked. It's unbelievable. It's complete injustice all the way around. It's disgusting".[38] A similar view was expressed by Tommy, who claimed, "this is not justice. We were convinced and are today that Gabe Watson murdered Tina … The fact of the matter is, there's no greater hardship than losing your daughter, your sister, your best friend for the rest of your life … [but] this [sentence] is not justice and this is not over".[39] Cindy similarly observed that this outcome reflected a widespread perception that she felt existed in the Queensland ODPP's handling of the case, that Gabe was treated more like a victim than Tina. She explained, "Tina had no rights there [in Australia] ... She didn't. She was nobody. Gabe was the victim". Thus, further to the consequences arising from the influence of the agreed summary of facts on the sentences imposed, the silencing of the victims' voices, combined with the sympathetic construction of Gabe, significantly

---

[34] *R v Watson; ex parte A-G (QLD)* [2009] QCA 279 (Chesterman J) 106.

[35] Ibid.

[36] Ibid.

[37] Tommy Thomas, cited in Amanda Bentley, "Great Barrier Reef Honeymoon Death: Diver's Jail Sentence 'Ludicrous' and 'Embarrassing'", *Sydney Morning Herald* (New South Wales), 5 June 2009.

[38] Alanda Thomas, cited in Mike Celizic, "Outrage over Sentencing in Honeymoon Drowning", *MSNBC News* (United States), 5 June 2009.

[39] Tommy Thomas, cited in Celizic, above n 38.

limited the capacity of the sentences imposed to provide justice, procedurally or subjectively, for members of the Thomas family.

In reflecting on the lack of consideration given to the victims throughout the Queensland plea bargain and sentencing processes, Flynn described the moment at which Justice Lyons sentenced Gabe as "gut-wrenching". He explained:

> The judge walks up in his garb and begins to extol on the courtroom how wonderful of a person Gabe is for coming back and facing an unknown—facing what he did wrong and that it's obvious that it's been so troubling and difficult for him, and we were listening to this just enormous pity pouring for him, and not a word about Tina. And not a word about her family and what they have had to go through and it's that judge's responsibility to impose a sentence as justice for those people's daughter. You know Tina was not a case number. Tina is not Charlie Oswald. That was Tina Thomas and when he gave the sentence for under 12 months, I just felt like I'd been kicked in the gut. I'm like you can't—at the time there was a professional American football player who had just been sentenced for illegally fighting dogs, and he had gotten a much longer sentence for fighting dogs than Gabe was going to get for being culpable in Tina's death ... And you think, well he got 12 months. That's all he's going to get after all of our work, that's all he's going to get. He's not even going to completely shake off his jet lag and he'll be on a plane back home. And I just felt gutted. It was just a huge slap in the face.

Gehringer similarly described his perceptions of the judge's sentencing remarks as being "all about Gabe ... and again nothing about the Thomas family. Nothing about what they've had to go through". He explained that the sentences focused on what "Gabe has had to go through" in terms of the "anguish" he had felt "over all these years". In describing his anger and disappointment in the sentencing process, Gehringer primarily attributed its inadequacy to the deal made on the agreed summary of facts between Brendan Campbell and Gabe's Australian defence lawyers. Gehringer explained:

> The judge was seeing an agreed set of facts ... and I don't hold anything against the particular judge because he obviously had to work on what was presented to him, but then for me it was the mental anguish because I was sitting right beside Tommy. The mental anguish of hearing [Steve] Zillman [the defence] hop up and give his verbal account of the agreed facts; of Brendan Campbell hopping up ... The way I interpreted it, the defence not only got themselves a watered-down set of agreed facts, but when it came down to the verbal side of it they poked it further ... [They said] poor old Gabe ... It was all Gabe, Gabe, Gabe, Gabe, Gabe. Then of course, that's

> what the judge has retired on and he's read the stuff and he's come back, and when the judge has come back, he said the same thing, well, you know, poor Gabe.

One of the reasons underpinning Gehringer's frustrations can be linked to the disregard given to the numerous requests that he and Gary Campbell made to the ODPP as to what should be incorporated into the agreed summary of facts. Discussing the meeting between Gary Campbell, Gehringer and Brendan Campbell—among others from the ODPP and the QPS—held in January 2009, Gehringer claimed:

> They discussed with us where we were at, and Brendan Campbell was obviously there, and the conversation was what do you think if they were to come back with some sort of a manslaughter—you know, wanting to plead [guilty] to manslaughter? ... And that was when Brendan Campbell trotted out the, if any sort of a plea [deal] was to be done and it was to do anything with manslaughter, it would have to be on a set of agreed facts and those agreed facts would be shown to you [Gary] and Kevin and everyone to make sure that it sufficiently covered what was going on.

Gehringer noted that during this meeting, he and Gary became quite agitated, and wanted to make sure that, if a deal were to be made with Gabe, it would be on a basis that they believed reflected Gabe's level of culpability in causing Tina's death. As Gehringer explained:

> Gary was hell-bent on this point about if there were to be any agreed facts, then it had to be within the facts that [there was] this interaction which we'd worked out [which] had happened between Gabe and Tina with the arms, you know, by her side, and they actually had physical contact before they parted. Gary mentioned in that video link-up that that would have to be a crucial aspect of any agreed facts.

Gehringer claimed that during this meeting he and Gary stressed that if a guilty plea were to be accepted, the prosecution's submission on sentence would have to be reflective of Gabe's culpability. He explained, "the other big thing was a timeframe thing, and if it was going to be manslaughter ... he [Gabe] would have to be looking at time served, around the seven-year mark, up to ten, maybe drop it back a year or so, that's what we told them". However, despite their insistence, neither of these requests were reflected in the agreed summary of facts or the verbal submission that Brendan Campbell gave to the court. In fact, in discussing Gabe's sentence as part of his verbal submission to the court, while acknowledging that "there are serious aggravating features, and the circumstances of the offending are such that a significant custodial sentence is required",[40] Brendan Campbell recommended that Gabe be required to serve "not less than 18 months in actual custody".[41] This recommendation was between 5.5 and 8.5 years below that proposed by the Queensland police investigators.

Further to the content of the agreed summary not reflecting the police's views or their January 2009 discussion with Brendan Campbell, the police were also denied access to the agreed summary of facts. This occurred despite Campbell advising them that they would be given access to the facts and would be able to provide some input into their preparation. As Gehringer explained, "Gary and I requested to see these agreed facts, and they'd promised if ever there was going to be anything, we would see these agreed facts. They just refused to show us what the agreed facts were, so we didn't know what the agreed facts were". Interestingly, despite several written requests, the QPS officers have still not been given access to a copy of the agreed summary of facts, even post Gabe's acquittal in Alabama in February 2012. As Gehringer stated, "the ODPP reneged and never supplied us with them".

In light of the events and concerns described above, there are some significant questions that the ODPP and Brendan Campbell in particular need to address in relation to their conduct in preparing and withholding access to the agreed summary of facts. In particular, their failure to provide the police involved in the investigation with a copy of the summary at their request appears at odds with the obligations on prosecutors to provide even confidential information to police investigators. As outlined in s 59 of the ODPP's *Director's Policy*:

> The ODPP has obligations in respect of confidentiality (section 24A of the *Director of Public Prosecutions Act 1994*) and privacy (*Queensland Government Policy*). Information about a case other than what is on the public record should not be released without authority from either the Director or Deputy Director subject to the following exceptions … the release of information to police as required.

This apparent breach raises further doubts over the legitimacy of the plea bargain, because if the agreed summary of facts were an accurate reflection of what the ODPP perceived was an appropriate overview of the offence and circumstances surrounding it, there remains a question as to why the details were not made accessible to the police involved in the case before, during or after Gabe was sentenced in Queensland. Perhaps this

---

[40] Brendan Campbell, sentencing hearing, 5 June 2009.
[41] Ibid.

decision to withhold access was made because the ODPP considered the policies were irrelevant in this particular case, or perhaps, as Brendan Campbell had explained to Tommy, the ODPP did not want the facts questioned or scrutinised, to avoid having to include anything that might legitimise the decision to proceed with a more serious offence. Alternatively, this decision might be related to the actual timing of when the plea deal was really made, as opposed to the timing suggested in the agreed summary of facts or presented by Brendan Campbell at Gabe's sentencing hearing.

When Was the Deal Made? The Importance of Timing

In his verbal sentencing submission to Justice Lyons, Brendan Campbell stated that Gabe was not presented with the option of a manslaughter plea until after he returned to Australia and was arraigned on 13 May 2009. Brendan Campbell explained, "at the time of the presentation of the indictment, that alternative basis was indicated to the defence and that was really the first opportunity for the accused to plead [guilty] to manslaughter on that basis".[42] However, it was over three months prior to Gabe's arraignment hearing, on 27 January 2009, when Gehringer and Detective Senior Sergeant Gary Campbell were first involved in discussions with Brendan Campbell during which the possibility of the Crown accepting a manslaughter plea was raised. Furthermore, Gehringer described a number of strange aspects of this meeting, such as he and Gary Campbell not being informed of the purpose of the meeting. He recalled that:

> Gary came to me saying you and I have been summoned to the ODPP office tomorrow in relation to Gabe, the [*Operation*] *Charlie Oswald*. And I said what's it about? And he said, I don't know. And then Gary sent an email to Michael Coward who's the head of the DPP in Townsville, to say what sort of material do you want us to bring? Because we were sort of thinking do they want to clarify something? And then of course in the back of our mind we're saying, is he going to come back voluntarily or is this the meeting to tell us that we're hopping on a plane to go over there and arrest him and extradite him? So they said, you don't need to bring anything … We even said do we need to bring a notepad? No, don't even need to bring a notepad, just come to the office.

By the conclusion of this meeting in January 2009, Gehringer believed that there was a strong probability that the ODPP had already spoken with

[42] Ibid.

Gabe's lawyers about the opportunity for a manslaughter deal, but he could not be entirely sure that this had occurred. As he explained, "Gary and I left that meeting and we still didn't, we were like, well, have they spoken to them [Gabe's lawyers]? Or are they going to speak to them?" Essentially, Gehringer understood that the purpose of the January meeting was to communicate that "there was going to be some sort of a manslaughter or some sort of a plea deal done, and that meeting with us was to initially gauge, for want of a better word, what our reactions were going to be to it". In expressing his frustration at the lack of engagement with his and Campbell's perspectives on the deal—the two main police investigators involved in the case—Gehringer professed, "I don't think it would have mattered what Gary and I had said, because I think [the] ODPP were going to do what the ODPP wanted to do, and what Gary and I thought as investigators didn't matter".

Coroner David Glasgow also suggested that he was aware that the ODPP might already have entered into a plea deal involving manslaughter before Gabe had returned from the US. He explained:

> Before he [Gabe] left America … I talked to [source from the ODPP] who works in Crown law ... I was going overseas … and he said to me, something will happen when you're away … And when I was away, things happened. The deal was done ... [I think] the deal was done not only on the plea, but the sentence, [and] before he left America ... I think he knew when he was coming back that he would face time, because he came back, [and] didn't apply for bail.

It has also been suggested by those most closely involved in the case that a decision on the plea bargain was made prior to Brendan Campbell flying to the US to meet with the Thomas family in May 2009, when he spoke with them about the process and intricacies of running a murder trial in Queensland. This view was largely informed by the content of the discussions between Brendan Campbell and the Thomas family, and because during the January 2009 meeting with the police investigators Brendan Campbell told them that if a plea deal were to be accepted, he would want to discuss this in person with the Thomas family. As Gehringer recalled:

> The other thing that was discussed was if there was any inclination that there was going to be any sort of a plea deal done, that they would have to, it was something that couldn't be done by phone call with the family. They needed, if they were looking or even considering that sort of option ... then they would need to get on a plane. [It was decided] that would have to be a discussion that was held [face to face].

Cited under both s 24 of the *Director's Policy* (Qld) and ss 12(a) and 13 of the *Victims of Crime Assistance Act 2009* (Qld) is the requirement that a prosecutor provide information to the victim in advance of the trial "so far as is reasonably practical … about relevant court processes". Under the premise of this requirement, Tommy recalled his initial discussion with Brendan Campbell just prior to Campbell's arrival in Alabama in mid-May 2009. Tommy explained that "Brendan called [and] said that they were planning a trip over here to meet with us, primarily to talk with us about our responsibilities as witnesses in a criminal trial and what we could expect in a criminal trial". Around the same time, Flynn also received a phone call advising him of the visit, but his call came from Gary Campbell, and at its conclusion, Flynn began questioning the true nature of Brendan Campbell's visit to Alabama. As Flynn explained:

> I get a phone call from Gary, this was like on a Tuesday night, out of the blue. He says, Brad, I'm on my way over there. I'm bringing some ODPP guys with me … They wanted to meet with everybody, have a meeting with the family and stuff and I said, okay, what's going on? And he kind of told me, he said, something's up. I don't like it, but he says, I don't have any information right now. I'll talk more when we land. And literally he was on a plane 24 hours later. So I called Tommy that night and the first thing that Tommy asked me, he says, what's going on? Something doesn't smell right here. I said, I don't know Tommy, they're coming under the guise of they want to sit down with all of us to prepare us for a trial to explain … So I said until we know something, let's take them at their word and let's just do what we need to do.

In addition to Brendan Campbell and Gary Campbell, a "media spin doctor from the ODPP"[43] also flew to Alabama to meet with the Thomas family on 14 May 2009, the day after Gabe had voluntarily arrived back in Australia. According to Tommy, the media person was brought "just in case. Because Brendan had stressed to me that they didn't need anybody knowing that they were coming, but their media guy was just in case I had tipped off the media or something, that they were here, so that they'd have somebody that could handle that".

In describing the details of this meeting, Flynn recalled that it initially began as though the murder trial was proceeding as planned:

> So they show up and … the first meeting is, okay, [they say] we're ready to go. We're gung-ho, we've got this. We want to prepare you for how the Australian judicial process is going to be ... We're there for you, we're going to get justice.

---

[43] Detective Senior Constable Kevin Gehringer.

But then, as Flynn described, the discussion somewhat unsurprisingly turned to the possibility of a plea deal:

> Kind of out of left field, Brendan Campbell throws into the pot, he says, well, you know, we're going to go with this [murder trial], but there's always a chance we may get backed into where we have to look at a plea deal just to protect the case … And so Tommy makes it clear, no plea bargains, no deals. It's a trial or nothing … So we continued talking. A little later, [Brendan] Campbell throws in another one, you know, we feel very strongly about this case, but there's an avenue here with this plea bargain where we can do this. And of course I again looked at Tommy and Tommy's looking at me and we were shaking our heads. And Tommy goes, no deals, no deals. So we progressed talking again and then [Brendan] Campbell throws it in again. By the time we leave that night, it's all but guaranteed there's going to be a plea bargain. We go from no, no deals, to him preparing us that it may be in a circumstance that they can't circumvent, that this is something that we have to take. And I remember me and Gary [Campbell] walked out of there and I said, well, it'll be a short trip to Australia because there's not going to be a trial. I said, they've made their mind up. They're going to cut a deal.

Tommy described this meeting in a similar vein. Like Flynn, he said that the discussion with Brendan Campbell suddenly switched from an explanation of the Australian trial process and what a murder trial would look and feel like to talk of the possibility of a plea deal:

> The first day that we met with them we spent most of the day talking about what a criminal trial would look like, you know, giving us a description of everything from the judge, the jury, the courtroom, how everything would go, what the procedures were, what the process was, what our duties and obligations were as witnesses and all this kind of stuff. I mean, it's sounding like, okay, well maybe we are going to trial. And then at the end of the day he changes the course of the conversation to, we are anticipating that his attorneys are going to request a plea [deal], and that's kind of what I was waiting for. I was just … I couldn't believe that he had wasted all this time to tell me all of this stuff just to get to this point. But then he starts trying to sell me on the idea of a manslaughter plea … He told me that manslaughter and murder were both major crimes in Australia … [and that] manslaughter's a very, you know, strong crime.

Tommy recounted that in attempting to "sell" the benefits of the plea bargain, Brendan Campbell referred to the deal as a "win–win for everybody". He claimed:

> He gets into this discussion of well you need to look at it from the standpoint of you and your family. This is a win–win for everybody,

> because if we let him accept a manslaughter plea then he's going to serve some time, your family doesn't have to go through the ordeal of coming back to Australia for a lengthy criminal trial, which may not start immediately, and so you'll save your family a lot of pain and anguish. He's going to go to prison and do time for what he did, and it'll save us from prosecuting the case and potentially losing it … My response to him was basically that he needed to understand something: first of all, it wasn't a win–win situation for everybody, because no matter what the outcome was, even if he went to trial, was found guilty and went to prison for the rest of his life, it's not a win for us … During this conversation [I asked], so have his attorneys contacted you about a plea deal yet? [And he said] no, we're just anticipating this … The way that he left it when he left Birmingham is that he was going back to Australia, he hadn't heard anything yet from Gabe's attorneys, but he would call me as soon as he did.

Somewhere between 24 and 48 hours after Brendan Campbell left the US, he contacted Tommy to advise him that a plea deal had been reached with Gabe. As Tommy described:

> He lets me know that Gabe's attorneys have made contact and they have offered to plead guilty to manslaughter … He said, well, we appreciate your position, but as I told you before it's ultimately our decision and we're going to take the manslaughter plea … He said, you need to understand, he's over here in jail and he's already serving time and it's going to count against whatever sentence he gets in the manslaughter plea, so we need to go ahead and get this done … He's going to be facing a sentencing hearing in June, and if you want to be there for the sentencing hearing then you need to make arrangements to get here.

While the content of these earlier discussions implies that a deal between Gabe and the ODPP had already been in motion before Brendan Campbell flew to the US and before Gabe left Alabama, perhaps the most compelling indication that a decision had been made before Gabe arrived in Australia was Brendan Campbell's admissions in a meeting held in Queensland just prior to Gabe's sentencing hearing, at which Tommy, Flynn, Gehringer and Gary Campbell were all present. The meeting was scheduled to discuss what would happen during the sentencing hearing and what the likely outcome would be. During this meeting, Tommy confronted Brendan Campbell about the plea deal, and as Tommy and Flynn describe below, Brendan Campbell admitted that Gabe returned to Australia with the knowledge that a manslaughter plea was on offer, and essentially, as Gehringer claimed, that "he'd lied to Tommy" during his earlier meeting with him in Alabama. Tommy explained:

> I got really angry in the room listening to Brendan Campbell … and I kind of got up out of my chair and went towards him and I told him, I said look, you've been lying to me all along. I told you in Birmingham not to lie to me, because I did, I had told him whatever you do, don't lie to me. And the fact is, you've lied to me about this plea deal. You knew about this plea deal before you even came to Birmingham. I want to know what was going on because you knew about it before he [Gabe] got off a plane in Brisbane or he'd have never come to Brisbane. And that's when Brendan basically said, in these words, I've repeated them a lot of times, because it's the way that he said it that really got me, but he said that prior to Gabe coming to Australia, they had to advise his attorneys on what basis they would consider a manslaughter plea and how that plea would be structured if he were to voluntarily return to Australia. So basically what I said was, so you've lied to me all along. You guys made a deal with him before he came to Australia? And he goes, no. I mean, he admits to lying, and then tries to make it look like he wasn't lying. He said no, no, no. You need to understand, there wasn't a deal, we told him on what basis we would consider a manslaughter plea deal and how that plea would be structured if he were to voluntarily come to Australia, and I said, okay, so what makes it not being a deal? [And he said] well, he had to come to Australia for it to be a deal. It's a matter of semantics, okay, they can play whatever word games they want to play, but the fact of the matter is, it was a deal that was made before he [Gabe] got on the plane [to Australia]. That's why he got on the plane to get there, and when he got there, he got exactly what he was expecting, which was a four-year sentence, to serve a minimum of a year.

Flynn similarly described Brendan Campbell's admission in the pre-sentence meeting in Queensland, claiming:

> So he finally agreed with us to sit down and he finally admitted what they had done and that he had lied to Tommy … He finally admitted that he had lied to Tommy, he had lied to us. He didn't really care. There was no emotion there. There was no, I wrestled with this, or it was a tough decision ... He didn't feel the case was winnable and that this was the best option that they could take.

Given Brendan Campbell's refusal to discuss the case with us, we cannot provide an explanation as to why he made such admissions, or whether these comments have been somehow misinterpreted by those present at the meeting. However, it is important to note that three separate eyewitnesses to the meeting provided markedly similar accounts of what occurred, without having knowledge of what the others were asked or the accounts that they provided to us. What is clear from these accounts is that some form of agreement and discussion about a deal involving a manslaughter guilty plea had likely occurred before Gabe left the US. It is also clear that Brendan Campbell provided misleading and inaccurate information regarding the plea deal to the secondary victims of this crime, thereby largely undermining his prosecutorial duty to treat victims with "courtesy, compassion, respect and dignity".[44]

Further to perceptions of Brendan Campbell's behaviour as an intentional deception of the Thomas family, the timing of the plea bargain is also significant because if a deal was struck prior to Gabe leaving the US, this brings further into question the validity of the initial and appeal sentences imposed on him. In particular, doubt emerges as to whether the sentences can be seen as offering just outcomes given the significance attributed to Gabe's voluntary return to Australia, purportedly under the threat of facing a murder trial. The voluntary nature of Gabe's return to Australia was identified in the prosecution's verbal sentencing submission and the agreed summary of facts as a primary reason for imposing a more lenient sentence. As Brendan Campbell stated in his submission:

> The accused voluntarily returned to Australia, thus avoiding the need [for Queensland] to pursue extradition proceedings, and his offer to plead guilty to manslaughter on that basis of the breach of the section 290 duty [of the *Criminal Code 1899* (Qld)] which the Crown has now accepted, are therefore both substantial matters in mitigation and should properly be given weight.[45]

Consequently, Gabe's voluntary return on the premise that he was to face a murder trial was a key mitigating factor identified by Justice Lyons in sentencing Gabe, whereby he noted that:

> You have voluntarily returned from the US and have surrendered yourself into custody in Australia. In my view, it is quite significant that at the time of your return you did not know that the Crown would not persist in charging you with murder, which carries a mandatory sentence of life imprisonment.[46]

If a deal was made with Gabe prior to his return to Australia, the mitigation attributed in his initial sentence to his voluntary return to face a murder charge is unfounded, and the resulting sentence therefore unjust. As identified by Gehringer, the fact that Gabe's voluntary return was highlighted so prominently by Brendan Campbell in his verbal sentencing

---

[44] *Victims of Crime Assistance Act 2009* (Qld) s 8.
[45] Brendan Campbell, sentencing hearing, 5 June 2009.
[46] *R v Watson* [2009] QSC 438 (Lyons J) 2.

submission was a significant concern in terms of the resolution of this case by plea bargain and its ability to provide a just outcome:

> A thing that really bugged me is that [Brendan] Campbell and [Steve] Zillman [the defence counsel] got up and said to the judge, and the judge clarified it, that Gabe had returned to Australia on a murder indictment and he had no idea that there was an option of manslaughter. That's a lie ... And [the judge] put a lot of weight on Gabe having returned for a murder trial, not for a manslaughter plea ... [The judge said] he's here, and he's come back voluntarily, and he's being so great because he's assisting. He's not causing the community costs because he's decided to come back voluntarily. [But] he's not incurring the costs of a trial because he's pleading to manslaughter ... That he came back for murder, that's a lie ... He returned for a manslaughter plea ... That was my lowest of lows as far as the whole investigation went, at that point there.

Gehringer's strong feelings of having been deceived, as evident in the above reflection, may also partly explain why the police were not given access to the agreed summary of facts either prior to or after the sentencing hearing. This is particularly so, given that Brendan Campbell's alleged admissions arguably contradicted key components of the summary that was provided to the court.

Another impact of the timing of the plea deal on the justness of the legal processes and outcomes in the *Watson* case is evident in the effect on the legal processes leading up to the capital murder trial in Alabama. In 2010, the assertion that Gabe had returned voluntarily to Australia to face a murder charge was again used in his favour, this time to support his bond application in Alabama. In explaining the reasons why Judge Tommy Nail should allow Gabe to avoid the compulsory remand applied to offenders facing capital murder trials in Alabama, Gabe's US defence attorney Brett Bloomston highlighted his voluntary return to face a murder charge in Australia as evidence of his "good" character. As Bloomston argued, "Gabe went back to Australia on his own volition when he was ultimately charged with murder … When he returned to Australia there was no deal. He was charged with murder".[47] Following these submissions, Gabe was granted a bond of $100,000—a highly unusual outcome given that he had been charged with a capital murder offence. Flynn also described Gabe's bond as "unjust" and non-reflective of the seriousness of the crime with which Gabe had been charged in Alabama. As Flynn explained:

---

[47] Brett Bloomston, bond hearing, 14 December 2010, 7.

> This was not good. The judge gives him, what was it? $100,000 bond I think is what they finally gave him, and said he would have to be monitored electronically. And I'm thinking to myself, oh, bond is one thing, but to let him out on $100,000? I've put drug users and serial burglary suspects in jail for more or had bigger bonds put on them … I really started getting a bad feeling.

Consequently, if the plea deal had been made with the Queensland ODPP prior to Gabe leaving the US, as was implicit in Brendan Campbell's admissions at the pre-sentencing meeting in June 2009, this fabrication impacted not only on the justness of the Australian resolution of the *Watson* case, but also on the legitimacy of the legal processes attached to the prosecution of Gabe in Alabama.

Is there Justice in this Outcome?

Despite the limitations of plea bargaining and the criticisms levied against the *Watson* plea deal and the resulting sentence imposed, in line with s 16 of the *Director's Policy* (Qld), we acknowledge that plea bargaining is a "legitimate and important part of the criminal justice system throughout Australia [with] the purpose [being] to secure a just result". However, as our analysis has shown, the *Watson* case demonstrates that when the processes through which plea bargaining is achieved do not uphold the expected and governed standards, justice is accordingly unobtainable for the key parties involved. In describing their perceptions of whether the plea deal offered a just outcome or any form of justice, the police as well as the secondary victims in this case provided the following responses:

> Gehringer: At the end of that [coronial] inquest, we had this job tied up in a little ribbon, bow, everything was there and then we'd got them the additional stuff they wanted. So back in 2009, all the ODPP had to do was fly everybody in and open up that little gift wrapped thing we'd given them, put it before a jury. To me, that would have been justice ... When the plea deal happened in Australia that was always what we used to say, we hadn't been given the opportunity to get in and fight for Tina.

> Flynn: It was just a huge slap in the face to us … I understand the need for plea bargains in some cases. It happens thousands of times a day up here [Alabama]. I understand it. I've been a part of it. Most of them I sign off on because I don't have a problem with them. But when you have a case such

> as this, that's gone on as much as it had, and you have a family who says all we want, win or lose, if you lose we don't hold it against you, we just want our day. That's all we want … Maybe it was the distance, maybe it was that they were cold and callous and indifferent to the family. I don't know … but it wasn't justice.

Tommy: This is a complaint totally against the ODPP, nobody other than the ODPP, and specifically Brendan Campbell and nobody else … They should never lie to the victim's family, or the victim. No matter how hard it hurts, they shouldn't lie … We had to go through a really long, painful, slow investigation to get to a deal … The only thing I'll tell you is if I had to do it all over again … the only thing that I would have changed is when Brendan Campbell pulled the stunt that he did with me over here, I'd have made sure the whole damn world knew that he was lying, before it happened, not afterwards ... And I'd have made sure the whole world knew that we were going over there for a plea deal. You know, that's the biggest thing that I'd change … But it doesn't matter. The thing about the ODPP is they don't answer to anybody. So since they don't answer to anybody—what do they care?

The common theme emanating from these reflections is a sense of regret and longing for what could have been had the ODPP pursued the *Watson* case to trial in Queensland back in 2009. Significantly, the key factor identified by each participant as leading to this breakdown in the attainment of justice involved the actions of the ODPP in accepting what was considered an unfavourable plea deal to a significantly lesser offence than that committed by Gabe on 22 October 2003.

Confusion and dissatisfaction surrounding the plea bargain, and the lack of any clarity from the ODPP on when and why the deal was made, contribute to the overwhelming perception that the handling of the *Watson* case in Queensland did not provide justice in either a subjective or procedural sense. This is particularly so, given Brendan Campbell's apparent indifference to his obligations to the secondary victims, leading up to and following the period in which the deal was made. Thus, in conjunction with the potential limitations of the plea deal for both Gabe and the Thomas family that were examined in this and the previous chapter, it is understandable why there exists a strong perception that justice was not obtained in any way, shape or form through the Queensland criminal justice system's handling and resolution of the *Watson* case.

PART II

JUSTICE IN ALABAMA

CHAPTER FIVE

PROSECUTING GABE ... AGAIN

> It may be the end of the road as far as the Australian legal system goes, but it's not the end of the road in terms of us getting justice for Tina ... He [Gabe] needs to stand in a criminal court for the murder he was charged with and face the evidence. At the end of that, whatever the jury decides will be justice as far as I'm concerned.[1]
>
> —Tina's father Tommy Thomas

In response to the perceived injustice of the Queensland Office of the Department of Public Prosecution's (ODPP) handling of the *Watson* case, Alabama Assistant Attorney-General (and lead prosecutor in the capital murder trial) Don Valeska, under the instructions of the then Alabama Attorney-General Troy King, sought to continue the pursuit for justice by initiating a capital murder prosecution against Gabe in Alabama. From one perspective, an Alabama-run trial provided an opportunity for justice to be attained in a form that was not possible in the Queensland handling of the case, by allowing all of the evidence to be tested in the presence of a jury—representing the community—who would then decide whether or not Gabe intentionally and with premeditation murdered Tina over eight years earlier. But to perceive that this trial would deliver justice, one would need to overlook the arguable breach of Gabe's due process rights that would occur as a result of running a second prosecution for his alleged involvement in Tina's death. As Gabe's US defence attorney, Brett Bloomston, commented in the lead-up to the Alabama trial, "it is a very distasteful situation when someone goes and takes responsibility for their actions in another country, serves his time and now he comes back to his home state facing nothing more than a lynch mob from the Attorney General's office".[2]

---

[1] Tommy Thomas, cited in Kathleen Skene, "Six Months Extra Jail", *Townsville Bulletin* (Queensland), 19 September 2009.

[2] Brett Bloomston, cited in Lisa Miller, "Watson Facing Alabama 'Lynch Mob'" on *ABC 621 Brisbane* (2 December 2010) <http://www.abc.net.au/news/stories/2010/12/02/3082507.htm?site=brisbane>.

Two of the unique and contentious legal issues that arose from Alabama's decision to prosecute Gabe relate to jurisdiction and the principle of double jeopardy. Traditionally, the law has defined jurisdiction by territory. Thus, if an offender commits a crime in Alabama, that state has the jurisdiction to prosecute; and conversely, if an offender commits a crime in the state of Queensland in Australia, the US state of Alabama should not have the jurisdiction to criminally prosecute that offender. On this basis, in terms of a traditional understanding of jurisdiction, the decision to prosecute Gabe in Alabama was considered controversial, and both Bloomston and Gabe's family and civil attorney, Bob Austin, consequently questioned the legitimacy of the prosecution proceeding. As Bloomston explained, "we thought the case was over [after Queensland]. We never thought that there would be a charge in Alabama. And that wasn't just my singular opinion; I spoke to judges, lawyers, law professors, who all thought that Alabama lacked jurisdiction". Austin further explained the problematic notion of establishing jurisdiction in Alabama, maintaining that:

> The question of jurisdiction ... I understand it's separate sovereignties, two different countries, two different laws ... [But] did the Alabama courts have jurisdiction? I don't think they did, under the circumstances. Even if they could have proved something, I don't think they had jurisdiction.

Although jurisdiction is traditionally defined in terms of geography and territory, in light of globalisation and the increasing need for criminal justice agencies and systems to be able to respond to transnational offences, there are exceptions to this conventional understanding of jurisdiction. One such exception, which was applicable in the *Watson* case, is referred to as extraterritorial jurisdiction. Thus, in the context of international law, because the victim and offender were both US citizens, there are two key principles that allowed Alabama to have jurisdiction in this case: nationality jurisdiction and passive personality jurisdiction. As research fellow, Dr Melanie O'Brien, from Griffith University in Queensland explains:

> States reserve the right to exercise jurisdiction over crimes committed by their nationals, even when committed outside their territory. Nationality jurisdiction is generally only enacted in the case of serious crimes, such as

> murder, treason, war crimes, and genocide ... Passive personality jurisdiction is when a crime committed results in harm to a national of that state.[3]

Specifically, within the State of Alabama, the right to claim extraterritorial jurisdiction is enshrined within the *Code of Alabama 1975*, which permits the state's laws to be applicable beyond its boundaries, in cases where some elements of the offence were committed within the state boundaries. In *Watson*, the Alabama Office of the Attorney-General proceeded with the charge of capital murder for pecuniary gain against Gabe by invoking ss 15-2-3 and 15-2-4 of the *Code of Alabama 1975*, which relate to an offence commenced in Alabama and consummated elsewhere, or an offence commenced elsewhere but consummated in Alabama. Jurisdiction was thus obtained on the basis that Gabe had planned and attempted to profit from the crime in Alabama—the pecuniary gain element of the offence—yet committed the murder element of the offence in Queensland. However, while recognising this potential to hold jurisdiction, Austin maintained that the prosecution would face difficulties in its attempt to prove that the alleged crime was planned in Alabama. As Austin explained, "if the charge was the plotting of this alleged crime, where did it occur? Did it occur in the Jefferson County division, or did he plot it at home? Or did it occur on the airplane to Australia? ... How could you prove that?" While "proof" would certainly become a central issue in the capital murder trial, particularly in relation to the pecuniary gain motive, the jurisdictional issues identified by Austin were not considered a sufficient basis to prevent the capital murder trial from proceeding. As Judge Tommy Nail stated on the first day of the trial, "this case started in this country and ended in Australia".[4] Thus, regardless of Austin's concerns, in legal terms Alabama possessed the jurisdiction to try Gabe for Tina's murder.

Aside from questioning whether Alabama held the jurisdictional scope to prosecute Gabe, a further concern regarding the justness of the second prosecution proceeding was raised on the basis of the double jeopardy principle. Double jeopardy refers to the protection that an individual should not be tried or punished twice for the same offence(s) arising from

---

[3] Melanie O'Brien, "Society is Entitled to but One Satisfaction: *Ne Bis In Idem* and Jurisdiction Questions in the Gabe Watson Case" (Speech delivered at *Crime, Justice and Democracy Conference*, Brisbane, Australia 26–28 September 2011) <http://crimejusticeconference.com/wp-content/uploads/2012/05/Conference-Proceedings-Crime-Justice-and-Social-Democracy-An-International-Conference.pdf> 64.

[4] Judge Tommy Nail, court observations, 13 February 2012.

the same conduct. In this context, there was a question over the legitimacy of the Alabama prosecution proceeding, given that Gabe was effectively being tried and possibly punished twice for the same conduct.

One of the most important protections afforded by the double jeopardy principle is that it offers a finality of criminal cases and upholds the integrity of jury acquittals, as well as sparing an accused from enduring the costs, trauma and anxieties that can arise from repeated prosecutions.[5] Double jeopardy protections are also seen as preventing excessive or oppressive prosecutions and discretionary decisions. As noted in the Australian High Court case of *R v Carroll*, "without safeguards, the power to prosecute could readily be used by the executive as an instrument of oppression".[6] Furthermore, as Sir William Blackstone explained back in 1789, it is "a universal maxim of the common law ... that no man is to be brought into jeopardy of his life more than once for the same offence".[7] Accordingly, the double jeopardy principle serves two key purposes: first, it prevents prosecutorial harassment and the negative implications that may arise in that context; and second, it promotes accuracy in criminal justice proceedings, "by preventing the state's representatives from simply retrying a defendant until they get a conviction".[8]

For these reasons, double jeopardy protections exist in various formal and informal ways at both the global and local levels, including within the jurisdictions of Queensland and Alabama. Under the Fifth Amendment of the *Constitution of the US*, no person shall "be subject for the same offence to be twice put in jeopardy of life or limb"—a requirement that applies to both state and federal prosecutions, as per the Fourteenth Amendment. Similarly, in Queensland, under s 16 of the *Criminal Code 1899* (Qld), "a person cannot be twice punished either under the provisions of this Code or under the provisions of any other law for the same act or omission". In 2007, however, Queensland introduced exceptions to this double jeopardy protection, whereby under ss 678B and 678C of the *Criminal Code 1899* (Qld), an individual can now be retried for a charge of murder where there is fresh and compelling evidence,[9] or for a crime

---

[5] Chris Corns, "Retrial of Acquitted Persons: Time for Reform of the Double Jeopardy Rule?" (2003) 27 *Criminal Law Journal* 80, 86.

[6] [2002] HCA 55 at 22.

[7] Sir William Blackstone, *Commentaries on the Law of England* (Clarendon Press, 1789).

[8] Paul Robinson and Michael Cahill, *Law without Justice: Why Criminal Law Doesn't Give People What They Deserve* (Oxford University Press, 2006) 166.

[9] Under s 678(D) of the *Criminal Code 1899* (Qld), fresh evidence includes where the evidence "was not adduced in the proceedings in which the person was

that would attract a sentence of 25 years or more, if it is decided that the original acquittal was tainted.[10] A provision exists within this statute, however, that an individual cannot be tried on either of these bases if the person has already been convicted of a lesser offence, even if they were acquitted of the more serious charge.[11] This means that in the *Watson* case, Gabe could never be tried in Queensland for the murder of Tina Thomas, because he was convicted (by guilty plea) of the lesser charge of manslaughter by criminal negligence. Gabe is also protected from a second prosecution in Queensland because the 2007 legislation does not apply retrospectively.

In establishing whether a double jeopardy protection applies, one of the primary determinative factors is whether the successive prosecutions or punishments would be for the same offence, or the same conduct. Under the *Criminal Code 1899* (Qld), murder and manslaughter are alternative verdicts; this means that they are not technically considered the "same" offence. While Gabe was convicted for his criminally negligent involvement in Tina's death in Queensland, Alabama was seeking to try Gabe for the different offence of capital murder, which involved his premeditated and intentional involvement in Tina's death. Thus, strictly speaking, Gabe was not being tried for the "same" offence.

In addition to the alternate offence rationale, there were three key arguments that allowed for the double jeopardy protection generally afforded to an accused to be overlooked in this case. These include the doctrine of dual sovereignty, the absence of a binding international standard or requirement on double jeopardy, and Australia's ability to deport rather than extradite Gabe. While the doctrine of dual sovereignty in the US has not been applied in an international context, it offers a framework to help explain why there was a strong perception that Alabama had the right to prosecute Gabe.

---

acquitted; and it could not have been adduced in those proceedings with the exercise of reasonable diligence". Under s 678D(3) of the Act, evidence is compelling if "it is reliable", "it is substantial" and "in the context of the issues in dispute in the proceedings in which the person was acquitted, it is highly probative of the case against the acquitted person".

[10] Under 678(E) of the *Criminal Code 1899* (Qld), a tainted acquittal is defined as a situation in which:

> The accused person or another person has been convicted in this State or elsewhere of an administration of justice offence in relation to the proceedings in which the accused person was acquitted; and it is more likely than not that, but for the commission of the administration of justice offence, the accused person would have been convicted.

[11] *Criminal Code 1899* (Qld) s 678A(2).

The doctrine of dual sovereignty, which was established by case law in *United States v Lanza*,[12] allows for two independent sovereigns to prosecute an individual who has violated the laws of both sovereigns, regardless of a prior acquittal or conviction. In *Lanza*, the accused was convicted of manufacturing, transporting and possessing intoxicating liquor by the State of Washington and was then charged for the same criminal conduct under federal laws. A federal district court initially prohibited the second prosecution, claiming that it breached the Fifth Amendment protection against double jeopardy. However, on appeal, the Supreme Court held that both the state and federal governments had the independent sovereignty to prosecute the case, stating that "it follows that an act denounced as a crime by both national and state sovereignties is an offense against the peace and dignity of both and may be punished by each".[13] This precedent consequently became known as the doctrine of dual sovereignty.

In applying the doctrine, the crucial consideration is whether the two jurisdictions that intend to prosecute the accused for the same course of conduct can be defined as separate sovereigns. This can be determined according to whether the prosecuting agencies derive from separate and independent sovereigns. Thus, because each state within the US is considered a separate sovereign, the double jeopardy protection does not apply when two different states decide to prosecute an individual for the same conduct, if it can be established that the individual violated the laws of both jurisdictions.

Within Alabama, the leading case to recognise the doctrine was *Heath v Alabama*.[14] In *Heath*, the accused hired two men to kill his wife. In adhering to a plan put together by Heath, the two hired men kidnapped Heath's wife from the family home in the state of Alabama, and her body was later found in the adjoining state of Georgia. Despite Heath accepting a plea deal in Georgia, in which he pleaded guilty to malice murder in exchange for a sentence of life imprisonment, Heath was subsequently tried and convicted in Alabama of capital murder by kidnapping, and was sentenced to death. This conviction was upheld by both the Alabama Court of Criminal Appeals and the Alabama Supreme Court, because even though the murder was carried out in Georgia, it was planned and commenced in Alabama. As a result, the accused had breached the laws of the two states; therefore, both Alabama and Georgia possessed the jurisdiction to try him for these criminal violations.

---

[12] 260 US 377 (1922).

[13] *United States v Lanza* 260 U.S 377 (1922) at 260.

[14] 472 U.S 82 (1985).

A similar premise can be applied in *Watson*. Queensland and Alabama are separate jurisdictions, whose prosecuting agencies derive from separate and independent sources, thus meeting the separate entities requirement of the doctrine. Furthermore, the offence for which Gabe was to be prosecuted in Alabama—murder for pecuniary gain—alleged that Gabe had planned Tina's murder in Alabama, and that he had attempted to benefit financially from her death upon his return to Alabama. Thus, while Gabe was accused of carrying out the offence of murder in Queensland, his alleged actions were in violation of the laws of both jurisdictions. As such, under the doctrine of dual sovereignty, Queensland and Alabama both held the power to try him for his alleged criminal conduct.

In recognition of the doctrine of dual sovereignty, Bloomston acknowledged that he did not believe double jeopardy was a concern, even though a defence motion was made prior to the trial commencing to dismiss the case on this basis. Bloomston explained, "I never thought we would get anywhere on a double jeopardy because of dual sovereignty. I never thought that was a good argument". From the prosecution's perspective, Valeska and Tina's father, Tommy Thomas, were also of the opinion that double jeopardy did not present a significant concern or a legitimate basis for the case not to proceed to trial in Alabama. As Tommy claimed:

> Double jeopardy was not an issue ... There's been too many cases here in the State of Alabama where it wasn't a state in another country, it was a state in our own country, but we retried people ... Plus there have been issues between state and federal prosecutions, you know you can be prosecuted, so that's not, that wasn't an issue ... Plus there's also plenty of evidence that he [Gabe] planned it here [in Alabama].

Similarly, Valeska noted, "they were arguing that Gabe had been tried in Australia, but it's not double jeopardy for different countries, or different states".

Another reason why the second prosecution was exempt from the double jeopardy protection was that Australia had the capacity to deport Gabe, rather than extradite him. As a result, there were no domestic legal requirements on Australia to consider the double jeopardy rule. The difference between an extradition and deportation is primarily that "the object of extradition is to restore a fugitive criminal to the jurisdiction of a state which has a lawful claim to try or punish him for an offence ... Deportation, on the other hand, is how a state rids itself of an undesired alien".[15] Had Australia extradited Gabe, based on the *Extradition Act 1988* (Cth), it would have had to take into account certain human rights considerations, including a double jeopardy protection which requires that an extradition objection be made when a person faces the prospect of a second prosecution or punishment for the same offence. Under s 7(e) of the *Extradition Act 1988*, an objection to extradition should be made when:

> The person has been acquitted or pardoned by a competent tribunal or authority in the extradition country or Australia, or has undergone the punishment provided by the law of that country or Australia, in respect of the extradition offence or another offence constituted by the same conduct as constitutes the extradition offence.

If this condition exists, the individual should not be extradited to the requesting country. However, because Australia was able to deport rather than extradite Gabe, this requirement was not applicable. As the Australian Immigration Minister Chris Bowen commented at the time of Gabe's deportation, "my role has been to ensure that we fulfil our treaty obligations [and] we've done that … Double jeopardy is not covered by our treaty obligations".[16]

A double jeopardy protection is, however, located in the *International Covenant on Civil and Political Rights 1966*, which both Australia and the US have ratified. Under Article 14(7), the covenant states that "no one shall be liable to be tried or punished again for an offence for which he or she has already been finally convicted or acquitted in accordance with the law and penal procedure for each country". The potential for the prosecution in Alabama to breach this international obligation was identified by a researcher working for Gabe's US defence team. However, as Bloomston explained, this was not a viable argument to make in front of an Alabama judge, particularly Judge Tommy Nail:

> We had a scholar who studied international law, saying, but this is violative of the treaty. I said, buddy, we're talking to Judge Tommy Nail, he's a cowboy ... I said, we're not going to win an international law motion to dismiss in front of Judge Nail. If you think you can win that at the Hague [International Criminal Court], go for it!

---

[15] Ivan Shearer, *Extradition in International Law* (University Press, 1971) 76.

[16] Immigration Minister Chris Bowen, cited in *Daily Mail*, "Honeymoon Killer Who Drowned Wife is Deported to US to Face Murder Trial after 18 Months in Australian Jail for Manslaughter", *Daily Mail* (United Kingdom), 25 November 2010.

While the "cowboy"-like nature of Judge Tommy Nail's character became evident at later stages of the trial—an issue examined in more detail in the next chapter—Bloomston's comments highlight the third rationale for the Alabama trial being able to avoid the double jeopardy protections: that although Australia's ratification of the covenant means that the nation has an international obligation to adhere to it, according to Australian High Court Justice Michael Kirby, international rules "do not bind as other 'rules' do".[17] Interestingly, this means that while Australia and the US have an obligation to act in accordance with the covenant, they are not legally bound to do so. Furthermore, the argument pertaining to the offences being different—manslaughter versus murder—could also be used to disregard this protection in the *Watson* case.

In overlooking the potential breach of Gabe's due process rights, Bloomston was able to identify one potential benefit of Gabe being prosecuted for a second time: that the defence had a significant, and detailed, insight into the prosecution's case. This was because Gabe's defence team had access to over 60 sworn statements from the coronial inquest held in Queensland, amounting to over 200,000 documents, several of which included the earlier statements of the prosecution witnesses who testified at the Alabama trial. As a result of this unique knowledge of the prosecution's evidence, Bloomston explained that the defence went into the trial with what he perceived to be a very strong case:

> While we weren't certain which witness was coming through the door next ... [we had] the coronial inquest testimony, and sworn statements, [so] we knew what everybody would say, we just had to be ready for it. And it certainly helped us ... Obviously to cross-examine a witness when you have a sworn statement, it's refreshing to have when you're a defence attorney, because in our system, we usually don't have the benefit of knowing what a witness says until it comes out of their mouth.

Interestingly, even in light of these potential benefits, the public's confusion as to whether the Alabama trial breached double jeopardy protections persisted throughout the case, evident within the comments of the potential members of the jury panel made on the first day of the jury selection process in the capital murder trial. As one potential juror proclaimed, "he's been tried already in another country and another continent, and I don't understand why he's being tried again".[18] Shortly after this comment was made, another potential juror stated, "I think he's already been tried. They came up with their verdict and it should stay on

[17] A*l-Kateb v Godwin* [2004] HCA 37 (Kirby J) at 173.
[18] Male potential juror #1, court observations, 13 February 2012.

that".[19] A third potential juror similarly professed that "he's already served time. They found him guilty of another criminal offence".[20]

While highlighting the extent of confusion surrounding double jeopardy in this case, these comments also highlight one of the reasons why this trial could arguably be perceived as failing to offer a just outcome to either Gabe or the Thomas family: because opinions as to Gabe's guilt or innocence had already been formed based on the international media's coverage of the case. Indeed, during our observations of the jury selection process, only four of the 67 potential jurors within the pool acknowledged that they had not heard something about the case prior to arriving in court on 13 February 2012. One potential juror went so far as to explain in front of all of the other potential jurors why she believed Gabe was guilty, describing the "evidence" she had read in newspapers, including that "he took out a life insurance policy ... and he casually swam to the top of the water after leaving her [Tina]".[21] Responding to this potential juror's comments, Valeska explained to the jury pool that:

> Everyone is entitled to their opinion, so Tina Thomas can have a fair trial and Gabe Watson can have a fair trial. This is the greatest justice system in the world, but it doesn't work if someone has a hidden agenda. The judge asked if anyone has a fixed opinion and we heard three people respond to this question, very vocally. Did what these three people say, I mean you can't un-ring a bell, so you have to tell us, if those comments influenced you, sitting here in the courtroom?[22]

While Valeska's question attempted to undo the damage that may have been caused by the "very vocal" comments of the potential juror, in terms of unduly influencing other potential jury members, the fact that Valeska needed to respond in this way further demonstrates how the trial process itself may be seen as unjust. This also illustrates the powerful influence of national and international pre-trial publicity on perceptions of guilt and innocence in high-profile criminal matters—an issue that is explored in more detail in Chapter Eight.

As evident from the above discussion, the second prosecution of Gabe in a different jurisdiction, but for the same conduct, was not only possible, but legally and technically just. Therefore, even in light of the concerns raised by the potential jurors, criticisms of the second prosecution proceeding based on jurisdictional or double jeopardy/due process

---

[19] Male potential juror #2, court observations, 13 February 2012.
[20] Female potential juror, court observations, 13 February 2012.
[21] Ibid.
[22] Don Valeska, court observations, 13 February 2012.

protections are not sufficient to doubt the capacity of the Alabama trial to provide a second chance for justice, even under a procedural justice framework. However, as explored in this and the following three chapters, even if one overlooks these issues, there are several key factors that emerged prior to and during the trial which ultimately prevented it from offering a procedurally just process or outcome.

Motivations for the Second Prosecution

A prominent factor that affected the capacity of the Alabama trial to provide justice related to the motivations underpinning the decision to prosecute Gabe in Alabama. Much like the uncertainty surrounding the motivations informing the Queensland ODPP's decision to plea bargain, similar concerns were raised in relation to the decision of the former Alabama Attorney-General, Troy King, to proceed with a capital murder prosecution of Gabe. While the public reason provided, and supported by those involved in the prosecution, was to offer a second chance to obtain justice, there was also a perception that a politically motivated Attorney-General was using the case to bolster his re-election prospects.

The decision to proceed with the charges in Alabama, even on the basis of a platform of seeking justice, was perceived as being somewhat questionable in light of the statements made in Australia by the Queensland ODPP Director, Anthony Moynihan, regarding the potential weaknesses in pursuing a murder charge against Gabe. In light of Director Moynihan's statement, Bloomston questioned the motivations for the prosecution proceeding in Alabama, explaining that "when the [Queensland] DPP came forward with its public proclamation that they never thought that they would be able to convince a jury beyond a reasonable doubt of Gabe's guilt, [you would think] that another prosecutor would pay heed, and would not seek charges". Austin expressed a similar view, asking why the decision to prosecute Gabe was made despite the fact that several Australian legal professionals publicly declared that he was not guilty of murder. Austin argued:

> They were wrong in indicting him ... the [Queensland] DPP said he didn't do anything deliberately. The [Queensland] trial judge [said] he didn't do anything deliberately. He [just] violated the dive buddy statute. Three appellate judges [in Queensland] said he didn't do anything deliberately. And the worst one wanted to do was to increase the sentence [by] another six months ... So why did it get to this point? Have any ideas?

While Austin's comments raise a legitimate question over the prosecution proceeding in Alabama, it should be clarified that in Queensland the appellate Justices were not examining the evidence or making a judgement on Gabe's guilt or the level of his involvement in Tina's death. They were instead determining only the validity of the prosecution's appeal against the manifest inadequacy of the sentence. This point was highlighted by one of the prosecutors at Gabe's bond hearing in Alabama on 14 December 2010, who stated that "Mr Watson pled guilty to manslaughter, and therefore, when the Supreme Court looked at this case that was on [the] appeal of sentence on a manslaughter plea. The appeal process did not go back and look at all of the trial because we never got to that".[23]

In accordance with Bloomston and Austin's concerns, one of the key accusations of injustice surrounding the Alabama prosecution was that the decision to proceed with the case was influenced by a political agenda, and the tough law-and-order stance that the then Attorney-General, Troy King, was known for. This stance was evident in 2007 when King publicly advocated the abolition of parole, on the basis that "crime victims expect criminals to serve the sentences they get in court, but that usually doesn't happen in Alabama".[24] In response, the Executive Director of the Alabama Sentencing Commission, Lynda Flynt, was quoted as stating, "Troy King's position [comes] from law and order, being tough on crime, and running for re-election".[25] While it can be posited that King's tough stance in relation to Gabe's prosecution was intended to uphold public interests, because Tina and her family were used as part of his re-election campaign, there exists a tension between whether the decision to proceed with the prosecution was motivated by the desire to attain a political advantage, or by the interests of justice. As former Vice President of the International Association of Prosecutors, Daniel Bellemare QC, notes, "where elected officials publicly call for charges to be laid, suggesting that crimes have been committed, there is a real danger that the public believes that the decision to charge or prosecute was influenced by these public statements".[26] Within this context, the distinction between making a

---

[23] Tina Coker Hammonds, bond hearing, 14 December 2010, 16.

[24] Troy King, cited in Phillip Rawls, "King Wants to Abolish Parole", *Tuscaloosa News* (Alabama), 22 October 2007.

[25] Lynda Flnyt, cited in Rawls, above n 24.

[26] Daniel Bellemare, "Accountability, Independence and Ethics in Prosecution Practice: Public Confidence and Accountability in the Exercise of Prosecutorial Discretion" (Speech delivered at the *International Society for Reform of Criminal Law: 18th International Conference*, Montreal, Canada, 10 August 2004) <http://www.isrcl.org /Papers/2004/Bellemare.pdf>.

decision to uphold public interests and making a decision to be politically savvy becomes somewhat blurred.

If the decision to prosecute Gabe was made to satisfy a political agenda, a range of ethical and legal concerns emerge, primarily because this brings the administration of justice into disrepute. As Bloomston explained:

> We had a very politically motivated and charged Attorney-General that pushed the case. He actually used [it] as part of his platform for running for a primary [election] ... He put flyers and banners all over her [Tina's] little city that said, "Remember Tina Thomas Watson, Vote for Troy King". And he used the Thomas family and used Tina's death to get attention. It got him on national television. He would get on Twitter and tweet when he was in New York City on the *Today Show*, [saying] that I'm heading to the big show, and doing God's work, and [he] just improperly used this case for his political gain. And then he lost ... What happened is after he lost the election, a new Attorney-General [Luther Strange] came in ... and I think it was probably a situation where if his prosecutors went forward and lost, he could always blame Troy King, his predecessor, he's the one who indicted this case, I inherited it and it's not my baby. And on the flip side, if they won, he would have taken credit for putting a murderer behind bars.

As implicit in Bloomston's comments, when a decision is made in accordance with an existing or even a perceived politically advantageous stance, questions are raised around the true motivations for the decision and the ability for the outcome to provide procedural justice. As Daniel Bellemare QC further claimed, "justice must be dispensed without regard to political consequences [and] the decision to prosecute must never be arbitrary or informed by improper considerations".[27] This is because if political, oppressive or harsh motivations frame the decision to prosecute, punitive, law and order–based political agendas may be allowed to infiltrate and control the entire prosecution process.

The concern that political gain motivated King's decision to prosecute Gabe formed part of the basis for the defence's motion for the charges against Gabe to be dismissed before the trial commenced, under the guise of a vindictive prosecution. In order to establish prosecutorial vindictiveness, the defence had to show either direct evidence of actual vindictiveness or facts that demonstrated the appearance of vindictiveness. This motion was dismissed by Judge Tommy Nail; however, in response the defence then sought to subpoena King as a hostile witness, to demonstrate the political motivations underpinning the prosecution. As

---

[27] Ibid.

Gabe's US defence attorney Joe Basgier argued during the pre-trial discussion on the first day of the capital murder trial, "it's vindictive. He used Tina as a political platform with campaigns like, 'remember Tina, vote for King'".[28] This subpoena request was also denied by Judge Nail, but it further highlighted the controversial nature of the second prosecution and the persistence of questions over the justness of the trial proceeding. As Gabe's father, David Watson, claimed:

> I do think the state of Alabama engendered a crime, an alleged crime, so they could bring charges. There was never any evidence that he attempted to collect any money, or attempted to have her change anything for that [monetary] benefit. That was all just conjured up to suit the government ... Troy King was running for re-election. I think he needed something to divert the attention away from his shortcomings, his problems. And I think he used the Thomas family, and I think he used the Watson family for his own selfish purposes. I think that's how it came to be in America. He just saw a golden opportunity to ride this thing all the way to re-election. I think had he been in the first year of a new term, he might have ignored it.

The possibility that a political advantage informed the decision to prosecute Gabe might also be implied by King requesting that Valeska keep abreast of the case while it was being responded to in Queensland, in the event that an unsatisfactory outcome resulted and the Alabama Office of the Attorney-General could then step in. As Lieutenant Brad Flynn recalled, Valeska first expressed an interest in the case, at the request of King, in early 2008:

> It was right in the middle of the [coronial] inquest when I got a call out of the blue from Don Valeska at the Attorney-General's Office, and he called to say, hey, I just wanted to let you know we're interested in this, we're watching it ... He [Gabe] may [also] be culpable in the US ... but [at this stage] we're not getting involved. This is strictly an Australian case. We'll be glad to help you however you need it behind the scenes, but he said we're not going to do anything.

Tommy similarly recognised that Valeska had an early interest in the case, one which included an interest in potentially prosecuting Gabe, even before the plea bargain and the perceived inadequate sentencing outcome of the case in Queensland was known. However, Tommy believed that this interest resonated from a desire to see justice achieved, as opposed to any political advantage it may have offered:

---

[28] Jo Basgier, court observations, 13 February 2012.

> During the coronial inquest ... I think it was the early part of 2008, Don Valeska had called us and wanted to meet with Brad and I, so Brad and I went down to Montgomery [in Alabama] and we had a meeting with Don ... And Don basically said we've been following the case, we've been monitoring what's going on in Australia, our concern is [that] she is a citizen of the State of Alabama, he actually is a citizen of the State of Alabama too, and we're afraid that you might not get justice in Australia. And I don't know why they had that fear. I don't know whether it was because of the length of the police investigation or whether it was because maybe they had done some research and found out that a lot of people get off over there. I don't know. But they offered to take the case, and I basically told Don that he [Gabe] did it in Australia, I really wanted him to face the evidence before a jury in Australia where he did it ... I told Don I wanted to take my chances in Australia, and he said, well, we're going to continue to monitor the case.

As reflected in Tommy's observations, Valeska's early interest could be interpreted as supporting the perception that the Alabama prosecution proceeded because justice was not attained in Australia. Indeed, the accusation that a political motivation informed the decision to prosecute was strongly denied by Tommy, who claimed:

> [Gabe's] attorneys, one of the big things that they've done is they've been talking about Troy King doing this as some kind of political ploy. Well this stuff started two years before the election. There was no politics involved in it. I really believe every politician looks for political advantages, but I don't believe in any way, shape or form, Troy was looking at this case as some type of political image case, because Don Valeska knew it was going to be a very difficult case, mainly because you don't have that proverbial smoking gun, okay, and so they knew that there were a lot of risks involved. So, you know, in no way, shape or form do I think it was political ... I've got nothing but the greatest amount of respect and admiration for both of them, and I will tell you this, neither one of them ever lied to me, which is a lot better than I can say for Brendan Campbell [the prosecutor] in Queensland.

This perspective was also supported by Valeska, who maintained that:

> If there had been what he [Troy King] perceived as justice for Tina [in Queensland], then he wouldn't have told us to go forward ... And of course had the jury verdict down there been not guilty ... we wouldn't have gone forward here ... But it was pretty obvious he was mad [with the outcome] ... Basically, the sentence of one year and they moved it up to six more months, so that wasn't, that didn't make him happy.

A commonly held view expressed by the police involved in the investigation into Tina's death was also that the Alabama prosecution would not have proceeded had the outcome in Australia been seen as delivering justice. As Detective Senior Constable Kevin Gehringer claimed:

> I don't think it would have been pursued over here if they'd [the Queensland ODPP] done their job properly in Australia. So if they'd taken it to trial in Australia ... win, lose or draw, I think that would have been the end of the matter. Or, [even with] him pleading [guilty] to manslaughter, if he'd got a decent term of imprisonment which reflected the proper facts, not the agreed facts that were watered down, but that he'd had so much more interaction with Tina when he separated from her, and he'd done, I don't know, but I sort of think ... if he'd spent four to six years in a jail in Australia, again I don't think the authorities over here [Alabama] would have run with it.

Flynn also believed that the Alabama prosecution proceeded because of the unjust outcome in Australia—an observation he based on his interactions with Valeska following Gabe's sentencing hearing in Queensland in June 2009. Flynn recounted:

> I called Don when we found out that the plea bargain was happening and I was going to Australia. And he said, do me a favour. He says, let me know how things work out, and he says, if you guys don't get what you think is justice, you let me know. And he says, I'm willing to drive this and see how far we can get with it. So I said, okay ... The first phone call I made after he [Gabe] was sentenced was to Don, and I said, Don, they gave him 12 months and he says, you have got to be kidding, because even Don thought if he was convicted of something like that in the [United] States, three to five years at a minimum he would have got, [but] he didn't even get a full year. And Don says, well, we're willing to look into this if the family wants it, and I said yes, I can tell you that the family wants it. So that's when, as soon as that happened, I jumped on a plane and came back and was in Montgomery [with Don] the next day.

Interestingly, and in line with our earlier observations of the complexities surrounding the definition of justice, Gabe's father David observed that justice would only have been perceived as being attained for the Thomas family had Gabe been found guilty of murder and then sentenced to a period of life imprisonment in Australia. From his perspective, David believed that, had any other outcome been reached in Australia, the decision to prosecute Gabe in the US would have proceeded because the Office of the Attorney-General in Alabama could make a jurisdictional claim to do so. He maintained that, "regardless of what the

Australians did or might have done, we would have ended up in the same place in America ... unless he had been sentenced to life in Australia, that would have been the only thing that would have appeased them". This perception mirrors Bloomston and Austin's views outlined earlier pertaining to the inevitability of the Alabama prosecution against Gabe, regardless of the outcome in Queensland.

In several interviews conducted after the resolution of the case in Queensland and the acquittal decision in Alabama, King has continued to defend his decision to prosecute Gabe on the basis that justice was not offered by the Queensland plea bargain and the subsequent sentence imposed. He claimed that Queensland "watered down"[29] its justice system and that Tina's family "didn't get justice in Australia".[30] Similarly, in an interview on the US *Today* show in 2012, King strongly denied that the decision to prosecute Gabe was in any way influenced by the potential political advantage of pursuing the case. He stated:

> One of the most sacred responsibilities an Attorney-General has is that which he owes to victims. That's not to win a popularity contest, it is to go to court and see justice done in every case possible ... [The Thomas family were] betrayed in Australia ... Now investigators and prosecutors [in Alabama] worked the case, came back and made the recommendation that we go to a grand jury, which we did. There is no politics involved in a grand jury. They don't run for election. The grand jury agreed with us that capital murder charges should be returned and they were ... I wasn't the one playing politics, I was the one doing my job ... And I'm proud of what we did. I believe we honoured Tina's memory. I believe we pursued justice.[31]

Problems with Running the Trial in Alabama

Regardless of whether the motivation was inherently or even partly political, or based on a desire to provide a second chance for justice, a number of additional factors arose during the Alabama trial that impacted on its capacity to ensure justice from any perspective. These factors can be divided into two primary categories: the cultural and logistical difficulties

---

[29] Troy King, cited in Greg Riesling and Ray Henry, "Honeymoon Killer Deported: Man Convicted in Wife's Death Sent Back to US", *Huffington Post* (United States), 25 November 2010.

[30] Ibid.

[31] Troy King, cited in *Birmingham News*, "Former Alabama AG Troy King Defends Decision to Pursue Gabe Watson Case", *Birmingham News* (Alabama), 24 February 2012.

of running a trial for a crime committed in a different country; and the costs and resources involved in running the trial, particularly given the precarious financial situation in Alabama leading up to and during the prosecution.

One of the primary problems identified in relation to trying the case in an alternate jurisdiction was the Alabama jury's understandably limited knowledge of scuba diving, the Great Barrier Reef and Australia in general. The city of Townsville is approximately 14,523 kilometres (9,024 miles) from Birmingham, Alabama. The region of Townsville itself spans 3,736 square kilometres and consists of coastal beaches, rainforests and outback/country areas. In contrast, the city of Birmingham spans approximately 393 square kilometres and is mainly considered a business hub. At June 2011, the city of Townsville's population stood at 189,931, while the city of Birmingham's population was approximately 212,237. Townsville is known for its central location to the Great Barrier Reef, which makes it a prominent location for scuba diving expeditions. Birmingham is located approximately 360 kilometres (224 miles) from the nearest coastline.

In our discussions with Valeska, he highlighted the difficulties he experienced in seeking to ensure an Alabama jury could comprehend some of the key elements of the prosecution's case, due to the significant differences between Townsville and Birmingham, particularly those pertaining to the diving industry. He explained:

> Dive expeditions, what happens, what doesn't happen. We were trying to understand it, learn it, but it's [diving] a major industry in Townsville. That would be like trying a case here about American baseball: everybody understands it, so we don't need an explanation. We can't be perplexed by the evidence presented.

Tommy similarly identified the difference between a Queensland jury and a jury comprising residents of Birmingham as a potential problem arising from running the trial in Alabama. He explained:

> Australia is where he did it. He should have been tried [there], the evidence should have been presented before a jury and it would have certainly been a jury of his peers because it would have been made up of a fair percentage of divers, which if you noticed in the trial here, they [the defence] made sure there wasn't a single diver on the jury ... Don Valeska and that team of prosecutors, they would have loved to have tried this case in Queensland. They would have loved to, because ... [it would have involved] members of the Australian public on a jury.

Alongside the problems regarding the make-up of the jury, Valeska also identified the limited capacity of the Alabama prosecution to offer the same depth of substantive justice as would likely have been offered by an Australian-run trial, because the prosecution was not able to present alternate charges. As outlined in Chapter Three, in addition to the murder charge, an alternative verdict of manslaughter would have been available for jury consideration in an Australian-run trial. As Valeska explained:

> In most capital murder charges, there are lesser included offences. You go from capital murder, to murder, to maybe manslaughter, depending on what the evidence is, or what the jury can reasonably infer from it. We definitely would have looked at a lesser [straight murder] charge. But being stuck with having to show a financial gain to even have a trial, we felt the evidence was there, but we could only have the capital murder charge.

As implicit in Valeska's comments, an Australian-run trial might have offered a more procedurally just outcome, not only because the jury would have perhaps better understood the circumstances surrounding a diving death in Australia, but also because the jury would have been able to decide whether to convict Gabe, and if so, on which homicide-related charge. Thus, despite the Alabama prosecution being projected as offering an avenue for justice—in the sense of running a traditional adversarial trial—even the prosecution and its supporters identified several limitations that hindered the trial's capacity from the outset to provide any true form of procedural, substantive and subjective justice. As Tommy explained:

> In reality, we should have never had a trial here, because we should have never had to have had a trial over here. It should have been a trial back there [in Australia]. And we knew that we would have a lot more difficulties with a trial here than we would over there, in every sense of the word.

Flynn similarly claimed that the limitations of having to try the case in Alabama, rather than Queensland, meant that the trial offered "justice [but] on face value only". In recognising the difficulties inherent to an Alabama trial, Flynn further claimed:

> This case should never be up here, we shouldn't have had to be doing this. That's the whole point. I didn't want to have to do it up here because I knew that we would be coming in with our right hand tied behind our back. So many issues; time, evidence, budgets ... We're not coming in with nearly the [witness] line-up we had in Australia.

Concerns surrounding the limited number of witnesses at the Alabama trial, an issue discussed in more detail in Chapter Seven, were also identified by Gehringer, who argued that the trial was only able to offer a partial opportunity for justice, as opposed to what might have occurred had the trial been run in Queensland in 2009. He explained:

> Yes it's justice to the extent that at least we're getting a trial, but ... we're now, whatever, eight years down the track, and ... they've [the prosecution in Alabama] had to cut back and use a skeleton witness list ... I suppose it is the best it can be for the circumstances that exist today, but is it true justice or complete justice? Not really.

Money, Money, Money: A Lack of Resources Strikes Again

As highlighted in Flynn's and Gehringer's comments above, another significant factor preventing the Alabama prosecution from being able to offer justice involved the limitations arising from the costs and resources required to run the trial. On this point, Tommy explained, "you notice money became an issue here too". In a similar vein to Queensland, the Alabama justice system was under immense economic constraints leading up to, during and post Gabe's February 2012 capital murder trial. Across the state of Alabama in the 2011–12 financial year, the justice budgets were reduced by $120 million.[32] This involved individual courts having to lay off staff and reduce court operating hours.[33] At the Jefferson County Courthouse alone, where the *Watson* trial was held, approximately 50 staff were dismissed between April and May 2011.[34] As a result of these economic and resource cut-backs, the *Watson* trial was initially postponed from 23 May 2011 until 13 February 2012, on the basis that there was an insufficient number of security personnel to staff the courtroom. As a *Birmingham News* reporter commented to us during the trial, they were "literally shutting down the courts to try this case".[35] Consequently, resource and cost constraints again infiltrated the *Watson* case, to the point where the potential for justice was delayed for a further nine months.

---

[32] National Centre for State Courts, *Alabama Overview* (2012) <http://www.ncsc.org/information-and-resources/budget-resource-center/states-activities-map/alabama.aspx>.
[33] Ibid.
[34] Ibid. See also, Peter Mitchell, "Gabe Watson Murder Trial Delayed", *Sydney Morning Herald* (New South Wales), 8 April 2011.
[35] US media reporter, court observations, 14 February 2012.

As argued in Chapter Three, the cost of attaining justice in Queensland was an influential factor in the decision to resolve the case by plea bargain in 2009. In February 2012, the cost of justice again impacted on a prosecution of Gabe Watson, this time by limiting the strength and depth of the prosecution's case. As Tommy claimed, "Jefferson County's broke, the state's broke, and because of that, we were limited on the number of witnesses we could bring over, we were limited on a lot of the other stuff that we could have done, and we would have had a stronger case with a few other people". In discussing the resource limitations facing the prosecution, Valeska highlighted costs as impacting not only on the trial, but also on the prosecution team's capacity to prepare for the trial, including the basic preparation of witnesses. He explained that because the Attorney-General's Office could only dedicate a certain, restricted amount of funding to the case, many of the witnesses were flown in within a day, sometimes even hours, of testifying. Valeska recalled:

> They were flying in, having to go [straight] on the stand and we didn't have time to prepare them, even though we'd read their statements from Australia, it just comes out different from what they write on a piece of paper as to what they say in front of a jury ... [Usually] when you're trying it [a case], all the witnesses are there [from the beginning] and you'll meet with them several times, but we couldn't [just] fly to Australia ... and we couldn't chase [witnesses] around the country.

Gehringer also identified the negative impact of the financial situation on the trial's capacity to provide justice, because the prosecution was not able to present all of the relevant witnesses. As he explained:

> Because Alabama is in a financial predicament and their resources aren't there ... we've got this trial where we're working with a skeleton witness list and not all the physical exhibits. And you're dealing with witnesses that are trying to recall stuff that's happened back in 2003 or 2004.

Gehringer's comments not only highlight the possible impact of financial constraints on the prosecution's case, but also illustrate the ongoing effect of the significant delays experienced in this case—an issue that is explored in further detail in Chapter Seven, specifically in relation to the prosecution's dive evidence.

Building on Gehringer's reflections, Valeska also described in detail a number of possible witnesses who could have been used to assist in proving the prosecution's case had the resource expenditure been available. Importantly, he observed that many of these Australian-based witnesses "would have been available [had] the first trial gone ahead" in Queensland in 2009. He explained:

> Gary Stempler, the man who took the picture [of Tina's body underwater] which would have been wonderful to have ... We would have brought the woman who heard Gabe say, I pushed her [Tina] away and she [Tina] was furious ... The other doctor that worked on the case, we didn't bring, we would have brought [him] if we had more money ... We would have brought the boat captain, just to say, look, they had plenty of briefings, they knew what they were doing, but we just couldn't justify that [given the budget allocation].

The extent to which such financial constraints impacted on the prosecution's case was particularly prominent in relation to the prosecution's capacity to present evidence pertaining to the fatal dive, as some significant pieces of evidence, such as the Queensland Police Service's (QPS) dive re-enactment video that showed significant inconsistencies and implausibility in Gabe's versions of what happened, could not be shown to the jury. This is because at trial, the evidence must be presented directly (first-hand), and any witness must be able to be cross-examined on their testimony. If a witness is not able to testify to the evidence, it cannot be used. As Gehringer explained, "all the evidence, the physical evidence, hasn't been able to be admitted [in the Alabama trial] because you haven't got those witnesses to be able to admit that evidence". Given these comments, significant questions arise as to whether the Alabama prosecution ever had the capacity to offer justice, since it was run without the full witness list and presentation of all of the evidence. As Gehringer claimed, "when it comes to that courtroom, you've got to prove the minutest [sic] points and if you don't have that person there in the courtroom to orally give that evidence, then it's not evidence ... it would have helped to have everyone".

Resource considerations also limited the ability of the trial to be run according to the basic expectations and principles inherent to obtaining procedural justice. In discussions after the trial, both Bloomston and Valeska identified occasions when there was the potential to take a certain course of action—such as requesting a mistrial, or appealing against Judge Nail's decisions—but neither of them took these avenues because of the potential costs involved should they lead to a retrial. As Bloomston explained, the US defence team considered the possibility of requesting a mistrial during the jury selection process:

> When jurors started standing up and blurting out opinions, we were shocked. We certainly could have moved for a mistrial at that time or for a

> new [jury] panel, [but it] would have been terribly difficult, because there's not that many jurors that are subpoenaed, or summoned to be part of the jury. It would have delayed the case, by weeks most likely. It would have been logistically a nightmare. And we have already expended for travel for our experts. It would have been awful.

Valeska also identified several occasions when he wanted to challenge Judge Nail's rulings, during both the pre-trial hearings and the trial, yet he "held back" on the basis that it might result in a perception that the prosecution had erred. This would have enabled Judge Nail to grant a defence motion for a mistrial, but the prosecution was not in a position to fund a second trial. As Valeska explained:

> When you try a case, you realise that the last person that gets to talk to the jury is the judge. So if you make the judge mad, he is the last person that the jury here is talking to. So we had to be weary of making him mad because ... in most trials, the defence is always asking for a mistrial, claiming that the prosecution did something wrong ... If we got a mistrial, we basically didn't have the resources to bring everybody back and start over.

The fact that resource limitations played a significant determinative factor in both the prosecution's and the defence's actions throughout the trial, propels the perception that the second prosecution of Gabe never had the capacity to provide justice. This is particularly problematic when contrasted with the capacity of an Australian-run trial to offer, at least procedurally, a more substantive and complete form of justice.

CHAPTER SIX

MURDER FOR MONEY: PROVING THE MOTIVE

> We had to show a financial gain so that's of course a motive, so that's what we tell the judge ... The father gets up there and says, yeah, there's $165,000 worth of insurance, and Amanda Phillips gets up there and said, Gabe said we're going to change your [Tina's] insurance policies and then Caesar Lamonica says, he came here looking for the life insurance money ... He's [Gabe's] the last one seen with Tina. He has the motive [and] she ends up on the ocean floor dead.
>
> —Alabama Assistant Attorney-General Don Valeska

The Alabama prosecution of Gabe Watson for the death of Tina Thomas began with two charges: capital murder by kidnapping and capital murder for pecuniary gain. These charges were determined seven years to the day that Tina died, on 22 October 2010, by an Alabama grand jury comprising 18 members of the Birmingham community. After listening to the evidence presented by the prosecution, the grand jury took less than five hours to decide that Gabe should be indicted to stand trial on both charges.

The Alabama grand jury provides a similar screening process to that of the pre-trial committal hearings run in many Australian jurisdictions, in that they are used to test the strength of the prosecution evidence prior to a trial being run, in order to determine whether there is a basis to indict the accused and on what charges—a decision that is informed by the various charging options presented by the prosecution. By subjecting the prosecution's case to some scrutiny at an early stage, weak or inappropriate cases can be identified. In theory, and much like an Australian-run committal hearing, the grand jury process provides a check on the discretionary powers of the criminal justice agencies involved in a case by ensuring that unjust or insufficient prosecutions do not proceed, thus supporting the basic due process rights afforded to accused persons. On a utilitarian basis, the grand jury process also works to prevent resources being spent on unnecessary trials. The significance or justness of grand jury indictments, however, can be somewhat questionable. One of the key reasons for this is that the decision to indict an accused is based on a much lower criminal standard: that of probable cause. This means that the grand jury must only possess "a reasonable amount of suspicion, supported by circumstances sufficiently strong to justify a prudent and cautious person's belief that certain facts are probably true".[1] Furthermore, within the grand jury setting, only the prosecution presents a version of the evidence. As such, the decision as to whether the facts presented are "probably true" is informed only by the prosecution's arguments. No rebuttal evidence from the defence is presented to, or considered by, the grand jury.

Concerns surrounding the perceived dubious nature of the grand jury's decision to indict Gabe on the two capital murder charges were raised at his bond hearing in Alabama on 14 December 2010, during which Gabe's US defence attorney Brett Bloomston and Judge Tommy Nail both appeared to disregard and even undermine the grand jury's decision. In comparing the coronial inquest indictment in Queensland to that of the grand jury's in Alabama, Bloomston stated, "the coronial inquest in Australia is a little bit more detailed, than at the eight-hour grand jury [hearing] that was convened by this AG's [Attorney-General's] office".[2] Casting doubt over the legitimacy of the process itself, Bloomston further stated that the grand jury indictment is "just some off-the-cuff proffer of probable cause".[3] In a similar vein, Judge Nail alluded to the insignificance of a grand jury indictment by stating, "you could indict a ham sandwich if you want to".[4] Perhaps somewhat in recognition of these perceptions, on the first day of the Alabama trial, the prosecution withdrew one of the charges determined by the grand jury—capital murder by kidnapping.

Interestingly, in light of the problems that emerged while attempting to prove the pecuniary gain motive of the remaining charge, Alabama Assistant Attorney-General and lead prosecutor in the capital murder trial, Don Valeska, identified similar "proof"-related problems as informing the decision to withdraw the capital murder by kidnapping charge on the first day of the trial. As he explained, the grand jury indicted Gabe on the kidnapping charge on the basis that "if Tina knew what was going on, she would never have got on an airplane … that's kidnapping". But given that proving this offence beyond reasonable doubt would have required the

---

[1] Jack Handler, *Ballentine's Law Dictionary: Legal Assistant Edition* (Delmar Publishers, 1994) 431.

[2] Brett Bloomston, bond hearing, 14 December 2010, 18.

[3] Ibid.

[4] Judge Tommy Nail, bond hearing, 14 December 2010, 17.

prosecution to break through preconceived views and stereotypes about what constitutes kidnapping, they decided to withdraw the charge. Valeska claimed that "the other lawyers helping me felt we'd be better off dropping it ... because of [the] confusion in having to explain to them [the jury] there's several types of kidnapping, it's not just I grab you off the street and throw you in the trunk of the car and race off". Thus, the Alabama prosecution proceeded on the basis that Gabe murdered Tina solely for financial benefit.

The need to prove the pecuniary gain motive beyond reasonable doubt placed a significant burden on the Alabama prosecution primarily because it is extremely difficult to establish beyond reasonable doubt why an individual does anything, given the speculative nature of seeking to understand an individual's decision-making processes.[5] The subjectiveness surrounding a person's state of mind, and the difficulty of identifying a potential motive in this case, was recognised during the coronial inquest in Townsville in June 2008 by Gabe's Queensland defence counsel, Steve Zillman. In arguing that Tina's death was accidental and could not be classified as murder, Zillman highlighted the absence of a clear motive in his closing verbal submission to Coroner David Glasgow:

> There is no logical and identifiable motive that might be able to explain this case as one of murder. To identify the circumstances of the death is to highlight the inherent improbability of such a thing occurring. Other than in extreme cases, it is not the way of the world, that a husband would kill his bride of 11 days.[6]

The difficulties that the Alabama prosecutors inevitably faced in establishing motive were also identified by Glasgow, prior to the February 2012 trial commencing, due to the multiple, but intertwined, motives that emerged during the coronial inquest in Queensland. As Glasgow claimed:

> There are issues about motive ... [because] it's all speculation, isn't it? ... They can say the motive is that he decided that she was the wrong bird and maybe she wasn't going to be as manipulative as he wanted ... [or] the fact that she had the so-called naughty weekend and whether it was a naughty weekend or not, but she went off with the ex-boyfriend, went to see him and he [Gabe] found out about it. There was also issues that came up about his attitude ... He was particularly selfish, not wanting her to have anything, also [making her do] the training [when] she was not wanting to

[5] See, for example, Asher Flynn and Nicola Henry, "Disputing Consent: The Role of Jury Directions in Victoria" (2012) 24(2) *Current Issues in Criminal Justice* 167.
[6] Transcript of Proceedings, *Inquest into the death of Christina Mae Watson* (19 June 2008) 16 (Steven Zillman QC).

> do scuba diving ... He had the intention, how they [the prosecutors in Alabama] establish it, that's really a difficulty.

While Glasgow ultimately identified financial benefit as a possible motive, and one that would justify proceeding with an Australian-run murder trial in his coronial inquest findings, his comments illustrate the difficulty of establishing a motive in this case. Accordingly, the need to prove Gabe's motive was considered by several of our participants to be one of the main reasons why the Alabama trial could not offer the same depth of justice that would have been offered by running a trial in Queensland in 2009, at which point, the Office of the Department of Public Prosecutions (ODPP) would only have had to prove that Gabe intended to kill Tina, and not have had to establish beyond reasonable doubt the reason(s) why. As a US attorney commented to us:

> Well, Australia, they had a less, lesser burden of proof than [Alabama] did because they didn't have to prove the insurance, that was the weak link, really, and they didn't have to even show that ... And I think that that's even summed up by the judge when he was starting out saying [in his acquittal judgement], we'll never know what happened under there. It shows that something happened under there, and if that was all Australia had to prove that something happened, well [*shrugs shoulders*].

Valeska similarly observed that the need to prove motive was a key limitation of the prosecution proceeding in Alabama rather than in Queensland. He explained that, "based on the burden of proof, ours was much stricter and a much higher one … I haven't been to court in Australia but I've talked to people that have. There wasn't much chance of a judge not letting the case go to the jury down there". The higher likelihood of the case proceeding to a jury verdict in Queensland, as identified in Valeska's comments, is particularly significant given that many of those involved in the ongoing prosecution and investigation of Gabe equated justice in this case with a jury verdict, as opposed to a half-run trial.

Further to the motive requirement creating an additional burden for the Alabama prosecution, another problem in relation to proving the motive was the central question of whether financial gain was the primary reason underpinning Gabe's alleged murder of Tina. All of those we spoke with who were involved in the investigation and prosecution of Gabe firmly believed that financial gain was a key factor fuelling his conduct, yet some participants described additional factors that they perceived had also motivated Gabe. While noting that money was certainly an incentive, these participants suggested that there was an additional burden on the prosecution to prove the pecuniary gain element of the offence, because there were other factors—still initiated in Alabama's jurisdiction, but not related to monetary gain—which they believed contributed to Gabe's decision to kill Tina.

The existence of such perceptions is problematic for two reasons. Initially, it suggests that the murder by pecuniary gain charge may not have been an appropriate offence to proceed with to trial, which not only jeopardises the capacity of the trial to offer justice, but also raises questions over the legitimacy of it proceeding at all. As Gabe's US defence attorney, Joe Basgier, explained, "I think they wanted to give Tommy Thomas an opportunity to get on the stand and testify and say what he wanted to say, [but] it's a violation of the Alabama code of ethics for attorneys, for a prosecutor to pursue a case, that does not meet the test of probable cause". Bloomston offered a similar perspective, claiming:

> [The motive issue] begs the questioning of their responsibilities as prosecutors, as Attorneys-General. That's not their job, to give a voice or to give a platform for everyone who feels like their son-in-law's a jerk. They have a duty, an ethical duty, to only prosecute those who need to be prosecuted.

The second reason why the claims of multiple motives are problematic is that they point to another reason why Australia would have been a more appropriate jurisdiction for the murder allegations against Gabe to be tested, as the focus of a Queensland trial would have been on the alleged criminal act, as opposed to speculations on the motivations that may have informed that act. As one participant explained:

> Motive-wise ... I'm sure he killed her, but I'm not too sure why he's killed her ... I know they're talking about it's for pecuniary gain or for monetary gain ... Yes, there's been some money to gain and I think he thought there was some money to be gained ... but there's other aspects [too] ... I'm quite certain that Gabe did find out that Tina went and had the weekend with Lorenz [a potential love interest] ... Tina had told Gabe that she was going away for a girl's weekend, which wasn't the case. She was going to hook up with him [Lorenz] and Gabe had found out about that and he was upset about that ... I sort of wonder to myself, is Gabe the sort of person who, because he'd gone out, for whatever reason, was Tina the trophy wife? But he's now upset with her, but it would be too embarrassing for him, or it would look bad on his character if he had to call the wedding off because of something that, even if it was something that she'd done wrong—but then that reflects poorly on him because he's chosen poorly, because he chose this girl that's then gone out and done these things ... Would he rather go through with the wedding and everything appear to be okay? But

> then in the back of his mind he's going, you bitch, you're not going to be around, and then he's committed the murder?

Offering a similar perspective, another participant identified jealousy, anger and psychological issues as possible additional motives fuelling Gabe's conduct:

> I think that mindset is what fuelled Gabe to make and do some of the things that he did. Like who in their right mind exhumes a body less than 30 days after you've buried it just because you want to put her in another plot? Then you get into the thing about the flowers [Gabe removing the flowers that members of the Thomas family placed on Tina's grave], and you get in about the material possessions and him showing up the day of the viewing ... [demanding] to pick up all of Tina's stuff ... Who in their right mind does that?

The questions raised in the above comments pertaining to Gabe's state of mind, and the character of someone who conducts themselves in the manner in which Gabe did following the death of his wife, are considered in more detail in Chapter Eight. But as the above reflections suggest, the prosecution's need to restrict its discussion of motive in the Alabama trial solely to that of pecuniary gain, appeared to be somewhat limiting to the strength of its murder case against Gabe.

Murder for Money?

In its attempt to prove beyond reasonable doubt that Gabe was motivated by financial gain in killing Tina, the prosecution presented testimony from four financial witnesses. In addition, the prosecution used the testimony of Tina's family members and closest friend to support the argument that Gabe had been aware that he would gain financially from Tina's death prior to departing for their honeymoon. However, as examined in more detail in the discussion below, the evidence of these latter witnesses was substantially limited due to the discretionary decisions made by Judge Tommy Nail throughout the trial.

Table 5-1: The Prosecution Pecuniary Gain Witness List (In order of the date of testimony)

Name and title	Referred to as	Role in the *Watson* case	Testimony date
Ms Stephanie Mercer	Mercer	Human Resource officer at Tina's place of employment (formerly known as *Parisian*).	Friday 17 February
Mr Eric Langley	Langley	Civil and business litigation attorney–Blach & Bingham LLP, Birmingham, Alabama; involved in Gabe's lawsuit against Old Republic insurance company.	Friday 17 February
Mrs Amanda Phillips	Phillips	Tina's best friend.	Monday 20 February
Mr Caesar Lamonica	Lamonica	Former manager at Tina's place of employment (Parisian).	Tuesday 21 February
Mr Sam Shelton	Shelton	Funeral director at Southern Heritage Funeral Home, the company used for Tina's funeral service.	Tuesday 21 February
Ms Alanda Thomas	Alanda	Tina's sister.	Tuesday 21 February
Mr Tommy Thomas	Tommy	Tina's father.	Thursday 23 February

In the prosecution's opening statement, Assistant Attorney-General Andrew Arrington explained to the jury that the financial benefits available to Gabe following Tina's death were threefold. First, Gabe was able to claim on Tina's Parisian employee life insurance policy, which according to the prosecution, Gabe believed to be valued at $165,000. Second, Gabe was able to claim $45,000 from Old Republic (Travelex), the insurance company from whom he had bought an insurance policy for the Queensland honeymoon. Further to this $45,000 claim which Gabe had made, the prosecution also established that Gabe had filed a complaint against this company of an alleged breach of contract and bad faith, which if successful would have meant he was eligible for mental suffering and punitive damages. While the amount to be awarded for such a claim is ultimately left to the discretion of a civil jury, Eric Langley, who testified during the Alabama trial, explained that from this claim, Gabe "could have received millions of dollars".[7] The third way in which the prosecution claimed that Gabe was able to obtain financial benefit from Tina's death was from acquiring all of her personal belongings as her next of kin. This included her engagement and wedding rings, as well as their wedding gifts, Tina's vehicle and other personal items.

In proving the financial motive, the prosecution also focused on the timing at which it alleged Gabe had tried to claim on the insurance policies. The prosecution argued that this was an indication of his guilt, noting that he "doggedly pursued it shortly after she died and then dropped it"[8] because it would have reflected poorly on his claims of innocence, had a criminal trial proceeded in Australia. Prior to the Alabama trial, Glasgow also identified Gabe's behaviour in dropping the civil lawsuit against Old Republic as suspicious and somewhat indicative of guilt, claiming that "the insurer went and got the thing set down for hearing and it was a hearing date before my [coronial inquest] hearing date and so he [Gabe] was forced to do something. He had to start giving evidence on oath over there or he had to withdraw it, so he withdrew the litigation".

Although this behaviour possibly indicates some level of guilt, the insurance evidence presented by the prosecution was pulled apart by Gabe's defence team during cross-examination, as they were able to establish from the testimony of the prosecution witnesses that even though Tina could have changed her life insurance policy during the open enrolment period—the set timeframe when all Parisian employees can change their insurance cover each year—she had not changed her policy prior to her death. Furthermore, the defence claimed that, had any changes been made, these would not have taken effect until a date that fell after Tina's death. As Bloomston explained:

> On the Parisian insurance, I think we were able to establish, in cross-examination, that Tina could have never increased her benefits in that period of time before her wedding, and before the honeymoon, and it would not have gone into effect until after she came back. So I think we did a good job of putting that to bed before our lawyers even had to testify.

Importantly, the defence also established that at the time of her death Tina's father Tommy Thomas, not Gabe, remained the sole beneficiary of her life insurance policy and that Tommy had sought to claim on this policy on 18 November 2003. Additionally, the defence showed that Tina could have changed her beneficiary at any time either at work or online.

---

[7] Eric Langley, court observations, 17 February 2012.

[8] Andrew Arrington, court observations, 14 February 2012.

From this, the defence argued that any inquiries Gabe had made following Tina's death about her Parisian insurance policy were made in his role as administrator of Tina's estate, rather than as the beneficiary of her policy.

In responding to the allegations that Gabe would have been able to claim somewhere in the realm of millions of dollars from Old Republic as part of his mental anguish damages, the defence also quickly established during cross-examination that in Gabe's first claim to the insurance company, made on 20 January 2004, he requested $10,134.92—an amount that would cover only the costs associated with the honeymoon and with flying his mother to Australia after Tina's death. Significantly, the defence was also able to confirm that had Old Republic paid this initial claim, Gabe would have signed a release precluding him from claiming anything further. As Bloomston explained:

> Gabe's lawyer Kit Bell sued the insurance company for bad faith, for not paying a claim, and for breach of contract. All of a sudden that became a multi-million dollar motive for Gabe, when he actually was just requesting $10,000. His lawyer sues, in a suit that could have included punitive damages, or damages above and beyond the breach of contract, which historically in Alabama could have been a lot of money. But for Gabe to have thought that process through and anticipated that the insurance company would deny his claim, sue him, he'd win, and then he could file suit? No one could have predicted that, and frankly, not Gabe. He's a box salesman; he's not a mastermind or any of that. Kit [Bell] would have testified on how that litigation came about, and I think it would have closed any potential motives on the travel insurance policy. Fortunately, we were able to get that very information out from the travel insurance company's lawyer, Eric Langley, who testified at trial ... The public perception of Gabe from 2004 was that there was a million dollar life insurance policy in play, and there never, ever was any life insurance in play.

A similar comment which also questioned the strength of the prosecution's evidence in demonstrating a financial motive was expressed by Gabe's family and civil attorney Bob Austin, who claimed:

> It just seems hard to imagine that anyone, the Thomas [family] included, would think that this young man would spend thousands of dollars on a honeymoon trip, take his bride halfway around the world, and on the first dive, the first day, undertake to commit murder in front of 50 potential witnesses ... They're saying that he's so smart, that he figured that on the trip insurance that they would deny it and then he would sue them? Now this is giving him a degree of intelligence that supersedes that of the average person. But yet, on the other hand, they're saying he's so stupid that he would undertake this [murder] in front of 50 witnesses, on the first day.

Thus, in addition to the limitations arising from the prosecution's need to prove Gabe's motive, it also appeared that the prosecution's evidence in establishing this motive was somewhat limited, further justifying the concerns discussed earlier in this chapter pertaining to the justness of this trial proceeding on the basis of the pecuniary gain charge.

An Early Judgement?

One of the key reasons identified by several of our participants as to why there was a perceived inadequacy in the strength of the prosecution's pecuniary gain evidence centred on the inadmissibility of evidence in the Alabama trial, in particular the inadmissibility of a significant portion of Tommy Thomas's testimony. Indeed, one of the primary concerns around the inadmissibility of this evidence involved the conduct of Judge Tommy Nail and the perception that he had predetermined his decision to acquit Gabe, which may have consequently impacted on the legitimacy and justness of this decision.

Judge Nail's negative perception of the prosecution's financial gain motive was evident prior to him granting the defence's motion for a judgement of acquittal on 23 February 2012. In the week leading up to this decision, Judge Nail made a number of comments during the trial, both in and outside the presence of the jury, which raised questions about his impartiality in hearing the case and making an acquittal determination. This conduct was highlighted in media commentaries of the trial, in which one US reporter noted that "the judge has been growing publicly skeptical of the prosecution's case in recent days".[9]

Specifically, on one occasion during the second week of the trial, Sam Shelton, the funeral director involved in Tina's memorial service, was testifying that Gabe had asked him to remove Tina's engagement ring prior to her burial. This testimony was used by the prosecution to support the pecuniary gain motive, on the basis that Gabe had sought to profit from Tina's death beyond the insurance policy claims, by also acquiring Tina's personal possessions, including her wedding and engagement rings. During Shelton's testimony in front of the jury, Judge Nail intervened, stating, "it's not uncommon … I don't think it's unusual practice. I have my mother's rings and she died in 1976".[10] Judge Nail's comment consequently lent undue weight to the evidence given by Shelton that "it is

[9] Nikki Battiste, "Honeymoon Murder Trial Charges Dismissed by Judge", *ABC News* (United States), 23 February 2012.
[10] Judge Tommy Nail, court observations, 21 February 2012.

very common [to keep rings], especially when there is someone to pass them down to".[11] Following the conclusion of the trial, Judge Nail's comment was described by Valeska as "uncalled for ... Judges are not supposed to make comments like that". Even Bloomston acknowledged that this comment provided an insight, in front of the jury, of Judge Nail's negative view of the prosecution's case. Bloomston noted that "when they alleged that Gabe took the ring as part of pecuniary gain … obviously you all saw what Judge Nail thought about that". The weight attributed to this comment in terms of assisting Gabe's defence and disparaging the prosecution's evidence was further demonstrated when the defence later relied upon the judge's statement as part of its motion for a judgement of acquittal, whereby in verbally arguing for this motion, Bloomston claimed that "even the court has recognised it's not uncommon [to take a ring]".[12]

Further to Judge Nail's comments regarding Gabe removing Tina's engagement ring, on the same day, but outside the presence of the jury, Judge Nail sternly outlined his view of the prosecution's pecuniary gain motive in stating, "your theory is that the defendant buys a ring, gives it to his future bride and planned it all here [Alabama], so he could take her there [Queensland], and kill her, so he could take the ring he bought back? You've got an uphill struggle".[13] This comment is particularly concerning as it implies that Judge Nail potentially had a preconceived view of the prosecution's case before they had rested, and prior to the defence filing a motion for a judgement of acquittal. This comment was made during a mid-afternoon break, between 2.45pm and 3.05pm, six days into the trial and two days before the prosecution finished presenting its evidence. This is highly problematic in that it suggests that the judge might have already made a decision on how the case would, or in this context would not, proceed.

A further indication of Judge Nail having predetermined his decision to acquit Gabe before the motion was presented by the defence was evident in comments made to us by his associate. During the first week of the trial, the judge's associate approached us during a break in the court proceedings to ascertain whether we were interested in interviewing Judge Nail. He then discussed our interest with the judge, and later informed us that the judge would be willing to discuss the key legal issues arising from this case at the conclusion of the trial. Prior to the start of court on Thursday 23 February 2012, however, Judge Nail's associate approached us and explained that the judge was no longer willing to participate in an

[11] Sam Shelton, court observations, 21 February 2012.
[12] Brett Bloomston, court observations, 23 February 2012.
[13] Judge Tommy Nail, court observations, 21 February 2012.

interview following the trial. When we enquired as to why he had changed his mind, his associate stated, "I can't say, but it will all become clear soon". In the post-acquittal period, Judge Nail refused to provide any public commentary on the acquittal, outside the judgement given in court, on the basis that it would be inappropriate to discuss the case. Consequently, the comment made to us by his associate is highly concerning, because it suggests that he was aware prior to the defence lodging its motion for acquittal, and prior to the prosecution resting its case, that Judge Nail had potentially already decided to acquit Gabe. A decision which would have made any discussion with us regarding the case inappropriate.

In addition to raising questions of justice and possible prejudice, if the judge had formed a view to acquit Gabe prior to the prosecution resting its case, this may also have influenced his decision not to permit key segments of Tommy's testimony on the final day of the trial. This testimony, which focused on a conversation that took place between Tommy and Tina prior to her wedding, could have significantly impacted on the strength of the prosecution's case. The conversation in question involved a discussion between Tina and Tommy about Tina's life insurance policy at Parisian, and Gabe's desire for her to have that policy increased. In his statement to the police in April 2007, Tommy described the conversation as follows:

> I recall on Friday the 26th day of September 2003 I had arrived home from my work. I had just flown back in from Akron, Ohio. At home was my wife Cindy and my daughter Tina who had dropped over knowing that I was on my way in from the airport. We exchanged greetings and just chatted for a while. We were standing in the kitchen around the island table ... Tina said to me that Gabe had told her that she needed to increase her group life insurance benefit to the maximum and change him to be the sole beneficiary for her insurance policy at work. I asked Tina, did Gabe say why he wanted her to do this? Tina said that Gabe had told her that now that they were getting married, any policies she had should have him to be the sole beneficiary. I told Tina that her re-enrolment was coming up in November and that she had enough going on with the wedding. I said to Tina that I was surprised that Gabe was thinking of such a thing with the wedding coming up. Tina asked me what she should tell Gabe as he might ask. I told Tina to tell Gabe that it was taken care of. Then I told Tina that we, Tina and I, would do it on the re-enrolment in November when she got back from her honeymoon.[14]

[14] Tommy Thomas, witness statement, 27 April 2007.

Tommy further described this conversation with Tina as "strange",[15] noting in his police statement that he had "been in insurance for 25 years and I had never come across a situation where a young soon-to-be-married couple were concerned about these matters at that time".[16]

The probative value of this evidence was identified by Coroner Glasgow in his findings at the coronial inquest in Queensland, whereby he described the importance of the conversation, stating that it could "provide a possible motive [for murder]".[17] However, prior to Tommy presenting his testimony on 23 February 2012, the defence objected on the basis that this conversation was double hearsay. Under Rule 800 of the *Code of Alabama 1975*, hearsay is defined as "a statement, other than one made by the declarant while testifying at the trial or hearing, offered in evidence to prove the truth of the matter asserted". Aside from some legislated and case law exceptions, such as allowing former testimony if the declarant is unavailable,[18] hearsay is deemed not admissible.[19]

In responding to this objection, the prosecution argued that Tommy could discuss, at the very minimum, what he had said to Tina in their conversation regarding changing her life insurance policy because the viability of his testimony could be tested by the defence upon cross-examination, and the victim's state of mind was not at issue. In this manner, the prosecution countered the defence's motion by claiming that the discussion was not hearsay. As Valeska explained, "the insurance [conversation] between Tina and Tommy ... it's very simple, what Tommy says back to her is not hearsay because he's here to be cross-examined". Citing the decision established by the Alabama Court of Criminal Appeals in *Brown v State*,[20] the prosecution also argued that Tommy's testimony would establish the fact that a conversation with Tina about changing her life insurance policy had occurred. The testimony was not being used to say that the substance of the discussion—as in, what Gabe had said to Tina—was true. Instead, it meant that Tommy could testify as to what he had discussed with Tina to establish that their conversation had taken place; and on this basis, had Gabe later testified, the prosecution would have been able to cross-examine him about the conversation he had

---

[15] Ibid.

[16] Ibid.

[17] Transcript of Proceedings, *Inquest into the death of Christina Mae Watson* (20 June 2008) 52 (Coroner David Glasgow).

[18] *Code of Alabama 1975,* Rule 804.

[19] Ibid, Rule 801.

[20] CR-07-1332 (2010).

allegedly had with Tina, to assess whether the conversation took place, and if so, what was said.

Ultimately, however, Judge Nail disregarded the ruling in *Brown v State* and granted the defence's hearsay motion, determining that the conversation was inadmissible. In making this judgement, Nail stated:

> It's the rankest hearsay ... There is no way anyone can cross-examine it and it undermines the Sixth Amendment. It is an out of court statement, not made under oath. It is hearsay because it involves other hearsay ... You may not like my ruling ... I don't care what your theory is, it's [the conversation] not relevant in this case.[21]

In addition to the judge's decision to disregard case law, Tommy also questioned the legitimacy of this decision on the basis that Cindy had been present during the discussion and therefore she could have provided evidence to corroborate the details of the conversation. As Tommy claimed, "the conversation about the insurance, if that had only happened with me, I wouldn't have been quite as upset [but] it happened with Cindy, because Cindy was with me when it happened here, but we couldn't talk about it [in court]". Cindy confirmed this point, stating, "I was standing at the island in my kitchen with my daughter talking to my husband about that insurance and Gabe …When Gabe left this country [in 2003] he thought the insurance was in his name".

In reflecting on the judge's decision to reject his testimony, Tommy questioned what kind of justice it offered, particularly from the perspective of his daughter, the victim:

> They want to call everything hearsay because Tina said things to myself, Amanda [Phillips—Tina's best friend], Alanda [Tina's sister] and other people. The thing that really aggravates me about that is if the victim is not there, and there are people that can speak for the victim, especially when this person has told more than one person the same story, why is it inadmissible? ... What was upsetting was the fact that there were so many witnesses that could have been Tina's voice that weren't allowed to speak. Not just me, but several others as well, and …. it doesn't seem right … It still appears that there were so many protections that are offered an accused, and so little consideration that's offered a victim. I mean, I've said that before, but that's exactly what it seems like to us.

Tommy's reflections illustrate a common frustration that victims and their families experience at the hands of the criminal justice system, whereby in attempting to ensure that the rights of an accused are upheld,

[21] Judge Tommy Nail, court observations, 23 February 2012.

the system is often criticised for failing to ensure that the rights of the victim are also considered. In critiquing this trend in both jurisdictions, Tommy commented that "the judicial system in both countries, if you're not careful, the judicial system will make the perpetrator the victim". This frustration was similarly expressed by Cindy, who perceived an imbalance between the consideration given to upholding the rights of the accused and the lack of consideration given to the victim. She claimed:

> Through this entire ordeal Tina had no rights … Tina had no rights in Australia, and she had no rights over here [Alabama], and that's the sad, sad thing … She just was not the victim in either country; Gabe was. And she had no rights, and she's the one who had to die a horrible death ... The victim is not the important person; the person that's treated more like the victim is the one who did it. And that's what happened, and that's what happened here [in Alabama] and it makes me angry.

Tommy and Cindy experienced emotional frustration not only regarding the inadmissibility of the conversation between Tommy and Tina, but also because this conversation was undoubtedly a vital component of the prosecution's case. Given the value attributed to Tommy's testimony by Coroner Glasgow as providing evidence of a motive, a question remains as to whether permitting this evidence in the trial would have meant that the prosecution case met the sufficient legal burden to send the matter to the jury for consideration. In Alabama, the decision as to whether a case should be submitted for jury consideration must be made by viewing the evidence in a manner most favourable to the prosecution. As Valeska explained:

> In a criminal case, it's beyond reasonable doubt. But it's not beyond reasonable doubt to get to the jury. It's just if there's any evidence that he killed her for money, then the jury's supposed to get it, and I don't see how any normal person could sit there and say there wasn't any evidence.

Significantly, had Judge Nail allowed this evidence to be presented at the Alabama trial, the strength of the prosecution's case may have been increased to a point where it would have been viable not to acquit Gabe, and instead the case would have been sent to the jury for consideration, or at least the defence would have been required to put forward its evidence before a second motion for a judgement of acquittal could be considered by the judge.

Importantly, in terms of the comparison between an Australian-run and an Alabama-run trial offering justice, Judge Nail's decision to rule Tommy's evidence as inadmissible is also problematic, given that in addition to recognising the value of Tommy's testimony in his findings, Coroner Glasgow also explained that this evidence would have been admissible in an Australian-run trial. He claimed:

> Mr Thomas's evidence is that he discussed with Tina shortly prior to her marriage to Gabe, Gabe's request that she not only increase her Company insurance to the maximum but make him the beneficiary. Mr Thomas said that it was resolved that Tina would tell Gabe that such had been done. Evidence was also given by Company officers of Gabe's inquiry to the company about Tina's insurance after her death. I am of the view Mr Thomas's evidence would be admissible in criminal proceedings against Gabe.[22]

The potential for this conversation between Tina and her father to be admissible in an Australian-run trial was also noted in our discussion with Tommy, who explained that:

> The whole deal in Australia, which is completely different from what we ran into here, is that the insurance conversation they didn't need to ask Alanda about it, they didn't need to ask Cindy about it over there. You know why? Two reasons: number one, it didn't matter whether he planned it here [Alabama] or not, but number two, the very fact that he went to Parisian to claim on it pretty much authenticated what I had told them.

The fact that Tommy's conversation with Tina would likely have been admitted had a trial been run in Queensland in 2009 further demonstrates the limited capacity of the Alabama prosecution to offer justice, as the prosecution's full case was not able to be tried. This is also evidenced by the judge's decision to acquit Gabe—a decision based primarily on the motive not being established beyond reasonable doubt. As Tommy explained:

> The judge really based his acquittal on the fact that there was no proof of any monetary gain, not that he didn't do it, [but] that we didn't prove the monetary gain portion of the indictment. That was the whole reason that this case was acquitted ... But that's what got us here. That wouldn't have got us in Australia, because it didn't matter. It would have been murder, and it wouldn't have mattered what he did it for.

Tina's father's reflections on the judge's decision to acquit Gabe highlights the key problems identified in this chapter in relation to proving a motive, and illustrate the frustration around the fact that such expectations

---

[22] Transcript of Proceedings, *Inquest into the death of Christina Mae Watson* (20 June 2008) 52 (Coroner David Glasgow).

to prove motive would not have been required in an Australian-run trial. It also further strengthens our argument that procedurally, subjectively and substantively, the Alabama trial was flawed in multiple ways, which ultimately prevented the process and outcome from offering a second chance for justice.

CHAPTER SEVEN

THE FATAL DIVE

> The State intends to prove that the defendant murdered his wife. She drowned seven minutes into the dive. He's the one that picked the dive. He's the one that set it up. And he's the one that abandoned her. He made no effort to save her … And he took her to one of the most dangerous dive spots in the world.[1]
>
> —Alabama Assistant Attorney-General Don Valeska

Providing an insight into what occurred between Gabe and Tina during the fatal dive was a central component of the prosecution's case in the Alabama trial. In presenting evidence pertaining to the fatal dive, the prosecution offered testimony from 15 witnesses to try to establish that not only was Gabe trained to perform a rescue on a panicked diver—and that he had previously assisted his dive training buddy Michael Moore in a panicked situation during a dive in Mexico—but also that the versions of events that Gabe had given, differed between individuals. Importantly, the prosecution sought to show that Gabe's different versions of what happened on the dive were not reflective of how a panicked diver would react, had Tina been panicking in the manner in which Gabe had described, and nor were they reflective of how a trained dive buddy would or should respond in such a situation.

[1] Don Valeska, bond hearing, 14 December 2010, 10.

Table 7-1: The Prosecution Fatal Dive Witness List (In order of the date of testimony)

Name and title	Referred to as	Role in the *Watson* case	Testimony date
Detective Senior Constable Kevin Gehringer	Gehringer	One of the primary police members involved in the investigation of Tina Thomas's death.	Wednesday 15 and Thursday 16 February
Mrs Paula Snyder	Paula Snyder	Fellow diver on board the *Spoilsport*; Gabe's support person during his first police statement.	Thursday 16 February
Dr Stanley Stutz	Stutz	Diver on board the *Jazz II*; witnessed an interaction between Gabe and Tina underwater; assisted with resuscitation attempts.	Thursday 16 February
Dr Douglas Milsap	Doug or Milsap	Fellow diver on board the *Spoilsport*.	Thursday 16 February
Mr Kenneth Snyder	Ken or Snyder	Fellow diver on board the *Spoilsport*.	Thursday 16 and Friday 17 February
Mr Michael Moore	Michael Moore	Gabe's childhood friend and dive training buddy.	Friday 17 February
Dr Farrell Mendlesohn	Dr Farrell Mendlesohn	Cardiologist at Baptist Medical Centre in Princeton; treated Tina in 2001 for pain she was experiencing as a result of heart palpitations.	Friday 17 February
Mr Adam White	White	Scuba technician and customer service manager of Oceanic Australia; performed tests on Gabe's and Tina's dive computers in 2004.	Monday 20 February
Mr Michael Hollis	Michael Hollis	Manufactures diving products including the Oceanic dive computer used by Gabe during the fatal dive.	Monday 20 February

Mr Uzi Barnai	Barnai	Diving assistant to the trip director on the *Spoilsport*; assisted with resuscitation attempts.	Monday 20 February
Mr Wade Singleton	Singleton	Trip director and dive master of the *Spoilsport*; rescued Tina from the ocean floor; assisted with resuscitation attempts.	Monday 20 and Tuesday 21 February
Senior Constable Joshua Kinghorn	Kinghorn	(Former) member of the Queensland Water Police Division; participated in the police re-enactment of Gabe and Tina's fatal dive.	Monday 20 February (to the judge only) and Tuesday 21 February
Dr David Williams	Dr David Williams	Performed the autopsy on Tina's body in Townsville.	Tuesday 21 February
Detective Senior Sergeant Gary Campbell	Campbell	One of the primary police members involved in the investigation into the death of Tina Thomas.	Tuesday 21 February
Mr Tom Jackson	Tom Jackson	Gabe and Tina's accredited diving instructor in Alabama.	Thursday 23 February

One of the main reasons why the accidental death investigation originally conducted by the Townsville Water Police Division became a homicide investigation within the Townsville CIB was the changing nature of Gabe's accounts of what occurred during the fatal dive, particularly regarding his direct interactions with Tina and how he responded to her alleged panicked actions. As Tina's father, Tommy Thomas, claimed, "he [Gabe] cannot tell the same story twice". Over the course of nearly five years, the police were able to confirm that Gabe had provided approximately 16 different versions of what happened on the dive. As previously noted, some of these differences were quite significant, such as his claim that he had approached two divers of Asian appearance on the access line, but then later acknowledging that this did not occur. Yet other variations were more minor, such as claiming that he grabbed Tina by the hand to swim towards the access line, as opposed to telling others that he grabbed Tina by her dive vest. Perhaps the strongest pieces of evidence demonstrating the variations in Gabe's account of events are the two statements that he gave to the Queensland police: the first of which took place on the night of Tina's death, and the second of which took place five days later. The differences between these two police statements—which was a key focus of the prosecution's case in the capital murder trial in Alabama—were initially recorded in an *Operation Charlie Oswald* report by Detective Senior Sergeant Gary Campbell in 2007, in which he stated, "also of concern is the evolving statements to witnesses and police over the period of time … his [Gabe's] statements appear to evolve as different questions are posed to him and he has had further time to consider his statements".[2] Accordingly, the audio recordings of the two statements given by Gabe in October 2003 were played in their entirety to the jury over the first two days of the Alabama trial. The jury was also given typed copies of the statements to read while the audio was played, after which Detective Senior Constable Kevin Gehringer then responded to questions about each of the statements.

In addition to using the police statements, the prosecution presented testimony from several of Gabe's fellow divers aboard the *Spoilsport*, which also highlighted inconsistencies in the version of events that he had given in the minutes and hours after he surfaced without Tina. Two of the prosecution's most influential witness testimonies were presented by Kenneth (Ken) Snyder and Douglas (Doug) Milsap, both highly qualified and internationally experienced open water divers. On 22 October 2003, Snyder and Milsap were travelling on board the *Spoilsport*, with their wives Paula Snyder (who was also called as a prosecution witness) and Virginia (Ginger) Milsap. At the time of Tina's death, Snyder had attained a Dive Master level of certification and had completed over 500 dives worldwide. According to PADI (the Professional Association of Diving Instructors), a Dive Master accreditation is one level above a certified rescue diver. It effectively means that the diver has acquired significant training and experience in a variety of dive environments. This qualification also enables individuals to supervise training and non-training activities, including planning, organising and directing dives. Milsap had also attained his Dive Master level of certification, and at the time of Tina's death, he had been scuba diving for over 30 years. During the trial, both Snyder and Milsap were admitted as scuba diving experts by the prosecution.

The evidence to which Snyder and Milsap could testify in the trial was primarily focused on the moments immediately after Gabe resurfaced from the *Yongala* dive site, without Tina. During this time, both Milsap and Snyder engaged in conversations with Gabe about what had happened on

---

[2] Queensland Police Service, "Investigation into the Death of Christina Mae Watson Nee Thomas whilst Scuba Diving off Townsville—22nd October 2003—Operation Charlie Oswald", *QPS Report* (Townsville) 15 November 2007, 38.

the dive, and both found the stories that Gabe told them to be far-fetched and largely implausible. In describing his reaction to Gabe's version of events in a police statement taken on the night of Tina's death, Snyder claimed:

> I said something like bullshit Gabe. That didn't happen. Something happened but that didn't happen. Gabe looked at me and I said, you may want to think that through. You left her and what you said didn't happen. I was a bit heated in my comments and Doug [Milsap] came over to see what was happening. Gabe relayed the story again to Doug and what confirmed my suspicions was that Doug, who had not heard the discussion between Gabe and myself, then said in reply to Gabe's story, that's bullshit Gabe.[3]

In expanding on the reasons behind this initial response, Snyder explained:

> When I originally said bullshit to Gabe, my meaning at that time was not that the story he was telling us was bullshit, but that he had deserted his wife, when he was only a couple of kicks away from saving her. The more I heard the story and thought about the situation, the more I believed that the story he was telling was bullshit.[4]

In a statement provided to the police in 2006, Snyder further elaborated on his perceptions of the implausibility of Gabe's story, claiming:

> It made no sense to a diver. There was no logic into what he was saying to us. It makes no sense that someone would elect to go to the surface and leave a live and breathing diver alone ... So he could certainly have rescued her, but he gave absolutely no assistance to her at that point and time. Even someone with a basic open water certification would have needed no assistance to rescue her. That made absolutely no sense to Doug [Milsap] or myself. There are about ten things he could have done prior to deserting her. Deserting her was not an option.[5]

Differing little from these statements, Snyder testified at Gabe's capital murder trial that "the story I had been told didn't make any sense to me, it wasn't possible … It wasn't a plausible story, it didn't make any sense, bells were going off in my head".[6]

---

[3] Kenneth Snyder, witness statement, 22 October 2003.
[4] Ibid.
[5] Kenneth Snyder, witness statement, 20 June 2006.
[6] Kenneth Snyder, court observations, 16 February 2012.

Further to the implausibility of Gabe's story of deserting Tina, Snyder also pointed to the implausibility of Gabe's description of Tina in the police statements he gave in 2006 and on the night of Tina's death. Snyder explained that Gabe's version "is not indicative of a panicked diver. A panicked diver will crawl over the top of others to get to the surface".[7] In the same statement, Snyder also explained that "my experiences are that I have been confronted with panicked divers in the past on about ten occasions. They will strip everything off to just get to the surface".[8] A similar comment was made by Doug Milsap's wife, Ginger, in her 2006 police statement, whereby she claimed that "none of that [Gabe's story] made any sense … No one in their right mind would leave a human being in distress … If she was alive, why wasn't she fighting? If you are in distress, you are going to be fighting to get to the surface".[9]

In discussing his suspicions about Gabe's version of events, Milsap made similar comments in the three statements he provided to the police in 2003, 2006 and 2007. In his 2006 statement, provided to Lieutenant Brad Flynn, Milsap explained that "Gabe told me what happened … [then] the story changed again later".[10] Further to his direct evidence regarding the changes in Gabe's version of events, Milsap also noted in both his 2006 and 2007 statements that he had heard "second-hand versions of the event after the fact that supposedly came from Watson, that vary from his initial account of what happened".[11] This included an account provided by Gabe in a diving magazine, which Milsap claimed "was greatly different from the story that he gave [me]".[12] In later discussing the inconsistencies in Gabe's stories with the police, Milsap recalled his initial conversation with Gabe:

> Gabe looked at me funny. I said, Gabe, underwater there is no sensation of weight, she couldn't have felt heavy. Gabe said, I was trying to hold her up. I was kicking and she was too heavy. I was trying to hold her up and I lost my grip on her. I again said, Gabe, that's bullshit. There is no sensation of weight underwater. Ken [Snyder] put his hand on my arm and said to me, Doug this is not the time. At this point we separated from Gabe … I am a trained Dive Master which means I have accomplished a Rescue Diver qualification … I don't believe the story that I heard from Gabe on the dive deck that day … From my experience diving, and my qualifications,

[7] Kenneth Snyder, witness statement, 22 October 2003.
[8] Ibid.
[9] Virginia Milsap, witness statement, 20 June 2006.
[10] Douglas Milsap, witness statement, 20 June 2006.
[11] Ibid.
[12] Ibid.

> I do not believe the version of events that were told to me by Gabe ... What I was told by Gabe is not correct, as are the other versions [he has told] that I have heard or read.[13]

Like Snyder, Milsap's testimony at the capital murder trial differed little from that given in his police statements. As Milsap testified, "he [Gabe] told two different versions [to me] in a matter of minutes".[14] In describing his first encounter with Gabe, Milsap testified that "I spoke to Gabe on the dive deck. I said, Gabe what happened? … I said, that's bullshit".[15]

Paula Snyder was also able to testify for the prosecution in Gabe's capital murder trial regarding a number of differences in the versions of the dive that she had heard Gabe provide. As explained in Chapter One, Paula Snyder was Gabe's support person at the police station on the night of Tina's death and was present for the entirety of the almost four hours in which Gabe provided his first statement to Gehringer. In describing the differences between the stories that Gabe had told her, those he had told Gehringer in his official statement and those he had told his parents—all of which occurred on the night of Tina's death—Paula Snyder recalled a significant difference relating to the state of Gabe's ears. In her statement to the police, Paula Snyder explained:

> When Gabe was talking to his mother he seemed to primarily talk about his ears and not about Tina. Gabe repeated several times about the pain in his ears. Gabe also [then] complained to me about his ears. This was the first time he talked about his ears to me. I did not recall him saying to Gehringer about his ears ... Gabe was quite insistent about his ears, it became evident out of the clear blue sky that his ears had become an issue, and it was at this point that I told him I would go and find [Dr John] Downie. I found Downie and he looked inside Gabe's ears. Downie said, I can't see any problem … On going back to continue the statement with Gehringer, I do not recall Gabe bringing up that his ears were a problem.[16]

In her trial testimony, Paula Snyder again described these differences, claiming that "when he was talking to his parents, he said he had hurt his ears … [but] Dr John [Downie] said he didn't see anything wrong with them … [I] was present for the whole interview [with Gabe and Gehringer] and he didn't mention the ears".[17] This testimony regarding

[13] Douglas Milsap, witness statement, 21 April 2007.
[14] Douglas Milsap, court observations, 16 February 2012.
[15] Ibid.
[16] Paula Snyder, witness statement, 21 April 2007.
[17] Paula Snyder, court observations, 16 February 2012.

Gabe's ears was considered an important variation in the initial accounts that Gabe had provided, particularly as there was no medical evidence to support an ear problem, and because Gabe later offered this as a reason to explain why he did not attempt to swim after Tina, in addition to the other accounts he had provided which included that even in swimming as fast as he could to reach Tina, she was sinking at a quicker rate, and that he did not attempt to swim after her because he decided the best way to respond would be to reach the surface help. Thus, by using these testimonies, the prosecution was able to emphasise the multiple variations in Gabe's versions of the fatal dive—variances that they argued implied a level of guilt. As Alabama Assistant Attorney-General Andrew Arrington questioned in the prosecution's opening statement, "Watson lied many times … He has given many stories, with details changing each time … Why? Why?"[18]

Further to highlighting the inconsistencies in Gabe's versions of events, the prosecution also utilised Milsap's and Snyder's testimonies to emphasise the dive buddy obligations that Gabe should have known of and adhered to given his diving qualifications. The most important obligation, as explained by the prosecution dive witnesses, is that under almost no circumstances do you leave your dive buddy alone. As discussed in Chapter Three, Gabe's breach of this rule formed the basis for his negotiated plea deal in Queensland in 2009, which allowed him to plead guilty to manslaughter by criminal negligence. As Snyder testified at the Alabama trial, the person you dive with is your "source of survival … you never leave your buddy".[19] Milsap similarly testified that the system of diving with a trusted person is "called the buddy system … [and] you don't leave your buddy".[20]

Throughout the trial, all of the prosecution's dive witnesses were asked about the dive buddy rules, and all confirmed that you do not leave your buddy alone. As Paula Snyder testified, "you don't leave your [dive] buddy ... You don't ever leave your buddy".[21] Of the prosecution witnesses, only "one acceptable reason for leaving your buddy"[22] was identified by Milsap, who claimed, you can breach this rule, "if your buddy is dead".[23] In creating this pattern across the divers' testimonies, the prosecution was able to further highlight the questionable decision that

---

[18] Andrew Arrington, court observations, 14 February 2012.
[19] Kenneth Snyder, court observations, 16 February 2012.
[20] Douglas Milsap, court observations, 16 February 2012.
[21] Paula Snyder, court observations, 16 February 2012.
[22] Douglas Milsap, court observations, 16 February 2012.
[23] Ibid.

Gabe had made to abandon Tina, which was particularly troubling given his rescue training and the fact that his dive buddy was also his wife of just 11 days.

The value of Snyder's and Milsap's testimonies in raising doubt over Gabe's versions of the dive was evident in our discussions with Flynn, who recalled his thoughts the first time he heard them explain their evidence:

> For them [Snyder and Milsap] to call him out, while his wife is being resuscitated on a boat 100 yards away, that itself lent a lot of credibility to what they were telling [me], because these guys knew. These guys had more dives cumulative than anybody I had talked to. These guys knew the sport inside and out, and for them to be able to say that, and say, you know, that's bullshit, in the middle of that tornado of emotion that [was] going around that boat. I remember thinking … these guys are onto something.

Media reports also highlighted the impact of Milsap's and Snyder's testimony at the trial in generating doubt over Gabe's story, with headlines such as "Diver testifies to doubts about Gabe Watson's story of wife's drowning",[24] and "Honeymoon drowning witness: Husband's version 'not plausible'".[25] As revealed within the media reports, what was perhaps most powerful in the testimonies of Milsap and Snyder was that the inaccuracies in Gabe's various accounts were not only based on their perceptions as witnesses, but were also informed by their roles as diving experts and their extensive experience in open water diving around the globe. Their status as experts thus further called into question Gabe's unusual and inconsistent accounts of what happened underwater, particularly his interactions with Tina.

Tommy reported a similar feeling when he first heard Snyder's evidence in November 2003, after Snyder had contacted him to discuss his feelings of doubt around Gabe's story. Tommy and Snyder met on 24 November 2003 from around 4pm until 7.30pm.[26] In discussing this meeting in an interview with the Australian ABC network's *Australian Story* program, Snyder claimed:

---

[24] Eric Velasco, "Diver Testifies to Doubts about Gabe Watson's Story of Wife's Drowning, Another Backs Parts of Account", *The Birmingham News* (Alabama), 16 February 2012.

[25] Nikki Battiste, "Honeymoon Drowning Witness: Husband's Version 'Not Plausible'", *ABC News* (United States), 16 February 2012.

[26] Tommy Thomas, witness statement, 27 April 2007.

> When we got back into Florida we were troubled by the events that happened. And I said, Paula, I'm going to call and try to get in touch with her [Tina's] parents ... What really rang one of the loudest bells is when Gabe said she was ten feet below him, arms outstretched and sinking looking up at him. I said, Tommy this is difficult because I've never heard of a diver in a full-out panic mode sinking serenely to the bottom of the ocean. A full-born panic attack in a diver will make that diver crawl right over the top of someone to get to the surface. And my experience tells me that live people don't sink; dead people sink.[27]

As implicit in Snyder's comments, he appeared to experience a significant internal struggle over whether or not to share his concerns with Tina's family; but the importance of his comments were described to us by Tommy as a key turning point in his understanding of the case. Tommy described how when he met with Gabe and his family and civil attorney, Bob Austin, in the days after talking with Snyder, "Gabe did exactly what Ken told [me] he had been doing on the boat. [He kept] changing the story, changing the story, and I knew then [that something wasn't right]". Tommy similarly explained in his *Australian Story* interview with the Australian ABC network, "He [Snyder] comes in and then we had a conversation about what he knew had happened and that really pretty much took Gabe's story apart … that really changed everything when he said that".[28]

In preparing to counter the evidence that would be presented by the prosecution showing the variations in Gabe's accounts of the dive, Gabe's US defence attorney, Brett Bloomston, asserted in the defence's opening statement that nothing about what Gabe has told authorities is "contradictory".[29] He further explained to the jury that the small inconsistencies in Gabe's accounts could be attributed to the fact that "the first statement was given on the day that she [Tina] died [and] he was in shock".[30] Indeed, given the timing at which the allegedly contrasting statements were made by Gabe to various other divers (in the moments immediately following him resurfacing without Tina, and after he had learnt of her death) and the timing of when he gave the two police statements (one on the night of Tina's death, and one just five days later) it

---

[27] ABC Television Network, "Unfathomable: Part One", *Australian Story*, 2 August 2010 (Kenneth Snyder) <http://www.abc.net.au/austory/content/2007/s2971395.htm>.

[28] ABC Television Network, above n 27 (Tommy Thomas) <http://www.abc.net.au/austory/content/2007/s2971395.htm>.

[29] Brett Bloomston, court observations, 14 February 2012.

[30] Ibid.

is possible that the variations are simply reflective of his state of shock rather than his guilt. It was this point that the defence sought to argue in countering the prosecution's dive evidence throughout the trial.

Further to his opening statement, and as discussed in more detail in the next chapter, throughout the trial, Bloomston was also able to rebut the testimony of the divers by drawing attention to the differences between their perspectives of Gabe on the night of Tina's death—which included perceiving him as being in shock and panic-stricken—and those they were presenting in court almost nine years later, after having been privy to numerous (mis)representations of Gabe's dislikeable character in the media. Additionally, in seeking to counter the testimony presented by the prosecution's dive witnesses, particularly that of Snyder and Milsap, the defence adopted a clear, consistent and effective strategy. When cross-examining each diver's testimony, the defence asked only a small number of questions specific to the evidence presented, and followed this by one question asked of all of the prosecution's dive witnesses that were present in Queensland when Tina died, with the exception of Stanley Stutz. The defence asked each of these witnesses whether they had any direct knowledge of what happened in the water during Tina's dive or in the moments preceding her death. Using this line of inquiry, the defence sought to highlight that the only two people who knew what happened during the dive were Gabe and Tina. Therefore, even though there were some variations in Gabe's account of what happened on the dive, which the defence attributed to the timing at which these statements were given, the defence effectively demonstrated that there was no direct evidence in the prosecution witnesses' statements to prove that Gabe's versions contradicted what actually happened. On this basis, the defence was able to effectively argue that the testimony provided by the prosecution witnesses was based on speculation and conjecture about what actions they would have taken themselves, had they been in the same position—none of which, the defence argued, provided sufficient evidence beyond reasonable doubt that Gabe was guilty of murdering Tina.

While this was certainly a strong strategy employed by the defence, and one that assisted Judge Tommy Nail in deciding to acquit Gabe, given the media responses to Snyder's and Milsap's testimonies, and the responses of Tommy and Flynn upon first hearing their evidence, there is a basis to question whether the acquittal outcome can be viewed as just. In acquitting Gabe of the capital murder charge, Judge Nail commented that the prosecution had failed to establish intent, claiming that there "is no evidence to suggest an intentional killing".[31] However, under Alabama case law, the importance attributed to circumstantial and direct evidence should be equal. As stated in *J.M.A v State*, where "circumstantial evidence points to the guilt of the accused, it will support a conviction as strongly as direct evidence".[32] On this basis, the strength of the testimony presented by the prosecution, particularly that of Snyder and Milsap, raises serious doubt over the validity of Gabe's versions of what occurred underwater, and why he needed to fabricate various stories. Indeed, in reflecting on his perception of the strength of the prosecution's dive evidence in terms of its impact on the jury, Tommy explained that:

> One of the things about the jurors that I noticed is [that] they listened very intently to his [Gabe's] first statement [to] the police, but they listened even more intently to his second statement, because they were taking a lot of notice, and the reason they were taking a lot of notice is [that] they were seeing a lot of differences ... And then of course you've got all the other versions that he told Ken Snyder and he told Doug Milsap.

While Tommy's comments suggest that the prosecution's dive evidence had a significant impact on the jury, its actual influence will never be known, as they were never given the opportunity to voice their verdict. However, if Tommy's reflections are in any way indicative of the jurors' views, then the justness of Judge Tommy Nail's decision to acquit Gabe is somewhat questionable in light of the perceived strength of this evidence. Furthermore, as argued in more detail in Chapters Ten and Eleven, this implies that the prosecution's evidence arguably provided sufficient doubt for the case to meet the hurdle required to progress at least to the defence's presentation of its evidence, as opposed to being thrown out when the prosecution rested its case.

The Only Eyewitness: Dr Stanley Stutz

As the only witness able to provide direct evidence of what happened between Gabe and Tina on the fatal dive, Dr Stanley Stutz, a diver from the *Jazz II* dive vessel, was considered the ideal witness. Stutz is an emergency room doctor, an accredited advanced open water diver and the only person, other than Gabe, who could provide a direct account of the underwater interaction that occurred between Gabe and Tina in the moments before she died. As Flynn described him, "this guy, he's not a

[31] Judge Tommy Nail, court observations, 23 February 2012.
[32] 74 So 3d 487 (2011) at 492.

flake. His credibility is, in my opinion, [well] he's a doctor. He has sound credentials. He's of very sane mind". Coroner David Glasgow expressed a similar view of Stutz's credentials as a witness, claiming that "he happens to be not only a medical practitioner, but a diver, a rescue diver ... [so he has] all that credibility". In addition to the sound nature of his character as a witness, the value of the evidence that Stutz could provide was recognised by several of our participants. Indeed, as outlined in Chapter One, Stutz's testimony provided one of the primary turning points for all three of the lead police investigators in considering Tina's death to be a homicide rather than an accidental death. Glasgow also recognised the value of Stutz's evidence, which he was privy to during the coronial inquest in Queensland, observing that "I don't think we would have got anywhere without Stutz really. It's his evidence and … he was very good". However, at the Alabama trial, Stutz's testimony provided at best a conflicted account of what occurred between Gabe and Tina in the last minutes of their dive, and as reported extensively in the media, his testimony was not perceived as assisting the prosecution's case.

Stutz was the second prosecution witness called at the Alabama trial. He took the stand at approximately 9:35am on 16 February 2012. In describing to the court the moment in which he first saw Tina, Stutz explained that:

> She [Tina] caught my eye because she was distressed, she was facing upwards … lying flat almost … Initially she was just floating … I was shocked, I was very concerned. She look liked she was in a lot of trouble … She was not thrashing, her arms were out and moving, and her legs were moving but she didn't have a lot of energy. She was not in any way swimming.[33]

In recalling the moments immediately after he first saw Tina, Stutz testified that he saw "a male diver in a black wetsuit swim over to her".[34] For the purpose of his testimony, Stutz identified the divers as Gabe and Tina; however, at the time of their interaction underwater, Stutz referred to Tina as diver one, and Gabe as diver two. Explaining what happened next, Stutz testified that the male diver, Gabe, "put his arms around her, under her armpits. It struck me, I thought that he was trying to save her. Then they split. He swam to the surface, and she sank rapidly".[35] It was this comment—"I thought that he was trying to save her"—that was utilised by the defence in its cross-examination to suggest that what Stutz witnessed

[33] Stanley Stutz, court observations, 16 February 2012.
[34] Ibid.
[35] Ibid.

was not Gabe murdering Tina, but indeed trying to assist her. During cross-examination, when asked to reflect again on what he saw, Stutz stated:

Stutz:	I thought Gabe was trying to save her.
Bloomston:	You don't think you saw a murder that day?
Stutz:	I was surprised when I got an email that it was a murder trial.[36]

In trying to counter the impact of this statement during its rebuttal, the prosecution attempted to establish that this view of Gabe saving Tina was reflective of what Stutz would have done had he been in the same position as Gabe, rather than of what he had witnessed. But it was this snapshot of Stutz's testimony that became a key focus for the media, with headlines such as "Witness thought Watson was helping wife",[37] and "Doctor thought Gabe Watson was trying to help wife on scuba dive".[38]

In discussing Stutz's testimony following Gabe's acquittal, Valeska expressed his frustration at the focus placed on the comments about Gabe saving Tina, when Stutz's evidence had asserted that Gabe had held Tina for between ten and 30 seconds underwater, before separating from her and swimming to the surface—testimony that conflicts with a number of the accounts that Gabe had provided as to what happened on the dive. Tommy also identified the importance of Stutz's testimony because it pointed to several inaccuracies in the versions given by Gabe. He explained:

> I think in most situations if you just took those 16 different versions of what he said and presented them to the jury, I think just about any jury anywhere for the most part would have convicted him, okay, just on that basis. But let's take that out, let's just take that out for a little bit. If you really look close[ly] at what Dr Stutz said he saw, and you compare it to any one version—not all 16 of them, but just one, it doesn't matter—I think that would also have convicted him [Gabe], because what Stutz saw was Gabe go down on top of Tina in a position that Gabe never put himself in, in a single version of any of his descriptions of what happened … So I

[36] Stanley Stutz and Brett Bloomston, court observations, 16 February 2012.
[37] Peter Mitchell, "Witness Thought Watson Was Helping Wife", *Sydney Morning Herald* (New South Wales), 17 February 2012.
[38] Australian Associated Press, "Doctor Thought Gabe Watson Was Trying to Help Wife on Scuba Dive", *The Australian* (Australia), 17 February 2012.

> think Stutz's testimony by itself, if you really take it apart, and just use any one of Gabe's 16 versions, you've pretty much got your choker, don't you?

In responding to criticisms of the veracity and usefulness of Stutz's testimony, Valeska acknowledged that "Stutz certainly wasn't the greatest witness", but he suggested that this was "because he's conflicted". As Valeska further explained, Stutz was basing his testimony on his own values and what he would have done in the same situation. It must also be considered, as in the case of most of the witness testimony presented at the Alabama trial, that Stutz's testimony was at least partially affected by the prolonged nature of the case, such that he was being asked to recall an interaction that he had seen in the water nearly nine years earlier. At no stage in his earlier police statements did Stutz suggest that the male diver he saw was attempting to save the distressed female diver. Indeed, in describing Tina to the police, Stutz claimed "I saw fear and distress on her face. The look on her face was awful and I had the belief that she knew that she was in danger".[39] Stutz also claimed in his 2007 statement to the police:

> While I had the two divers under observation I observed no interaction between the two where either of the diver's masks or regulators came loose or appeared to come loose ... When the two divers separated, diver one's [Tina's] limb and body movements did not change. There did not seem to be any organised structure in her body movements. When they separated, diver two [Gabe had] ascended. While I had diver two [Gabe] under observation, he did not change his direction of swimming and did not go after diver one [Tina].[40]

Given the significant differences between this statement and his testimony at trial, it would appear that the extensive delay between Tina's death and the Alabama trial affected the validity and reliability of Stutz's testimony. This provides further evidence of the limited capacity of the 2012 Alabama trial to provide a just process or outcome.

The Missing Pieces of the Puzzle

In addition to the impact of delays, the *Watson* case was plagued by resource limitations and financial constraints in both Queensland and Alabama. Gehringer claimed that because of Alabama's "financial predicament" the trial did not present the "whole picture". The prosecution's

[39] Stanley Stutz, witness statement, 18 April 2007.
[40] Ibid.

case was restricted in a number of ways, including that it was only able to present a minimal representation of all of the evidence and witness testimony that had been collated since 2003 as part of *Operation Charlie Oswald*. On this basis, and as briefly discussed in Chapter Five, it can be argued that the Alabama trial failed to ensure a process through which justice could be achieved, as it did not provide a forum for all of the evidence both in favour and against Gabe to be heard, tested and evaluated by a jury of his peers within the confines of a court of law.

A significant example of the consequences of the lack of resources available to sufficiently fund the prosecution's case arose during the second week of the trial, when Judge Tommy Nail ruled that the prosecution would not be able to present the results of a re-enactment dive conducted by the Queensland Police Service (QPS) and the Australian Customs Service in September 2006. The re-enactment attempted to recreate Gabe and Tina's fatal dive, and was considered by the Australian and many US participants to be an influential piece of evidence as it demonstrated a significant difference between where Gabe claimed he and Tina were diving, and where her body was found. As Gehringer explained:

> Josh Kinghorn, whilst he wasn't female, wore all Tina's equipment [and acted as Tina] in the re-enactment. We did all these test dives and every time that Josh and the other divers that were there would follow Gabe's version, as to going down to that depth that we had factual information from his dive computer, and then letting the current take them over the top of the wreck ... Every time they did it, out of the three tests that they did, Josh was always landing either on the deck of the *Yongala* itself or on the sand right beside the deck ... Wade [Singleton] was able to pinpoint, and Wade had no hesitation in going to where he picked up Tina from the ocean floor, and being able to identify it with the geography or what was on the ocean floor, to be able to say this is the exact spot where I picked her up from ... So then they [the re-enactment team] took it one [step] further and said, well what would we have to do to end up where Wade pointed it out? And that's where, the only way they got close to ending up to where Wade said, is by swimming out from the descent line, the diver access point, at right angles away from the wreck, and if anything a little bit forward. And then the drift was taking them down, and Josh was coming within the vicinity of where they found Tina.

The findings of the re-enactment, which involved tests based on Wade's version of events, also reflected a photograph that had been taken by a fellow diver on the *Spoilsport*, Gary Stempler, who had inadvertently captured a graphic image of Tina's body lying flat on a sandbank towards the bottom of the ocean.

Subsequent to the re-enactment, a report produced by the QPS in 2007 showed that the results of the re-enactment cast significant doubt over Gabe's versions of events, particularly in relation to where Tina's body was found, and the rate at which Gabe ascended to the ocean surface. As noted by Detective Senior Sergeant Gary Campbell in the report:

> The husband of the deceased claimed to have left the deceased in a certain area above the shipwreck within a certain distance of the diver access point when he last saw her. The test drifts conducted by the members of the Brisbane dive squad show that this statement is unlikely to be true … The husband of the deceased claimed to have risen to the surface on leaving his wife as quick as he could … The husband rose 15 metres to the surface in two and a half minutes which was [as] quick as he could go by his words. Bearing in mind that it was his wife of 11 days and it was a matter of life and death and he was a certified rescue diver, Singleton rose 30 metres in less than one and a half minutes carrying the body of a person only known to him by one day. A police diver replicated the ascent of the husband and it was recorded on video. The actions of the police diver appear pedestrian under the known circumstances by which the husband ascended.[41]

In describing the value of the dive re-enactment, Gehringer explained:

> I used to think to myself, well, if I was a member on the jury and I've seen all the evidence, if up until that point I wanted to give him [Gabe] the benefit of the doubt, either being a coward or he panicked, that [the dive re-enactment] was probably the clincher for me. Why would you take someone that distance away?

Despite its potential significance for the prosecution's case, the defence described the re-enactment as "fraught with problems",[42] and they successfully objected to the video being shown to the jury and to witnesses being permitted to discuss the re-enactment. Judge Tommy Nail ruled that the re-enactment evidence was inadmissible because two of the key individuals involved in the scientific elements of the re-enactment, which included determining currents and information on the *Yongala* dive site, were not present to provide evidence at the trial and face cross-examination. Interestingly, this ruling was made despite several witnesses who were involved in the re-enactment being present and able to testify at the Alabama trial, including Senior Constable Joshua Kinghorn, a former member of the Queensland Water Police Division who had played the role of Tina in the re-enactment tests.

---

[41] Campbell, above n 2, 36.
[42] Brett Bloomston, court observations, 15 February 2012.

The two witnesses that Judge Nail wanted to testify to allow the re-enactment video to be admissible were Dr Thomas Stieglitz and Dr Richard Brinkman. Stieglitz is a scientist at the Marine Geophysical Laboratory, School of Maths, Physics and IT at James Cook University in Townsville. As part of his research, Stieglitz generated a scientific 3D model of the *SS Yongala* wreck, which was used to inform the re-enactment conducted by the QPS. Brinkman's role in the re-enactment was to use his expertise in physical oceanography—specifically, his expertise in the study of currents between Bowen and Townsville on the Great Barrier Reef—to provide possible timeframes "in which the conditions may be as similar as possible to the dive conditions at the time of the death of the deceased".[43] Accordingly, Brinkman provided three timeframes in August, September and October 2006.

In reflecting on the restrictions placed on the prosecution's case as a result of the minimal financial support available, Valeska acknowledged resources as a concern, but identified the decisions made by Judge Nail, such as the inadmissibility of the video of the dive re-enactment, as more problematic for the prosecution. As Valeska explained:

> I don't know … I could have brought every witness from around the world … [but] if the judge was going to throw [acquit] it … and if he wasn't going to believe who we had. There is no better eyewitness than Stutz and I mean Stutz said the mask was on both of them, and they just separated. And in most justice systems around the world, a jury is supposed to make that decision as to, like Snyder said and Milsap [said], dead people sink. A lot of people float and she [Tina] was not floating anymore.

Significantly, this comment reflects two key issues that have emerged in relation to the capacity of the Alabama trial to provide a forum for justice. Initially, it demonstrates that a jury was not given the opportunity to evaluate the value of Stutz's evidence; instead, it was only evaluated by a single judge, which limits the achievability of justice in a traditional and procedural sense. Second, Valeska's comment suggests that the conduct and decisions of the judge throughout the trial led key players involved in the investigation and prosecution of Gabe to question whether any evidence presented at the trial could have been able to influence the judge away from his decision to acquit Gabe at the earliest available opportunity. As explored in Chapters Six and Eleven, the possibility that Judge Nail had predetermined his decision to acquit Gabe before the prosecution case

---

[43] Richard Brinkman, witness statement, 26 October 2007.

had rested, and before the defence had even filed the motion, further fuels this argument, and the potentially unjust nature of the Alabama trial.

Displacing Responsibility: The Mike Ball Counter Argument

Perhaps one of the most significant pieces of evidence that was missing from the prosecution's case, as a result of resource constraints placed on the Alabama trial, was an email sent by Gabe to Mike Ball Diving Expeditions (Mike Ball) on 20 May 2003. The email was inadmissible, because the person who had read and responded to the email was not present to directly testify to the details of its contents, or to be cross-examined to check the validity of their testimony. In describing his frustration upon learning that the email was not going to be presented as part of the prosecution's case, Tommy recalled the explanation given to him by the prosecution team:

> The person that received the email was an employee of Mike Ball. She wasn't here [in Alabama], so she had to be here in order to say, yes, I got this email, and I'm going—you've got to be kidding me. And they said, Tommy, we didn't realise it at the time, but now it's too late to do anything about it.

The email in question was sent by Gabe almost five months before he and Tina left for their Australian honeymoon, and it specifically asked about the *Yongala* dive, stating:

> I'd also like to know about the *Yongala* dive. I had my rescue certification, however, Tina only has her beginner's certificate. I've noticed on the booking form it says anyone with less than 15 long dives in the past 12 months, must pass a rec[reation] orientation. Is this something you guys do on the trip so she would be able to dive it?[44]

In describing to us the email response that Gabe received following this initial enquiry, Tommy explained that "Mike Ball has sent a response back [which said] … with her level of experience we would recommend that she either go on an orientation dive or she sit this dive out".

The significance of this email interaction to the prosecution's case was very strong, given that it would have illustrated to Judge Nail, and the jury,

[44] Email from Gabe Watson to Mike Ball, cited in Transcript of Proceedings, *Inquest into the death of Christina Mae Watson* (21 January 2008) 1163 (Admitted by Harvey Walters).

the contradictions between Gabe's claims that he had only a limited awareness of the difficulty of the *Yongala* dive, and that he did not realise, or appreciate, the need for Tina to be given an orientation dive. Indeed, since providing the police with his two statements in 2003, Gabe has repeatedly denied being aware of either the difficulty of that specific dive site or that Tina required an orientation dive. This is demonstrated in his second statement to the police, in which he claimed:

> I didn't know anything about the dive before we did it … it's not what I would consider a dive that a beginner, which is what Tina was, just was not a dive that they, I don't even know if they should be allowed to do it with somebody … All I know about the *Yongala* was basically what Wade had told us, you know, which you know gave us a brief history … But no, I had no knowledge prior to it.[45]

In the same statement, in response to several questions from Senior Constable Glen Lawrence, Gabe also denied that Tina was offered an orientation dive for the *Yongala* dive:

> Lawrence: So after the dive instructor questioned you about your experience, level, number of dives and Tina's, did um, anyone then, any of the dive instructors offer to go with you like, come down with you on your first one?
>
> Gabe: No, no.
>
> Lawrence: Ok, did um anyone mention to you anything about orientation dives or—?
>
> Gabe: The only thing that was said about anything and I remember this from the night, the night before we left and we, you know I was telling you guys, we're filling out the paperwork and all that.
>
> Lawrence: Yep.
>
> Gabe: And I asked him [Wade Singleton] ah, you know, do we, do we [do a] night dive. Cause he, I mean, I think that at point he said, we'd be there [at the *Yongala*] all day. And I asked him if he did night diving and he said, "well yeah" and that's when he'd asked if we'd done one and I said well I have but Tina hasn't, and he said, "well Tina I'd like to ... do that first night dive with you".

[45] Gabe Watson, witness statement, 27 October 2003.

Lawrence: Mmm.

Gabe: But there was no [orientation dive], you know, and they knew when we filled it [the form] out, you know, he asked how many dives she'd done and she put them down and it had, well actually the different types of dives so there was, so they knew where her level was, but there was no orientation dive.

Lawrence: So there's [sic] was, was there an orientation dive offered to anyone on board or to yourself or—?

Gabe: I don't know if it was [to] the other people, there wasn't anything directly to us.[46]

These excerpts from Gabe's statements contrast not only with the emails that Gabe had sent and received from Mike Ball in May 2003, but also with the initial statements that Singleton provided to the police, in which he claimed:

> I discussed the dive matters with them [Gabe and Tina] and I remember advising them that due to her not having done a night dive before, her first one would be completed with one of our dive instructors. I also suggested to Tina to have an initial orientation dive with one of our instructors. I recommended this simply because she had done a low number of dives. She advised me that she felt confident in her ability to dive without an instructor and that she would take one for a night dive ... [The next morning] I then went down to the dive deck to inquire if Tina was attending the orientation dive [for the *Yongala* dive], and both her and Gabe were there. They stated that they were not attending this orientation dive as was mentioned the previous night, but would attend the night orientation dive. Tina reminded me of this in that she said that she would hold my hand during the orientation night dive. I said, "You don't have to wait, enjoy your dive". I then hugged her.[47]

In denying that he was aware of the difficulty of the *Yongala* dive, Gabe appeared to be displacing responsibility from himself onto the diving company in charge of the expedition. Indeed, at several stages throughout the investigation and prosecution of this case, and even in media interviews following his acquittal, Gabe and his defence team have repeatedly criticised Mike Ball for not advising divers of the difficulty of

[46] Gabe Watson and Senior Constable Glen Lawrence, cited in Gabe Watson, witness statement, 27 October 2003.
[47] Wade Singleton, witness statement, 22 October 2003.

the *Yongala* dive site and for allegedly not offering or insisting that Tina have an orientation dive. In the defence's opening statement, for example, Bloomston explained that the *Yongala* dive site is an "extremely difficult and dangerous place. It's a red flag dive … and Gabe and Tina were taken there on the first day of a seven day dive trip".[48] To further support the assertion that Tina should not have been diving at the *Yongala*, Bloomston also claimed that "Tina was predisposed to have issues underwater ... She was terribly inexperienced".[49] Interestingly, this picture of Tina painted by the defence during the Alabama trial contrasts with the statement that Gabe provided to the police on the night of Tina's death, where in describing her diving history he stated that, "in total, I would say she had done about 12 dives. Tina would always get a little nervous before diving but once she was in she was okay. I have not known her to have panicked in the water before".[50]

In advancing the defence argument that Mike Ball, not Gabe, was responsible for Tina's death, the defence referred to the Industry Code of Practice (ICOP), which provides standards for the regulation and oversight of the dive industry. Reading from these standards during the trial, Bloomston noted that the ICOP requires that the diving company "should ensure conditions of the dive site are appropriate to the certifications and experiences of the divers".[51] In describing the conditions of the *Yongala* dive site in his first police statement, Gabe explained the ocean current as "coming over pretty good. By that, I mean from my experience it was a strong current".[52] However, Gabe's description of the current differed from that offered by his fellow divers, including Doug Milsap, who described it as only "a little strong",[53] and Ken Snyder, who said the current was "moderate"[54] and "invigorating … but not something you would lose control of".[55] Gabe's description was used by the defence team throughout the trial as it lent support to their argument that part of the reason why Tina panicked during the dive and subsequently knocked Gabe's mask and regulator out was her lack of experience diving in such strong current conditions.

[48] Brett Bloomston, court observations, 14 February 2012.
[49] Ibid.
[50] Gabe Watson, witness statement, 22 October 2003.
[51] Brett Bloomston, court observations, 21 February 2012.
[52] Gabe Watson, witness statement, 22 October 2003.
[53] Douglas Milsap, witness statement, 22 October 2003.
[54] Kenneth Snyder, witness statement, 22 October 2003.
[55] Kenneth Snyder, court observations, 16 February 2012.

To further support Gabe's explanation for why Tina might have panicked, the defence also drew upon the police statements given by Singleton, who described the dive in his first statement as having "a strong current".[56] What the defence did not mention was that Singleton also explained that Mike Ball had "catered for this [current] by informing the passengers that we would transfer them to the far end of the wreck by tender and they could simply drift back with the current toward the stern of the wreck and therefore back to the *Spoilsport*".[57]

In advancing the defence's rebuttal of the prosecution's case during his cross-examination of the dive witnesses, Bloomston also drew attention to the internal guidelines that Mike Ball used to govern its dives at the time of Tina's death, which stated that the dive site should be suited to the experiences of the diver—a suitability that is gauged during the diver's initial interview with the trip director and dive master at the beginning of the expedition. In outlining these internal guidelines, the defence attempted to place significant responsibility on Singleton for Tina's death.

At the time of Tina's death, Singleton held a Master Scuba Diver Trainer certification, which he explained consisted of "an open water scuba instructor's ticket and a number of specialty instructor ratings".[58] In testifying at the trial, Singleton estimated that he had completed between 4000 and 5000 dives, of which at least 500 were at the *Yongala* dive site. Describing his role as the trip director and dive master on the *Spoilsport*, Singleton explained in his first police statement that "I would say that in my job capacity, I am a capable and experienced dive instructor. I am good at my job and I am respected amongst my peers".[59] However, it was his capability and thoroughness in his role as trip director and dive master that was called into question by the defence to support its counter-arguments against the prosecution's case.

On the night that Gabe and Tina boarded the *Spoilsport*, Singleton was responsible for interviewing them in order to check their "diving certifications, dive history, [to] check insurance and medical evacuation details, and to inquire as to any concerns they may have with regards to their diving and a basic assessment of their abilities as a diver".[60] As Singleton explained in his first police statement:

---

[56] Wade Singleton, witness statement, 22 October 2003.
[57] Ibid.
[58] Ibid.
[59] Ibid.
[60] Ibid.

> During this interview, the subject of [dive] buddies is considered. If the person is travelling with a companion, they basically have a buddy and I concentrate more on their ability rather their pairing … If it is two inexperienced divers, I would recommend strongly to those persons, to participate in an orientation dive. It is based on their abilities, their comfort level and the dive site … I remember that Tina produced an open water certification card that had been obtained in the last 12 months … I discussed the dive matters with them and I remember advising them that due to her not having done a night dive before, her first one would be completed with one of our dive instructors. I also suggested to Tina to have an initial orientation dive with one of our instructors.[61]

During cross-examination at the Alabama trial, Bloomston questioned why Singleton did not insist that Tina take an orientation dive, given that the Mike Ball safety manual expressly stated that "novice divers must undertake a safety orientation dive".[62] In his response, Singleton testified that "the fact that her dive buddy [Gabe] was a rescue diver … had a big influence"[63] on his decision to allow Tina to undertake the dive without an orientation. Despite this justification, Bloomston also drew attention to the Mike Ball waiver form, which all novice divers who refuse an orientation dive are meant to complete, and he extracted an admission from Singleton that Tina had not signed this form prior to her dive with Gabe. In pointing out the perceived flaws in Singleton's actions in relation to the orientation dive and his pre-dive interview with Gabe and Tina, Bloomston attempted to present Singleton as negligent, for not properly following the rules and procedures. In doing so, the defence sought to further strengthen its attempts to shift the blame for Tina's death from Gabe to Singleton and Mike Ball.

The prosecution was able to counter some of the negative perceptions of Singleton presented by the defence by highlighting the role that he played in the attempted rescue of Tina, by bringing her rapidly to the surface and assisting with the resuscitation attempts on the *Jazz II*. In describing the attempted rescue in court, the prosecution clearly demonstrated the gallant efforts of Singleton and the ease with which he was able to surface with Tina, at a rate that was between 30 and 90 seconds faster than that of Gabe when he surfaced alone, allegedly in a panicked state to seek help for his wife. As Singleton testified at the trial, "all her equipment was in place, there was no reaction from her [and] her eyes were open … I dropped my weight belt and pushed a button … it was

[61] Ibid.
[62] Brett Bloomston, court observations, 21 February 2012.
[63] Wade Singleton, court observations, 20 February 2012.

a fast assent".[64] The prosecution also adopted a number of somewhat dramatic tactics to further counter any negative perceptions of or blame attributed to Singleton, while simultaneously challenging the validity of Gabe's versions of events. This included physically marking out in the courtroom the 16 metre distance between where Singleton found Tina and where Gabe claimed they were diving. The prosecution also asked Gabe and Singleton to both stand up before the jury, to demonstrate the obvious differences between their height, weight and general size. This was a powerful moment in the prosecution's case, as it raised questions as to the legitimacy of Gabe's claims that Tina was too heavy for him to keep hold of her underwater, given that this smaller person (Singleton) was able to swiftly lift her up and bring her immediately to the surface.

The prosecution was also able to counter the defence's argument attributing blame to Singleton for not insisting that Tina have an orientation dive by Singleton testifying that "you can't force someone to take an orientation dive".[65] The impact of this statement, however, was somewhat reduced—perhaps indicative of a clever strategy—as the defence objected to the style of questioning employed by the prosecution, in response to which Judge Nail told the prosecution to "move it along",[66] and stop the "repetitive nature of the questions".[67]

Retaining their focus on Mike Ball as a party responsible for Tina's death, the defence was also able to establish during their cross-examination of Singleton that Mike Ball was prosecuted under s 28(3) of the *Workplace Health and Safety Act 1995* (Cth) in Australia for breaching the code that requires inexperienced divers to be accompanied on an orientation dive by a qualified diver. In doing so, the defence sought to strengthen its attribution of blame onto this company. This argument was also used by Bloomston at Gabe's bond hearing on 14 December 2010, in an attempt to show that Gabe was not guilty of murder and should be entitled to bond. As Bloomston claimed:

> It's important to note, your Honor, that the *Mike Ball Dive Company* was cited for the Australian equivalent of an OSHA [Occupational Safety and Health Administration] violation for failing to provide her [Tina with] a dive master on her very first open water dive, failure to provide her [with]

[64] Ibid.
[65] Wade Singleton, court observations, 21 February 2012.
[66] Judge Tommy Nail, court observations, 21 February 2012
[67] Ibid.

> an orientation dive and generally through their negligence in putting her on a very advanced dive for her very first dive in open water.[68]

In attempting to counter the significance placed on this civil prosecution by the defence at the Alabama trial, the prosecution sought to explain that what Mike Ball had pleaded guilty to in May 2007 was not a criminal act or even a breach of external diving regulations; it was a guilty plea to breaching its own internal code of practice, which was set at a higher level than was the norm for the industry. The punishment for the company's admission of negligence was a $6500 fine—less than the cost of Tina's and Gabe's fares for the diving trip.[69] As Gehringer explained:

> Mike Ball could have very easily contested that [prosecution] because it wasn't the industry standards that they'd breached. It was higher standards that they'd imposed upon themselves that they had breached … [But], for whatever reason, they accepted to take the fine even though the fine related to a breach of their standards, not the base industry standards.

While the prosecution was able to address some of the rebuttal arguments presented by the defence, its inability to present all of the available dive evidence, particularly the dive re-enactment video which disputed Gabe's claims as to what happened underwater and the email evidence which countered the defence's allegations of misconduct against *Mike Ball*, represents another point in the *Watson* case where the influence of resource and financial constraints arguably prevented the achievement of procedural, substantive or subjective justice. This is particularly so, given that this evidence would likely have been used as part of a prosecution against Gabe had the case proceeded to trial in Queensland in 2009.

A Typical Accidental Diving Death?

While the Alabama trial concluded abruptly and without the defence being required to present any of its evidence pertaining to the fatal dive, in our discussions with Gabe's legal team and in the various comments they have made to the media, the defence has strongly argued that Tina's death was typical of an accidental diving death. In explaining this argument, Bloomston stated to us that at the Alabama trial the defence intended to

---

[68] Brett Bloomston, bond hearing, 14 December 2010, 5.

[69] Michael McFadyen, "Tina Watson's Death" on *Michael McFadyen's Scuba Diving Website* (2012) <http://www.michaelmcfadyenscuba.info/viewpage.php?page_id=791>.

present evidence from two key diving witnesses—Dr Carl Edmonds and Michael McFadyen—whom he claimed would have been able to demonstrate to the court, the public and the Thomas family "what happened ... to Tina underwater", specifically, that her death was accidental. As discussed in more detail in Chapter Eleven, the inability of the defence to present the testimony of these key witnesses within the confines of the court, as opposed to within media outlets only, is one of the key reasons why the Alabama trial did not provide a just outcome, procedurally or subjectively. This is particularly the case given Bloomston's strong conviction about the value of the testimony in fully explaining Gabe's version of events.

The first of the defence's proposed dive witnesses, Dr Carl Edmonds, has a significant history in the Australian diving field. Edmonds was a co-founder and director of the Australian Diving Medical Centre for 30 years, and has researched and published widely in the field of diving and dive medicine. One of Edmonds's 14 books, *Diving Medicine for Scuba Divers*, which examines a significant number of diving fatalities, was used to support the defence's accidental diving death theory at the coronial inquest in Queensland. Given his background, Edmonds was described by Bloomston as "the foremost expert on dive medicine in Australia". Importantly, Bloomston explained that Edmonds would have testified at the Alabama trial, had a defence been required, that:

> Tina's death ... [was] typical of every accidental dive death that he's [Edmonds] ever done. It's the same set of facts: an inexperienced diver panics, no air in the BCD [buoyancy control device], at the bottom of the ocean with the weights on.

After the Alabama trial, having not had the opportunity to testify for the defence, Edmonds publicly discussed his views on the *Watson* case in various media interviews, including with the Australian Nine Network's *60 Minutes* program and the US ABC network's *20/20* program—the same two television programs on which Gabe and his defence team also appeared. Edmonds used these forums as an opportunity to criticise and dissect the dive evidence presented by the prosecution at the Alabama trial, and in doing so, publicly disclose his personal views as to what happened on the fatal dive. A reporter on *60 Minutes* asked him: "It's absolutely clear, based on all the information, the data you have, that Gabe Watson did not murder his wife"?[70] In response, Edmonds explained:

---

[70] Nine Network Australia, "Deep Trouble" on *60 Minutes* (23 March 2012) (Liz Hayes) <http://sixtyminutes.ninemsn.com.au/stories/8440110/deep-trouble>.

> Of course not, he tried to rescue her. He did his best and he failed in the rescue. This is a common tragedy. It's terrible but it's so common. We're not looking at anything exceptional in this case. There's not one unusual aspect to this case, not one.[71]

In a similar vein, and much like the testimony Bloomston claimed that Edmonds would have provided for the defence, Edmonds noted in his *20/20* interview that Tina's death was typical of the accidental dive–related deaths that occur around the world each year. Justifying his perspective and mirroring the comments of Gabe and his defence attorneys, Edmonds claimed that "she [Tina] was doing a dive to a depth that she had never been to before, in conditions she'd never experienced before. It all fits together … A very common drowning accident".[72]

The second key dive witness who would have been presented by the defence, Michael McFadyen, is a scuba diver based in the Australian state of New South Wales, also considered by Bloomston to be an expert in scuba diving. As of March 2012, McFadyen reported that he had completed over 3,250 open water dives.[73] McFadyen developed an interest in the *Watson* case, due to his personal experience of dealing with two panicked divers on one of his first dives, in which he had to assist them by rapidly ascending to the ocean surface. For this reason, McFadyen kept an online blog detailing his perspectives on what happened on Gabe and Tina's fatal dive—a perspective that the defence argued supports the versions given by Gabe.

The value of McFadyen's evidence, Bloomston explained, would have been his testimony that there was not enough time during the dive for Gabe to have carried out the lethal actions alleged by the prosecution. Bloomston stated that:

> Some of the important things that he [McFadyen] would testify to is that there just wasn't enough time for Gabe to do what the state alleged, underwater. The ascent of a minute to three minutes, and their descent of four minutes to where her trouble started, left only a minute or so for Gabe to be able to do anything intentional, and that's just not enough time to drown someone, to cut off their oxygen and drown someone … So Michael

---

[71] Nine Network Australia, above n 70 (Carl Edmonds).
[72] Shana Druckerman, Nikki Battiste and Edward Lovett, "Honeymoon Killer: Gabe Watson Breaks Silence on Details of Wife's Death" on *ABC News 20/20* (2 March 2012) (Carl Edmonds) <http://abcnews.go.com/US/honeymoon-killer-gabe-watson-breaks-silence-details-wifes/story?id=15819106>.
[73] McFadyen, above n 69.

> [McFadyen] was prepared to testify about that, and the currents and issues such as that.

The significance of this evidence to the defence's case, and in supporting what Gabe claimed happened during the fatal dive, was also identified by Gabe's family and civil lawyer, Bob Austin, who highlighted the importance of timing in disproving the prosecution's case. Austin claimed:

> There's not time for anyone to have turned off her air, let her die, turn her air back on, and do it within the timeframe that they took to go down to 15 [sic, 16] metres, do whatever they did, her sink to the bottom, and Singleton bring her up in a minute and a half. There was just not sufficient time to do it.

While Austin's and Bloomston's comments reveal their perceptions of the strength of McFadyen's evidence regarding timing, as Tommy explained to us, this strength only exists if one accepts Gabe's version of events. Tommy argued that if you contrast the defence's claims with the evidence presented by Stutz, not only does it suggest that Gabe "had her [Tina] in his grasp long enough to turn her air off or turn it back on, which we believe he did, turn it back on as he'd turned it off earlier", but it also raises questions as to why Gabe did not ascend with Tina while he was holding her. As Tommy explained:

> The question in my mind, because she's not fighting anymore, he [Stutz] was very clear, she [Tina] was not fighting. She was either losing consciousness or already unconscious, but she wasn't fighting anymore. So she was too weak to fight. All of his [Gabe's] stuff was on, so he'd already gotten his mask back on [if Tina had knocked it off]. Gabe had her in his grasp long enough to turn her air ... back on ... He also had her in his grasp long enough to take her to the surface. And he did one or the other. We know which one he didn't do, for a fact. He didn't bring her to the surface, so you know, whether he wanted to say she was too heavy, whether he wanted to say she was ten feet below him, or whether he wanted to say she was falling faster than he could go down after her and he was kicking as hard as he could. No matter what version he wanted to do, he had his arms around her, and she was not fighting him, and all he had to do was take her to the surface, and he didn't.

Such concerns and questions raised by Tommy's comments further highlight the frustrations that emerged from the defence not having to present its evidence within the context of a criminal trial, where it would have been revealed, tried and tested according to the law, and not simply exposed in the media. This points to an additional concern surrounding the resolution of the *Watson* case, in both Alabama and Queensland: that the acquittal and the plea bargain removed any opportunity for the legal outcomes to provide any sense of closure or a more concrete understanding of how Tina died, largely because no defence was ever tested within the confines of the law. The implications of this are not only felt by the Thomas family, but also Gabe, because there remain a significant number of unanswered questions surrounding his involvement in Tina's death. This is evident in an article posted by Edmonds in which he expressed his views on the dive, and the justness of the two prosecutions against Gabe, on the *Divers Alert Network* (DAN) online newsletter in August 2012, as follows:

> Tina died from drowning and/or air embolism—the two commonest causes of diving fatalities. She had both. The question of why Tina died was easy to answer, and now has been. The more difficult one is: how did this case get so out of hand that a grieving husband and a despairing family can have their lives torn apart by such an incompetent investigation.[74]

Two key issues arise from Edmonds's post-acquittal analysis of the *Watson* case. Initially, it raises concerns of justice for Gabe, in the sense that if Tina's death was indeed accidental, the legal processes and public scrutiny that he faced for almost nine years demonstrate a significant injustice against him, financially, legally and emotionally. However, perhaps what is most concerning about Edmonds's proclamations of Gabe's innocence and his personal perspectives on how Tina died, which reflect the frustrations and questions identified earlier by Tommy, is the need for these comments to be made, nearly six months after Gabe was acquitted of murder, and therefore legally cleared of having any premeditated or intentional involvement in Tina's death.

While according to the law, Gabe has been acquitted of murdering Tina, the fact that the trial did not follow a traditional and procedurally normative process means that the acquittal outcome was not able to offer procedural justice. It also limits the validity of the public claims made by Gabe, his defence team, Edmonds and McFadyen, because they did not have to present their testimony within the confines of a criminal court, and have their evidence subjected to the same rules of evidence, scrutiny and cross-examination that were applied to the prosecution's case. This is particularly so, given that the prosecution could have provided evidence to

---

[74] Carl Edmonds, "The Honeymoon Death Chronicle" on *DAN Divers Alert Network–Asia Pacific* (6 August 2012) <http://www.danasiapacific.org/main/honeymoon_chronicle.php>.

rebut the defence witnesses' testimony. While Edmonds's and McFadyen's accounts of what occurred are reflective of common diving deaths, in outlining the results of his autopsy of Tina, Dr David Williams stated that "there was no evidence that her death was caused by an arrhythmia ... In my opinion, she had deprivation of oxygen before she died".[75] Similarly, in his statement to the police in 2007, medical practitioner Dr David Griffiths, who performed a number of tests as part of the police investigation, explained that the autopsy of Tina produced no evidence that she had died as a result of "a heart conduction defect, or death due to abnormal cardiac rhythm".[76] Griffiths further explained that:

> Evidence of a gas embolism throughout Christina's body ... is likely to be a consequence of the attempted cardiopulmonary resuscitation that Christina received upon retrieval to the surface, together with the post mortem release of nitrogen gas bubbles into her blood vessels from her stores of body tissue gas, from air absorbed at greater than atmospheric pressure whilst breathing under water. A severe anxiety attack causing Christina to pull off her husband's mask is unlikely to be a satisfactory explanation of events ... Panic alone would be likely to cause hyperventilation, but not unconsciousness. Death would only be likely following panic, if the victim lost her SCUBA regulator or ascended to the surface while breath holding. Christina's dive computer confirms her continual descent to the bottom where she was found by Wade Singleton with both her SCUBA regulator and mask undisplaced.[77]

Consequently, and as examined more extensively in Chapters Eight and Eleven, the absence of a defence being presented to counter the prosecution's dive evidence has not only had negative consequences for the Thomas family in terms of the decision of guilt being made by one authoritative representative of the criminal justice system, as opposed to a jury's decision following a trial, but has also had implications for Gabe, as significant questions around his guilt continue to linger in the public realm.

---

[75] Dr David Williams, witness statement, 11 May 2005.
[76] Dr David Griffiths, witness statement, 18 February 2005.
[77] Ibid.

CHAPTER EIGHT

JUDGING "THE CHARACTER" OF GABE

> They [the Alabama prosecution] wanted to call a lot of character witnesses [to say] that Gabe did strange things, that their relationship was not as it's portrayed to be, that Gabe controlled Tina, that he was cruel to her, teased her with her engagement ring, her wedding ring and things like that ... When you don't have the facts on your side, you have to demonise the defendant. So we anticipated all that bad character evidence would be out there.
>
> —Gabe's US defence attorney Brett Bloomston

At all stages of the almost nine-year duration of the *Watson* case, Gabe's initial response to Tina's death and his actions in the years following have fuelled questions and criticisms of his character. In turn, these have strongly impacted on perceptions of his guilt or innocence among those closest to the case, as well as members of the public and international media. In particular, questions have often been asked about Gabe's treatment of Tina's family in the aftermath of her death, which among other examples included failing to personally contact her family to inform them that Tina had died, requesting that all of Tina's belongings be handed over to him on the day of her funeral, and engaging in a number of unusual behaviours, such as removing flowers placed by the Thomas family on Tina's grave, and having Tina's body exhumed and reburied approximately 188 metres (200 yards) from her original gravesite.

While evidence regarding the character of an accused is generally not admissible in a criminal prosecution, unless it is in the context of a mitigating factor during the sentencing hearing or if it relates specifically to questions of their guilt or innocence, perceptions of Gabe and whether his character is that of someone capable of murdering their wife have undoubtedly influenced various aspects of the *Watson* case, both within and outside the confines of the courtroom. As a consequence, the perceptions and negative depictions of Gabe and his conduct in the wake of Tina's death further diminished the capacity of the Alabama trial to provide substantive, subjective or procedural justice.

Perhaps the most prominent and indeed public example of Gabe's behaviour that has influenced perceptions that he is a person capable of murdering his wife was the footage filmed by Lieutenant Brad Flynn on 7 November 2005 in the Southern Heritage Cemetery in Alabama. This footage showed Gabe using bolt cutters to remove the flowers that were placed by the Thomas family on Tina's grave, and was taken in response to numerous reports of missing flowers that had been made by members of the Thomas family to their local police station in Pelham between February 2004 and November 2005. As Tommy explained in his 2007 statement to the Queensland police:

> The week of 9 February 2004 was also the first time our flowers had been removed from Tina's grave … From that time forward, every weekend or two until sometime in May 2004, I would put new flowers on Tina's grave because someone would come by sometime during the week while I was out of town on business and take them … Generally by Tuesday or Wednesday of the following week they would already be gone.[1]

As discussed in Chapter One, under Rule 403 of the *Alabama Rules of Evidence* and the US *Federal Rules of Evidence*, the video footage of Gabe removing the flowers was deemed inadmissible in the Alabama trial, on the basis that it was overly prejudicial. The rules state that "although relevant, evidence may be excluded if its probative value is substantially outweighed by the danger of unfair prejudice".[2] Accordingly, by ruling it inadmissible Judge Nail must have believed that the video footage might unfairly prejudice the jury against Gabe, due to the emotional reaction they may have had to it. This decision was strongly supported by Bloomston, who believed the evidence was not only prejudicial but was "not relevant". Bloomston further claimed that "Judge Nail, properly, did not allow character evidence to come in. [He] did not allow things such as, well, before the wedding he did this or at the funeral he did this". Since his acquittal, Gabe has also questioned the relevance of the video, claiming, "I don't understand what this has to do with what happened in 2003. This was a year or two later—I can't grasp the relevance of that to Tina's death".[3]

The potential prejudice that could be caused by Gabe's behaviour at the cemetery was highlighted by Coroner David Glasgow prior to the

---

[1] Tommy Thomas, witness statement, 27 April 2007.

[2] *Alabama Rules of Evidence*, Rule 403; *Federal Rules of Evidence* (US), Rule 403.

[3] Gabe Watson, cited in Nikki Battiste and Alice Gomstyn, "Gabe Watson Defends His Behaviour at Wife's Grave", *ABC News* (United States), 29 February 2012.

Alabama trial, in which he explained the possible emotional reaction that could arise from hearing about Gabe's actions. He claimed:

> You've got to remember that the emotion that comes from someone chopping off some flowers off her grave site and throwing them to the ground and moving the body, preventing the parents from even going, all these sorts of things. I just think that he was the architect of his own misfortune.

The powerful influence that Gabe's actions at the cemetery had on questions of his guilt were also particularly evident in Flynn's reflections on filming the scene. In describing the video footage, Flynn explained how it gave him a unique insight into Gabe's character, "a glimpse" into who he really was. From Flynn's perspective, this behaviour demonstrated that Gabe was capable of engaging in more controlling, criminal conduct. As Flynn explained:

> One thing that people do not take away from watching that video, everybody wants to focus on him pulling out the bolt cutters and him throwing the flowers in the street. Okay, that's an important part, but … there is absolutely no—at no time during that video—where he stops to pay any kind of respect to Tina. He doesn't drop a knee, you don't see any emotion. It's a cold, robotic act. He shows up; he looks at the flowers; he sees they're from Tommy; he goes back to get his bolt cutters; cuts them off and throws them in the street … At that one moment … I'm sitting here witnessing the biggest disrespect that somebody could do to somebody else ... I'm like who are you? What in the world are you doing? I'm already having to file an injunction against you in court from digging her [Tina's body] up and moving her for absolutely no valid reason. You got this issue with them [the Watsons] now demanding to have every material that she [Tina] owns. Then you get the incident with the flowers on the gravesite. What innocent, normal person does this?

After Flynn provided the Pelham Police with the video evidence of Gabe removing the flowers in 2005, the police contacted Gabe and he denied having any involvement in their removal. At this stage, the Thomas family decided not to pursue the matter, largely due to concerns that it may have hindered the progress of the police investigation that was continuing in Queensland.

As explained in Chapter One, the footage was shown during the coronial inquest in Townsville, Queensland, in 2007–08, following which Gabe admitted that he had removed the flowers. But, his explanations as to why he did this have varied between 2007 and 2012, ranging from Tina's grave being his property so he could decide what was and was not kept on the grave, to the cemetery dictating that those types of flowers could not be displayed, and also that the cemetery had requested that he move the flowers so that they could mow around the area. In his interview with the US ABC network's *20/20* program following his acquittal, Gabe was also asked to explain his behaviour in the video footage, to which he responded:

> When I would go out to Tina's grave I always left fresh flowers … and it struck a nerve with me that what I considered, and what I think Tina would have considered, big, gaudy, plastic arrangements that would sit out there and get faded in the sun … It definitely wasn't my finest hour ... [but] I'd just been accused of murder … I was still dealing with the death of Tina. I wasn't thinking clearly on everything that I did.[4]

However, based on the timeframe within which the flowers were reported as missing, this explanation is not credible. The video footage was captured by Flynn in November 2005, and the Pelham Police reports of missing flowers began in early 2004. Both of these dates precede Gabe being formally charged or accused of murder by at least 24 months. Furthermore, in illustrating how these inconsistencies in Gabe's various explanations for why he removed the flowers affected perceptions of his character, Tommy commented:

> The guy can't tell the truth about anything … not ever did we ever put cheap plastic flowers on that grave. We always put silk flowers like what we put on my dad's and Cindy's mum's [graves], the same kind Tina used to help us pick out for my dad.

Similarly, Tina's mother, Cindy Thomas, claimed, "he says that we're not allowed to go there and put anything on her grave because it's his property. His property … It's the body of our child. It's not property … it's horrible, and it's a new story every time he opens his mouth".

In line with Cindy's description of Gabe perceiving Tina's grave as his property, an excerpt from one of the *Operation Charlie Oswald* reports includes a comment from Detective Senior Sergeant Gary Campbell that Gabe's behaviour at the cemetery demonstrated "controlling behaviour on

---

[4] Shana Druckerman, Nikki Battiste and Edward Lovett, "Honeymoon Killer: Gabe Watson Breaks Silence on Details of Wife's Death" on *ABC News 20/20* (2 March 2012) (Gabe Watson) <http://abcnews.go.com/US/honeymoon-killer-gabe-watson-breaks-silence-details-wifes/story?id=15819106>.

the part of Mr Watson, of the deceased".[5] This interpretation, which aligns with the possible motives identified by some of our participants as to why Gabe might have killed Tina, as discussed in Chapter Six, demonstrates the important role of Gabe's character not only within the police investigation, but also in the trial from the prosecution's perspective, in revealing that Gabe was a man capable of committing the capital murder offence. The importance of the judge and jury being able to gain an insight into Gabe's character, in order to assess his guilt or capacity to commit murder, was identified by Flynn, who claimed:

> The defence is real quick to try people out, to cry, to show emotion in a courtroom. I think it's just as important that the judge and the jury know what the actions of the defendant [are] ... This is the defendant inflicting this on the family after the fact. You can fight about it and say that it's irrelevant, but I'm going to make you fight to keep it out of court because I believe it is relevant.

In addition to having the flower footage deemed inadmissible under the prejudicial rule, the defence was also able to successfully block the admission of other character evidence, including a Christmas card that Gabe had sent to Tina's best friend, Amanda Phillips, two months after Tina's death. Phillips explained in her statement to the police in April 2007 that she "received a Christmas card from Gabe. It had a wedding picture of Gabe and Tina on the front [and] there was a handwritten note from Gabe on the inside".[6] In describing the content of the handwritten note in her interview with the Australian ABC network's *Australian Story* program, Phillips claimed, "on the inside of it, [it] said, who's that sexy guy next to Tina? Oh yeah, that's me. And he put a smiley face on it. I just threw it down on the counter top in disgust and I said, there is something weird going on here".[7]

As evident in Phillips's emotional response to the card described in her *Australian Story* interview, and as supported by Coroner Glasgow's comments earlier regarding the cemetery footage, this behaviour sheds light on a very negative side of Gabe's character—one that even the judge believed was so abhorrent that it would be impossible for the jury to view

---

[5] Queensland Police Service, "Investigation into the Death of Christina Mae Watson Nee Thomas whilst Scuba Diving off Townsville—22nd October 2003—Operation Charlie Oswald", *QPS Report* (Townsville) 15 November 2007, 37.

[6] Amanda Phillips, witness statement, 21 April 2007.

[7] ABC Television Network, "Unfathomable: Part One", *Australian Story*, 2 August 2010 (Amanda Phillips) <http://www.abc.net.au/austory/content/2007/s2971395.htm>.

Gabe in anything other than a negative light. This is particularly interesting given the "good" character description that was attributed to Gabe in Queensland by the Justices who sentenced him in 2009. Importantly, these same Justices disregarded the victims' views of Gabe, which align with the more negative picture that Judge Nail feared could overly prejudice the Alabama jury. This negative depiction is further supported by the description of Gabe's behaviour leading up to Tina's funeral provided by Tommy in his statement to the police in April 2007:

> Gabe said something about releasing a number of doves at the funeral. Cindy got real upset and said that was something that Tina was against, that Cindy and I had offered to do something like that at the wedding but Tina was against that as she was against birds being caged … At this point Gabe got upset, got up and made a comment that we needed to realise that this was not about us and it was about him. I thought it was about Tina and this really pissed me off … Gabe also said that it would have been easy for him to have her cremated and buried in Australia if he wanted to, and we should be thankful that he bought [sic] her back for us ... The comment about it being easier to cremate and bury Tina in Australia and that we should be thankful alarmed me as it was another little thing that told me that things were not right.[8]

While the behaviour described by Tommy, Amanda Phillips and Lieutenant Brad Flynn certainly does not constitute evidence of Gabe's guilt, it does contribute to the perception that Gabe was the type of person who might be capable of inappropriate and harmful conduct. Importantly, the influence of these assessments of character illustrates the subjective nature of justice, whereby perceptions can be based on individual evaluations of a person's character and informed by knowledge of details of legally inadmissible evidence.

The impact is also evident in the perceptions that Tina's family had of Tina and Gabe's relationship. In describing the manner in which Gabe asked for Tina's hand in marriage, Tommy explained in his 2007 police statement that:

> Gabe told me that this relationship with Tina just felt right. I asked him if he loved Tina and he responded by telling me that he thought that was a "little corny". Gabe told me he felt they were comfortable together and, once again, their relationship just felt right for him. Gabe did not, at any

[8] Tommy Thomas, witness statement, 27 April 2007.

> time, tell me that he loved her, which, as her father, was what I was looking for.[9]

Although this behaviour is not inherently relevant to questions of guilt or innocence in the official legal context, Gabe's unusual behaviours have undoubtedly influenced perceptions of his guilt and provided a basis for some to suggest that he has the character of someone who is capable of wrongdoing. Therefore, while it may be argued that Judge Nail's decision to rule much of the character evidence inadmissible in Alabama was because Gabe's "character" was not on trial, his decision further highlights the potential injustice of the outcome of the case in Queensland, in light of the favourable and sympathetic representation of Gabe's character, which was strongly reflected in the sentences imposed on him.

The Actions of a Grieving Husband or a Murderer?

As discussed in Chapter Six, the prosecution faced significant obstacles in trying to establish a motive of financial gain, particularly given that some of its key evidence pertaining to Tina's insurance was deemed inadmissible by Judge Nail, on the basis that it was hearsay. Another major obstacle the prosecution faced was the need to establish that Gabe was a man capable of killing his wife, given the constraints of the admissibility decisions being applied to most of the character evidence presented.

At several points during the capital murder trial, the prosecution attempted to introduce evidence pertaining to Gabe's character, arguing that it would help to establish the financial gain motive. While many of these attempts were overruled by Judge Nail, using the evidence that was permitted the prosecution sought to highlight the unusual behaviour of Gabe immediately after Tina's death as a means of establishing his guilt and portraying him as a man who cared little for his bride of 11 days. One example of this behaviour was disclosed in what was deemed admissible in the testimony of Tina's sister, Alanda Thomas, in which she described how Gabe demanded that he be given all of Tina's personal belongings in the days surrounding her funeral because "he was done with the grieving process".[10] This testimony mirrored Alanda's 2007 police statement, in which she recounted a conversation with Gabe about Tina's belongings that took place in the week of Tina's funeral:

---

[9] Ibid.

[10] Alanda Thomas, court observations, 21 February 2012.

> When I spoke to Gabe I said to him, why are you doing this? Why do you need this stuff now? Gabe told me that we had to understand that he had already completed the grieving process and we were just starting. I was appalled at this and could not understand what he was saying and why he was doing this. I became really upset and dad took the telephone from me. This was the last time I spoke to Gabe.[11]

Another significant piece of evidence regarding Gabe's character that was allowed to infiltrate the Alabama trial was his decision not to be present on the *Jazz II*, while attempts were made to resuscitate Tina. In order to demonstrate this negative side of Gabe's character and thus imply some level of guilt, throughout the trial the prosecution asked those witnesses who were aboard either the *Spoilsport* or the *Jazz II* on 22 October 2003 to confirm whether Gabe had been present on the *Jazz II* during the 40 minutes in which attempts were made to resuscitate Tina. In response, several of the prosecution dive witnesses testified that not only was Gabe not present, but also that he did not ask to be taken to the *Jazz II* until after he was told by Dr John Downie that Tina had died. This was despite Gabe having told the Thomas family in their first interaction following Tina's death that he was with her "the whole time".[12] As described by Alanda in her statement to the Queensland police:

> Gabe was asked by mum if he was with her while they tried to revive her and he said he was by her side the whole time. We all told him that we were sorry for him and I felt very sorry for him knowing that he would have that mental image with him forever.[13]

The fabrication that Gabe was present throughout the resuscitation was also described by Alanda at the trial, when she testified that Gabe "promised he was with her the whole time, he said he never left her the whole time".[14]

Over the nearly nine-year duration of the *Watson* case, Gabe's decision not to assist, watch or comfort Tina during the 40 minutes while attempts were made to resuscitate her has been a strong influence on people's perceptions of his character and his level of involvement in her death. This is illustrated by the headline of a *Courier Mail* article published during the Alabama trial, which read, "Gabe Watson 'hung out and asked for hugs'

---

[11] Alanda Thomas, witness statement, 30 April 2007.
[12] Ibid.
[13] Ibid.
[14] Alanda Thomas, court observations, 21 February 2012.

on other dive boat as others tried to save Tina's life".[15] A similar view was expressed in the comments of the divers present on the *Spoilsport*, who described Gabe's decision as unusual and not reflective of a grieving or concerned husband. In her statement to the police on the night of Tina's death, Virginia (Ginger) Milsap, a fellow diver aboard the *Spoilsport*, commented that, "I remember seeing someone performing CPR upon Tina. I couldn't understand why Gabe wasn't over there with her. I would have swum over there if they would not have taken me".[16] In a second statement given as part of the ongoing police investigation in June 2006, Ginger further stated that, "I thought it was strange that he was even on the boat [*Spoilsport*]. Why isn't he over there with Tina the whole time? You couldn't have peeled me away from my husband, especially a newlywed. It was difficult to understand that. It didn't make any sense to me at all".[17] Offering a similar view, Kenneth (Ken) Snyder, another diver on the *Spoilsport* who was with Gabe while attempts were made to resuscitate Tina, commented in his second police statement in 2006 that:

> I thought he didn't behave as a husband should behave. At no time did he ask to go over to the other [boat] … and I thought that was bizarre. If it were my wife and they were doing CPR on another boat and there was traffic on those boats going back and forth bringing the first aid kits and the doctor back and forth, I would have been on one of those dinghies to see what was going on with my wife. No one could have stopped me. If someone would have tried to have stopped me, I would have jumped overboard and swam over … I would have expected him to be much more frantic and want to get on the dive boat and go over and see what happened. He didn't even climb the steps to the upper deck to see what was going on. I just thought he didn't appear excited over it or distraught. He was somewhat calm.[18]

When testifying at the Alabama trial in 2012, Snyder also commented on the ease with which Gabe could have reached Tina had he wanted to. As Snyder claimed, "you could swim the distance [between the *Spoilsport* and the *Jazz II*] in minutes. There were rafts transporting people back and forth ... A raft left taking the doctor to the other boat ... No one was

[15] Tuck Thompson, "Gabe Watson 'Hung Out and Asked for Hugs' on Other Dive Boat as Others Tried to Save Tina's Life", *The Courier Mail* (Queensland), 16 February 2012.
[16] Virginia Milsap, witness statement, 22 October 2003.
[17] Virginia Milsap, witness statement, 20 June 2006.
[18] Kenneth Snyder, witness statement, 20 June 2006.

stopping Gabe going over ... [but] Gabe was just talking to Paula [Snyder]".[19]

To further support the portrayal of Gabe as failing to display the normative and socially acceptable behaviour of a grieving husband, the prosecution asked several of the dive witnesses during the trial to describe Gabe's reaction when he first saw Tina's body aboard the *Jazz II*. Uzi Barnai, one of the Mike Ball Dive Expeditions (Mike Ball) employees who assisted on the *Spoilsport* during Gabe and Tina's diving trip, and who was also involved in Tina's attempted rescue and resuscitation, testified that when "Gabe went onto the boat, it was really strange ... he didn't look like he was crying".[20] This testimony supported earlier commentary that Barnai had made, in which he claimed that:

> [Gabe] took an eternity to come and see her [Tina] ... When he did, he did not collapse in grief like a heartbroken husband might. This was the first dive of their honeymoon after all … His face was empty. He just sat there, making funny sobbing sounds. I don't know if it was for show or genuine.[21]

Building upon this testimony, the prosecution also sought to highlight the differences between Gabe's behaviour and the conduct and actions that the witnesses said they would have engaged in had it been their partner who was in trouble or had died on the dive. In questioning Snyder, the prosecution asked, "What would you have done to save yourself and your wife?", to which he responded, "you'd go straight to the top [ocean surface]".[22] Similarly, in his response to the prosecution's questions regarding what one needs to do to assist a panicked diver, Douglas (Doug) Milsap testified that "the logical thing to do is inflate your BC [buoyancy control] and go straight to the surface ... We wouldn't be here today [if] he'd [Gabe] pressed the BC, it would've taken her to the top ... You'd do it in a heartbeat ... Once learnt, never forgotten".[23]

This type of commentary on Gabe's behaviour, including evaluations of how he "should" have behaved as a grieving husband, has surrounded the case since 2003, such that members of the public and those most involved in the case have often questioned whether Gabe was a coward or a killer. As Wade Singleton explained in his second police statement:

---

[19] Kenneth Snyder, court observations, 16 February 2012.
[20] Uzi Barnai, court observations, 20 February 2012.
[21] Uzi Barnai, cited in Peter Mitchell, "Witness Thought Watson Was Helping Wife", *Sydney Morning Herald* (New South Wales), 17 February 2009.
[22] Kenneth Snyder, court observations, 16 February 2012.
[23] Douglas Milsap, court observations, 17 February 2012.

> I do not see myself in a similar situation leaving someone who is close to me; however, everyone acts differently. Gabe also made a comment to me on our return to Townsville in the hours following the death. Gabe did state that he would prefer to return to the vessel [*Spoilsport*] that night and spend the night on board. Again, in similar circumstances I would not wish to go anywhere near the vessel again.

This view was also evident in media headlines such as, "He is a coward: Cousin of wife in scuba drowning rips bizarre antics of cleared husband",[24] and "Watson a 'coward' but not a killer".[25]

While Gabe's actions may be perceived as contradicting traditional and normative understandings of how a grieving husband should behave in the aftermath of his new wife's death, such behaviour is not necessarily indicative of guilt. As Gabe described in his post-acquittal interview with the US ABC network's *20/20* program, he was "devastated" and "collapsed" upon learning of Tina's death.[26] Furthermore, in explaining his reasons for not being present on the *Jazz II* during the resuscitation attempts, Gabe stated, "that's not something I can handle … I don't ever want to see one of my loved ones being worked on like that, ever".[27]

In an attempt to counter the seemingly negative portrayals of Gabe's character, and his behaviour immediately before and after Tina's death, the defence used its cross-examination opportunities during the trial to extract statements from various witnesses to offer their perceptions of Gabe on the night, as opposed to their perceptions nearly nine years down the track after they had been subjected to and potentially influenced by various portrayals of Gabe in the media. This can be seen in the cross-examination of Singleton, whereby the defence asked him to clarify the comments he had made in the statement he had given to the police on the night that Tina died, in which he described Gabe as being "definitely distressed",[28] noting "that he was crying".[29] At the trial, the defence also reminded Singleton of a statement he had given to the police in November 2004, in which he described Gabe's emotional reaction to the death of his wife as being "quite natural and appropriate under the circumstances".[30]

---

[24] Holly Aguirre, "'He is a Coward': Cousin of Wife in Scuba Drowning Rips Bizarre Antics of Cleared Husband", *The Daily* (Australia), 26 February 2012.

[25] Australian Associated Press, "Watson a 'Coward' but Not a Killer", *The Age* (Victoria), 22 April 2011.

[26] Druckerman, Battiste and Lovett, above n 4.

[27] Ibid.

[28] Wade Singleton, witness statement, 22 October 2003.

[29] Ibid.

[30] Wade Singleton, witness statement, 4 November 2004.

A similar tactic was used in the cross-examination of Barnai, whereby the defence was able to show a significant difference between the statement he gave to the police in Queensland on the night of Tina's death, and the testimony he gave at the Alabama trial on 20 February 2012. In particular, the defence pointed to Barnai's conflicting statements regarding the absence of water in Tina's mouth when he pulled her from the water. In his testimony at the trial, Barnai stated that "after taking off her regulator and mask, I started CPR".[31] He then testified that "I thought it was unusual that no water was coming out of her mouth".[32] This differed significantly from the statement he had given to the police on 22 October 2003, when he explained that "I tilted her head and cleared foam from her mouth. I also saw a lot of water and a little bit of blood come out of her mouth".[33] To demonstrate these inconsistencies, Gabe's US defence attorney, Brett Bloomston, asked, "So which is it? Your first testimony, or what you've told us now?",[34] and then asked Barnai to read from his police statement. This was a powerful moment for the defence, particularly as Barnai was a charismatic witness for the prosecution, drawing people in with his likeable nature and his discussion of Gabe's "strange" behaviour, including making "clucking noises" over Tina's body.[35]

The importance of this moment was recognised by Bloomston in our discussions following the trial, as he claimed, "Uzi [said], oh, she didn't have any water coming out ... He lied, and we had him ... When witnesses get up on the stand, like Uzi Barnai and lie ... It was good ... It certainly helped us". In addition to benefiting the defence, the differences between Barnai's two statements highlighted the limitations of the Alabama trial in providing an appropriate forum for justice because of the extent of the delays and their potential impact on the accuracy and viability of witness statements. This impact was identified by Gehringer, who explained that "time is of the essence ... [with] witnesses, the longer it takes before you can get a matter in front of a court, the harder it is".

The defence used their cross-examination of the prosecution's dive witnesses to demonstrate that the differences between statements given on the night of Tina's death, during the protracted police investigation, and those presented at the February 2012 trial, were the result of hindsight and Gabe's later actions, including his treatment of the Thomas family, rather than accurate reflections of witnesses' actual perceptions of Gabe on the

---

[31] Uzi Barnai, court observations, 20 February 2012.
[32] Ibid.
[33] Uzi Barnai, witness statement, 22 October 2003.
[34] Brett Bloomston, court observations, 20 February 2012.
[35] Uzi Barnai, court observations, 20 February 2012.

night that Tina died. In the cross-examination of Paula Snyder—a fellow diver on the *Spoilsport* who also acted as Gabe's support person while he gave his first statement to the police—the defence was able to extrapolate several comments to show that on the night of Tina's death, Paula Snyder believed that Gabe was displaying the normal behaviour of a man who had just lost his wife, including that he seemed "shocked", "sombre", "dazed" and that he "was crying" and appeared in "a trance".[36] Thus, despite Paula testifying during the prosecution's questioning that Gabe's demeanour was "calm",[37] the defence was able to suggest that this was not in line with her earlier views of Gabe, expressed shortly after Tina's death—thus somewhat countering the prosecution's portrayal of Gabe as a man who cared little for his new wife.

Defending Gabe's Character

Gabe's defence team in the Alabama trial faced an arguably harder task than the prosecution in terms of substantiating Gabe's character, as they were required to effectively change the negative portrayals and labels applied to Gabe into a depiction of him as a grief-stricken husband, wrongly accused of murder in two jurisdictions. The prejudicial rule assisted the defence team in that they did not have to explain Gabe's actions in the wake of Tina's death in court, and the insurance motive did not lend itself to requiring them to address specific questions around Gabe's character or his relationship with Tina before her death. However, in our discussions with Bloomston following the acquittal, he explained that had Gabe not been acquitted, these issues would have required some response within the defence they presented in court, in order to combat prejudicial and preconceived juror opinions. As Bloomston explained, "he was portrayed and given the moniker as the honeymoon killer. We knew we had an uphill battle with media and public perception".

A response to the negative representations of Gabe's character would also have been needed had a defence been run, to counter the strategy utilised by the prosecution during the trial to humanise Tina in the eyes of the jury. The prosecution achieved this by providing the jury—wherever possible and when not objected to by the defence as irrelevant—with some insight into who Tina Thomas was. In questioning the witnesses who had some direct interaction with Tina, whether members of her family or the dive witnesses on board the *Spoilsport*, the prosecution asked for a

[36] Paula Snyder, court observations, 16 February 2012.
[37] Ibid.

description of Tina. In describing meeting Tina the night before the dive, Snyder testified that "she was excited, she was smiling, she was exuberant".[38] Similarly, Paula Snyder described her perceptions of Tina upon first meeting her, commenting that "she was adorable … She just kind of grabbed our hearts right then".[39] While these witnesses were only able to provide quite brief comments about Tina, a clear picture emerged for the jury of who Tina was. This picture was reflected in the comments provided to us by Flynn:

> [In the course of the police investigation] I began to see a side of Gabe that was unanimous, in that everybody described Tina as the sunshine and everybody described Gabe as the black cloud. And that he was the last person that anybody would ever expect her to end up with ... So I had established that Tina was a bright and bubbly person and Gabe just tried to snuff that out in so many different ways, both verbally [and] in some physical actions.

Given the picture of Tina that had emerged from the statements of the prosecution witnesses, while brief and legally not relevant to Gabe's guilt or innocence, it was important that had a defence been offered, a "good" image of Gabe was also presented. As Bloomston acknowledged, had the jury been given the opportunity to return a verdict, he was concerned that they would have convicted Gabe, not based on the strength of the prosecution's evidence, but because they perceived him as "a jerk." This comment, made by a member of Gabe's own defence team, illustrates the subjective nature of justice, and the difficulties that emerge accordingly, in that decisions pertaining to guilt or innocence, which should be made based on an unbiased evaluation of the admissible evidence presented in a criminal trial, can be made and influenced by prejudicial assessments of an individual's character—a factor that was strengthened by the significant delays inherent in this case.

In describing the ways in which the defence team intended to address the potentially negative, preconceived views of Gabe, Bloomston explained that they planned to call two of Tina's bridesmaids—Susanne Warren and Amy Bach—to testify. Bloomston believed that this testimony would have showed that "Tina and Gabe had a wonderful relationship ... a loving and sweet relationship ... [that] he cared for her, he doted on her, and he protected her." Bloomston further described the testimony as including comments such as, "Tina looked to Gabe as her rock and her security".

---

[38] Kenneth Snyder, court observations, 16 February 2012.
[39] Paula Snyder, court observations, 16 February 2012.

From Bloomston's perspective, this testimony would have disputed the inaccurate picture painted by the prosecution of Tina and Gabe's relationship, and also that it would have stood in sharp contrast to the picture of Gabe, and particularly of Gabe and Tina's relationship, that had been promoted in the media and by members of the Thomas family in the lead-up to and during the Alabama trial. Bloomston also explained that the defence had planned to call the Australian licensed grief therapist, Candia Bruce, whom Mike Ball had organised to meet with Gabe in the days following Tina's death. Bloomston commented:

> She [Candia Bruce] would have testified that Gabe was devastated, that he was in shock, that he grieved, that she helped him with some tips on how to handle it and prepared him to come back to the [United] States … Alanda's spin on it was that Gabe said he was finished grieving, but that's not the case, he wasn't finished grieving and his mother will tell you, she had to get him out of bed for the next three months, because he was still completely depressed and withdrawn. But Candia would have testified that she helped Gabe through the process and she certainly indicated by everything she said, that he was devastated by his wife's death.

The beginning of this counter-portrayal of Gabe, and the defence's attempt to humanise him to the jury, was evident in the defence's opening statement in which Gabe's US defence attorney, Jo Basgier, sought to remind the jury that Gabe should also be seen as a victim in this case, commenting that he "lost her [Tina], just like the Thomas family did".[40] This depiction of Gabe as a victim rather than an aggressor was further promoted in the same opening statement, when Basgier commented that "this is a tragic case, and what is even more tragic is the blame of Gabe".[41] However, because the trial ended without the defence having to present any of its evidence, the opportunity to disclose this "other" side to Tina and Gabe's relationship, or even to present the alternate side of Gabe's character, was limited to these brief comments in the defence's opening statement. As a result, questions around the nature of Tina and Gabe's relationship, and negative perceptions of Gabe's character, remain strong within the public realm. As Gabe's father, David Watson, commented in the wake of the acquittal decision, "the proof of Gabe's character and

[40] Joe Basgier, court observations, 14 February 2012.
[41] Ibid.

nature will be how he lives the rest of his life ... Hopefully people will look back and see that he was a good person".[42]

[42] David Watson, cited in Katie Kindelan and Nikki Battiste, "Gabe Watson's Father 'Relieved' after Son's Murder Case Dismissed", *ABC News* (United States), 24 February 2012.

PART III

ACHIEVING JUSTICE

CHAPTER NINE

GABE'S ACQUITTAL

> By no means is any justice system perfect, but I guess as the English decided at the Battle of Runnymede, they wanted a jury trial. They were tired of the Sheriff deciding who was guilty and who was going to jail … Justice isn't necessarily a conviction; justice is putting it into court, letting everybody know the evidence.
>
> —Alabama Assistant Attorney-General Don Valeska

In the US, an accused has the constitutional right to have their case heard by a jury. This applies to all cases where the punishment could involve a term of six months or more in prison. An accused can waive this right prior to the trial commencing by pleading guilty, or, with the consent of the prosecution and the court, by electing to have the matter heard and determined by a judge alone.[1] Interestingly, however, even once a jury has been empanelled and the trial has commenced, an accused maintains the right to request that the decision of guilt be removed from the jury to instead be determined by the trial judge. This can be achieved by the defence filing a motion for a judgement of acquittal.[2]

A motion for a judgement of acquittal can be made before or after the case is submitted to the jury, for any offence in which the defence believes the prosecution's evidence is insufficient to sustain a conviction. Generally, an acquittal motion is made at the close of the prosecution's case, after all of the evidence from both sides has come to a close (or within 14 days of the jury being discharged), or after a jury has returned a guilty verdict. Regardless of when the motion is made, the judge can reserve making a decision on whether to grant the motion until any time before or after the jury returns its verdict, or until the jury is discharged if a verdict cannot be reached. However, if the judge does reserve their

---

[1] *Federal Rules of Criminal Procedure* (US), Rule 23a.

[2] In Alabama, this right exists under Rule 29 of the *Federal Rules of Criminal Procedure 1986* (US) and Rules 20.1(a-b) and 20.2(a-c) of the *Alabama Rules of Criminal Procedure*.

decision, they must decide the motion based only on the evidence that had been presented up until the time at which the motion was first made.

When determining whether to grant an acquittal, the judge must consider whether the evidence that has been presented in the case is sufficient to sustain a guilty verdict. This essentially requires the judge to decide whether any reasonable jury, properly instructed, could find that the essential elements of the offence were proven beyond reasonable doubt. As discussed in Chapter Six, this decision must be made by viewing the evidence presented in the most favourable light to the prosecution. This requirement is outlined in case law, which states that:

> In determining the sufficiency of the evidence to sustain a conviction, a reviewing court must accept as true all evidence introduced by the State, and accord the State all legitimate inferences there from, and consider all of the evidence in a light most favourable to the prosecution.[3]

Case law further dictates that the "test in determining the sufficiency of evidence to sustain a conviction is whether, viewing the evidence in a light most favourable to the prosecution, a rational finder of fact"[4] could find the accused guilty beyond reasonable doubt.

If the motion is denied, the jury must then make a determination of guilt. If the motion is granted after a jury has returned a guilty verdict, the prosecution can appeal against the acquittal. If this appeal is successful, the jury's guilty verdict is reinstated. If the appeal fails, the acquittal stands. If, however, the motion for acquittal is granted before a jury delivers a verdict, the double jeopardy protection enshrined in the Fifth Amendment of the *Constitution of the US* prevents the prosecution from appealing the judge's decision.

A Motion for Judgement of Acquittal

In *Watson*, the motion for a judgement of acquittal was filed with the court at the close of the prosecution's case, immediately after lunch on 23 February 2012. In presenting its motion, the defence prepared a 17-page written document and orally argued the key elements of the motion in the courtroom before Judge Tommy Nail and the prosecution, outside the presence of the jury. The defence had supplied the prosecution with a copy of its written motion one day earlier, on 22 February 2012. The underlying premise of the defence's motion was that at the close of its case, the

---

[3] *Ballenger v State* (1998) 720 So 2d 1033 at 1034.
[4] *J.M.A v State* (2011) 74 So 3d 487 at 498.

prosecution had failed to present sufficient evidence that Gabe had murdered Tina for pecuniary gain, to the required criminal standard. In its written motion, the defence stated that:

> Before the jury could convict Gabe Watson of an intentional murder committed for pecuniary or other valuable consideration as set forth in Count One of the Indictment, the State of Alabama would have to prove the following facts beyond a reasonable doubt:
>
> a) Tina Watson is dead; and,
> b) Gabe Watson caused the death of Tina Watson by drowning her; and,
> c) That in committing the act which caused the death of Tina Watson, Gabe Watson intended to kill Tina Watson; and,
> d) That the intentional murder was committed by Gabe Watson for a pecuniary or other valuable consideration. [5]

Following this, the defence motion stated that "the evidence and testimony presented by the Attorney General's Office in this trial is insufficient to support a finding of guilt beyond a reasonable doubt and the State has failed to make out a prima facie case as to the intentional murder of Tina Watson".[6]

This argument was mirrored by Gabe's US defence attorney Brett Bloomston's verbal arguments to the court, in which he claimed, "the key elements of the offence—that he caused her death by drowning with an intent to gain money—were not met. There is insufficient evidence to support guilt beyond reasonable doubt".[7] The defence's motion provided a critical analysis of and rebuttal to individual witness statements, and key pieces of evidence that the prosecution had presented in relation to the cause and circumstances surrounding Tina's death. The defence team's analysis was detailed and thematic, addressing the prosecution's failure to prove that Gabe caused Tina's death and that he did so motivated by a potential financial gain.

Beginning with the prosecution's dive evidence, the defence motion drew attention to the only "direct evidence" presented: the testimony of Dr Stanley Stutz, the diver from the *Jazz II* who witnessed an interaction between Gabe and Tina underwater before she died. The defence highlighted that in his testimony, Stutz indicated that he believed Gabe was "trying to save his wife, before rapidly ascending to the surface", and

---

[5] Defence Motion for Judgement of Acquittal, 23 February 2012, 2-3.
[6] Ibid.
[7] Brett Bloomston, court observations, 23 February 2012.

that Stutz was "shocked it was [being called] murder".[8] On this basis, the defence claimed that the prosecution's only direct evidence "in no way proves Tina's death was intentional".[9] In further disputing the dive evidence presented by the prosecution, the defence noted that in the testimony given by Wade Singleton—the dive master and trip adviser of Gabe and Tina's seven-day expedition on the *Spoilsport*—he admitted to having "no personal knowledge" of how Tina died, and his comments were "speculation, conjecture and opinion ... circumstantial at best".[10] The defence also argued that Singleton's testimony provided another avenue of blame independent of Gabe's actions, claiming that Singleton effectively acknowledged that he held "some responsibility" because he had "failed to ascertain Tina's diving inexperience" prior to their dive at the *SS Yongala* wreck.[11]

In addition, the defence motion identified limitations in the evidence provided by Gabe's fellow divers, Kenneth (Ken) Snyder and Douglas (Doug) Milsap, and the diving assistant on board the *Spoilsport*, Uzi Barnai, on the basis that none of these witnesses had "direct knowledge" or "first-hand evidence" of how Tina died or of Gabe's diving training.[12] Instead, the defence claimed that their testimonies were based purely on what they believed they would have done had they been in Gabe's position. As Bloomston orally argued in relation to these witnesses' testimonies, "convictions cannot be predicated on opinions and speculation".[13] Similarly, in discussing the details of Tina's death, the defence motion pointed to the testimony of Adam White (the scuba technician and customer service manager of Oceanic Australia who performed tests on Gabe's and Tina's dive computers) that Gabe had "ascended in a rapid manner",[14] and the admission of Dr David Williams (the doctor who conducted Tina's autopsy) that he "couldn't state how Tina drowned",[15] to further illustrate the failure of the prosecution to prove the capital murder charge against Gabe.

In verbally arguing the motion before the judge, Bloomston claimed, "based on these witnesses, guesswork is not enough for a jury conviction ... Suspicion and guesswork should not override the presumption of

---

[8] Ibid.
[9] Ibid.
[10] Ibid.
[11] Ibid.
[12] Ibid.
[13] Ibid.
[14] Ibid.
[15] Ibid.

innocence".[16] This supported the written submission that surmised the prosecution's dive evidence as relying "upon testimony that can only be described as speculation, conjecture, and opinion by witnesses who have no first hand or personal knowledge to support a finding of guilty beyond reasonable doubt and a conviction for intentional murder".[17] The written motion also drew from existing case law to strengthen the premise underpinning the speculative testimony argument. Quoting from three cases,[18] the submission stated:

> While a jury is under a duty to draw whatever permissible inferences it may from the evidence, including circumstantial evidence, mere speculation, conjecture, or surmise that the accused is guilty of the offense charged does not authorize a conviction ... A defendant should not be convicted on mere suspicion or out of fear that he might have committed the crime ... While reasonable inferences from the evidence may furnish a basis for proof beyond a reasonable doubt ... mere possibility, suspicion, or guesswork, no matter how strong, will not overturn the presumption of innocence.[19]

The defence team's motion for a judgement of acquittal then turned towards addressing the problems they perceived in relation to the pecuniary gain element of the prosecution's case, again referring to individual witness testimonies to highlight potential flaws and weaknesses within them. In critiquing the insurance policy evidence, the defence drew attention to the acknowledgement made by Eric Langley—the civil lawyer for the defence in Gabe's lawsuit against Old Republic insurance company—that had Gabe been awarded the $10,134.92 he sought in his original insurance claim, "the matter would've been settled".[20] Consequently, in its written motion the defence claimed that the prosecution "incorrectly relies upon the testimony of Langley to support their pecuniary gain arguments".[21] The motion further stipulated that:

> Mr Langley's testimony reflects an attempt by Gabe Watson to collect on a travel insurance policy that was intended to cover the costs and expenses which he had already paid in the event that his honeymoon was cut short for a covered event. This was not an attempt to obtain a pecuniary gain, but

---

[16] Ibid.
[17] Defence Motion, above n 5, 9.
[18] *Harnage v State* (1972) 274 So 2d 333; *J.M.A v State* (2011) 74 So 3d 487; *Royals v State* (1951) 56 So 2d 368.
[19] Defence Motion, above n 5, 17.
[20] Brett Bloomston, court observations, 23 February 2012.
[21] Defence Motion, above n 5, 32.

was instead an attempt to recovery money that he and/or his family had already spent on the honeymoon.[22]

The defence also cited the testimony of Stephanie Mercer—the human resource officer at Tina's place of employment—in which she stated that "Tina could've got three times her salary, but she didn't",[23] and "any changes made would only have taken effect from January 2004".[24] This point was emphasised to the judge in both the verbal and written submissions, with Bloomston stating that the prosecution's evidence showed "in no way, shape or form, [that] an additional policy [was] in place prior to the honeymoon".[25] In reiterating this point, the written motion similarly stated:

> Mercer testified (1) that Tina Watson had a life insurance policy and her father was the beneficiary, (2) that Tina Watson had an option to purchase more life insurance which she could not do until returning from her honeymoon, and (3) that Tina Watson had the option to change the beneficiary on her life insurance policy at any time but had not done so. Mercer's testimony in no way establishes proof beyond a reasonable doubt that Gabe Watson killed his wife with the belief that he would benefit from her employer-provided life insurance policy following her death.[26]

The defence also identified the testimony of Caesar Lamonica—the former manager at Tina's place of employment—as "providing no evidence [that] Gabe was seeking to benefit"[27] from Tina's death. Instead, the defence suggested that Lamonica's statement only proved that Gabe had visited Parisians one month after Tina's death, when he was referred to human resources to discuss any issues relating to Tina's insurance policy and other matters. As argued by the defence, this visit did not prove a financial motive. Bloomston similarly stated that the testimony of Tina's best friend, Amanda Phillips, that Gabe "joked about changing the policy ... doesn't prove intent [or] any pecuniary gain".[28] As the written motion explained:

> The testimony of Phillips establishes only that Gabe and Tina Watson joked about insurance prior to their honeymoon. It does not establish proof

---

[22] Ibid.
[23] Brett Bloomston, court observations, 23 February 2012.
[24] Ibid.
[25] Ibid.
[26] Defence Motion, above n 5, 39.
[27] Brett Bloomston, court observations, 23 February 2012.
[28] Ibid.

> beyond reasonable doubt that Gabe Watson initiated the purchase of insurance or forced Tina Watson to increase her life insurance coverage prior to their wedding in an effort to realize a pecuniary gain from her death.[29]

Further to this claim, the defence pointed to the fact that Tina's assets were worth $3,000 yet her liability was valued at $24,000, thus providing direct evidence that Gabe could not have gained financially from her death.

In summarising its arguments for an acquittal, the defence's written motion again drew upon relevant case law to emphasise the speculative nature of the prosecution's case and what the defence perceived to be the prosecution's inability to present sufficient evidence to support the capital murder charge.[30] The motion stated:

> Based on the testimony and evidence presented to this jury, the State has failed to present sufficient evidence to prove a prima facie case that Gabe Watson intentionally murdered Tina Watson for a pecuniary gain or other valuable consideration beyond a reasonable doubt. The testimony and evidence presents mere possibilities, suspicions, and guesswork about what might have occurred and what Gabe Watson should have done differently on that day.[31]

Furthermore, the written motion argued that in light of the prosecution's failure to prove that Gabe intentionally killed Tina or that he sought to gain financially from her death, Alabama had no jurisdiction to continue the prosecution. The defence argued this on the basis that the prosecution:

> Failed to present evidence or testimony, direct or indirect, which links this offense to the Birmingham Division of Jefferson County … The State has utterly failed to show that Gabe Watson ever received any economic gain, or attempted to receive any economic gain, as a result of Tina Watson's death.[32]

Similarly, in concluding his verbal submission to the judge, Bloomston argued that the prosecution "had failed to present evidence directly or indirectly to prove their case, or any testimony that supports [that] Gabe

---

[29] Defence Motion, above n 5, 35.
[30] *Harnage v State* (1972) 274 So 2d 333.
[31] Defence Motion, above n 5, 41.
[32] Ibid, 42.

Watson killed Tina and collected money ... There was no economic gain proved ... There was no evidence".[33]

In later discussing their motion for acquittal and their perceptions as to whether it would be successful, Gabe's US defence attorneys Joe Basgier and Brett Bloomston suggested that they were somewhat confident, but not convinced that the acquittal would be granted. As Basgier explained:

> We prepared [almost] a 20-page brief when we made our motion, which is not typical. It's not typical to have a written motion for judgement of acquittal, and we did that because we thought we had very strong grounds on which to make that motion. But we didn't allow ourselves to become convinced that was going to happen ... I mean, we did a lot of work; we interviewed all these witnesses, we knew or anticipated how they were going to testify ... We had to continue to expect that we would have to put on our own case and put on our own witnesses.

Bloomston similarly noted:

> When we filed the motion with Judge Nail, and the questions that he was posing to the prosecutors and his clear opinion as to their theories, I felt optimistic, I wouldn't say confident. My first witness was in the conference room outside of the court. And I called him at lunch, I said that they may rest after lunch ... He was our first witness, and he was there and ready to go.

Following the defence's verbal motion for acquittal, the prosecution provided a verbal response immediately in court, commencing with a reminder to the judge that he was required to view the evidence in the most favourable light to the prosecution. Drawing upon comments made by individual prosecution witnesses, Alabama Assistant Attorney-General and lead prosecutor in the capital murder trial Don Valeska argued that "the State proved Gabe Watson killed Tina and his purpose has been proven to be monetary gain, whether he got anything or not".[34] Valeska stressed that motive had been proved regardless of what money or proceeds Gabe had actually received, because it was his anticipation and expectation of potential gain that demonstrated financial motive. In concluding the prosecution's response, Valeska stated that in addition to the strength of the evidence presented by the prosecution providing a reason for jury consideration of the case, the verdict should be determined by a jury for the simple reason that Tina was last seen in the company of

[33] Brett Bloomston, court observations, 23 February 2012.
[34] Don Valeska, court observations, 23 February 2012.

the accused. As such, "intent was a jury question".[35] As Valeska later explained to us:

> In America, the law is [that] the judge must consider the State's case in the most favourable light. If there's any evidence, well, after eight days there was plenty, he's supposed to let it go to the jury, even the defence said that. So when I said, well, judge, even the defence said you have to consider the evidence in the most favourable light to me, I assumed he was going to let it go [to the jury] ... In Alabama, if you're the last person seen with the victim and the victim ends up dead of non-natural causes, then the jury's supposed to be able to vote on it ... At the bond hearing, the judge said, she's going to get her trial ... [and] during the week his comments [like] you decide the facts, that's your job, to the jury, we'd just assumed that ... he was going to let it go [to the jury].

From the comments made by both the prosecution and the defence, it appears that neither side was anticipating that the motion for acquittal would be successful, at least not at this early point in the proceedings. Furthermore, in drawing upon their own legal experiences following the acquittal, these stakeholders reflected on the rarity of a successful motion. As Bloomston explained:

> I've only had two judgements of acquittal by a judge in 16 years of practice, and some lawyers have never had any ... Most of the time, that motion is just a formality. We have to make it upon the state resting, but most of the time we don't get it; most of the time it's not granted. So normally, the judge rules from the bench: congratulations, that's a good argument, Mr Bloomston, but I think they've met their prima facia burden and now it's your turn to present your defence.

From the prosecution's perspective, Valeska similarly noted that in his 41 years of working as a prosecutor in Alabama, he had "never had a judge acquit" at any stage of a criminal trial. Further highlighting the significance of Judge Nail's decision to acquit, Gabe's civil and family attorney, Bob Austin, also attested to the rare nature of acquittals in criminal cases, commenting:

> It's unusual to the extent that most prosecutors will not bring a case that they don't think that they can win ... So it's unusual, because it doesn't happen. I'm aware of several cases [where acquittals have happened], but a lot of times it happens in civil cases. It is less likely in criminal cases ... [even though] a motion for judgement of acquittal is made in every

[35] Ibid.

> criminal case. That's the procedure, you just do it ... I've only had it happen once in a plaintiff's case.

Tina's father, Tommy Thomas, also described his perceptions of the unlikelihood of an acquittal at this early stage of the trial, explaining that:

> I had been prepared going into it that once the prosecution rests, his [Gabe's] attorneys were going to ask for an acquittal and we were going to face it then. I had been prepared that once the defence presented its case and rested that there would be another request for an acquittal and they could have got it then. And I'd also been prepared that once the prosecution offered any rebuttal witnesses to the defence, and also either before or after the closing arguments, I can't remember which, but there would be even a third attempt by the defence for an acquittal. So I knew that we had to get through all three of them ... So I was thinking, as we were moving through the second week, okay, we'll get through the first acquittal, I mean we'll get through the first opportunity for them to get an acquittal. Don [Valeska] warned me about it the night before, but I'm still thinking, from the first week, well, we ought to get through the first one ... The judge even said there in the first week that, you know, they [the jury] didn't need to pay attention to what the attorneys on either side said, which I was kind of glad he said that because I was thinking, yeah, because I've heard them [the defence] lie a lot. And he said, you don't even need to pay attention necessarily to what I say, because it is up to you to determine the interpretation of the law and his guilt or innocence and ... what the actual evidence shows.

However, in reflecting on the power of the defence's motion for a judgement of acquittal, Tommy went on to explain that his perception shifted dramatically as the defence began presenting their verbal arguments. He explained, "when his attorney started talking, my heart sunk, because I was sitting there thinking, this is not going to go well. It's like all of a sudden I just woke up and said, this is not going to go good".

Despite the rare occurrence of criminal acquittals, almost immediately following Valeska's oral rebuttal to the defence's motion for a judgement of acquittal, Judge Tommy Nail looked from one side of the courtroom to the other, as he provided his decision. In explaining his judgement, it quickly became clear to those within the courtroom that the judge had begun outlining the reasons why he was granting the defence's motion and acquitting Gabe Watson of the capital murder charge.

Judge Nail said:

> I have listened to the evidence and have to view it in the most favourable light to the State ... There is a sufficient basis there if I was trying a civil negligence case, but it is my opinion the evidence is sorely lacking in an

> intentional case. The only way the jury can find him guilty is to do so based on speculation and conjecture ... The State has failed to establish an intentional killing ... It stretches the bounds of credibility that financial gain is proved. It doesn't make any sense; even your own witnesses state that. He was not a beneficiary on the insurance policy. He asked whether she had insurance after her death. It doesn't establish any intent to get a financial gain ... I don't think anyone knows for sure what happened in the waters down there and they probably will never know ... You have to speculate, there is no evidence to suggest an intentional killing. I'm going to grant the defence's motion to acquit.[36]

As the realisation of the acquittal sank in, tears of sadness, happiness, desperation and contempt spilt across the courtroom, as Bloomston publicly declared "we got justice today".[37] The image of the acquittal depicted by the media within almost minutes of the decision was that of Gabe and his legal team celebrating. As one reporter who had been present in the courtroom described in his written commentary, there was an "eruption of cheers from Watson's supporters".[38] In his televised interview on the US ABC network's *20/20* program following the acquittal, Gabe similarly described the elation he felt at this moment, claiming, "as soon as he [Judge Nail] said, I am going to grant the defendant's motion for acquittal, oh, I was in shock. It's been so long and these two sentences just ended everything".[39]

Little was shown in the media of the initial reactions of the prosecution, the police investigators or the members of the Thomas family, as they quickly exited the courtroom, heads bowed, defeated. Outside the courthouse over an hour after the decision was made, Valeska addressed the waiting media pack, stating that with the case now "over forever", he felt "sorry for the people in Australia and the US who worked so hard. They don't do it for money, they do it for justice".[40] In an emotionally

---

[36] Judge Tommy Nail, court observations, 23 February 2012.

[37] Brett Bloomston, court observations, 23 February 2012.

[38] Eric Velasco, "Watson Acquitted of Wife's Murder: Charges Dropped in '03 Honeymoon Drowning", *Birmingham News* (Alabama), 24 February 2012.

[39] Gabe Watson, cited in Carol Robinson, "Interview: Gabe Watson Looks to Leave Shadow of his Wife's Honeymoon Death and His Murder Trial" on *Birmingham News* (Alabama) (3 March 2012) <http://blog.al.com/spotnews/2012/03/interview_gabe_watson_looks_to.html>.

[40] Don Valeska, cited in Tuck Thompson, "Gabe Watson Freed Due to Lack of Evidence at Alabama Murder Trial", *The Courier Mail* (Queensland), 25 February 2012.

charged moment, with the weight of the acquittal decision on his shoulders, Valeska firmly stated, "Tina did not get justice today".[41]

[41] Don Valeska, observations, 23 February 2012.

CHAPTER TEN

(IN)JUSTICE FOR TINA? (IN)JUSTICE FOR GABE?

> Injustice anywhere is a threat to justice everywhere.[1]
>
> —Martin Luther King Jr.

For all involved in the *Watson* case, Judge Nail's decision to acquit Gabe brought the capital murder trial in Alabama to an abrupt and somewhat unexpected end. The responses of those most intimately involved in the case were polarised. Was it a just outcome? Was it the right decision? Was it a fair decision? And, importantly, did it offer justice? Like the many questions that linger around the justness of the outcome of the *Watson* case in Queensland, there is no immediate or simplistic response to these questions surrounding the Alabama trial. While in the legal context, both the negotiated manslaughter plea in Queensland and the judicial acquittal in Alabama cleared Gabe of any intentional involvement in Tina's death, whether this tragic story is finished, and whether the processes leading to these outcomes provided justice or closure from any perspective, remains doubtful.

As we have discussed so far, the problems inherent to the legal processes, both in Queensland and Alabama, jeopardised the capacity of either outcome to provide procedural justice. Simultaneously, the perceptions of bias and the various concerns that have engulfed both prosecutions of Gabe, particularly in relation to the power that was held by individuals to make finite determinations of guilt outside the traditional, normative justice process, meant that subjective justice was also not wholly achieved in either jurisdiction. Significantly, even in light of Gabe's acquittal, the destructive representation of him within the media, alongside the absence of a defence being presented within the confines of a criminal trial, has resulted in questions of guilt and injustice still lingering, reducing the level of substantive justice offered by either legal

---

[1] Martin Luther King Jr., *Letter from Birmingham Jail*, 16 April 1963.

outcome. Thus, even though subjectively one could argue that Gabe's acquittal provides justice from the Watson family's perspective and injustice from that of the Thomas family, we believe that in this case, from both perspectives, justice was difficult, if not impossible to attain. There was no black and white; no one person's justice equating with another's injustice. There were instead glimmers of justice hidden among obstacles that ultimately prevented both the Queensland and Alabama justice systems from procedurally or even wholly subjectively and substantively providing their namesake—justice.

Throughout its almost nine-year duration, one of the key features of the *Watson* case was its representation as a quest for justice—in particular, as the Thomas family's quest for justice. At each of the legal milestones in the case, from its initial investigation, through to the plea deal and sentence in Queensland, and then to Gabe's prosecution in Alabama, Tina's father, Tommy Thomas, who became the spokesperson for the family, has publicly declared his desire to achieve justice for his daughter. As Tommy claimed in response to the Alabama grand jury's decision to indict Gabe on two counts of capital murder in October 2010, "this is not about me. This is about my daughter, Tina, and the fact [that] we wanted to, from the very beginning, just know the truth about what happened to her, and get justice for whatever reason may have caused her death".[2] Following Gabe's acquittal 16 months later, Tina's mother Cindy and Tommy expressed markedly similar motivations for wanting the second prosecution against Gabe pursued in Alabama, despite its earlier finalisation in Queensland. In describing their reasons, both Tommy and Cindy portrayed their quest as inherently driven by their memories of Tina, and what she would have wanted them to do:

Cindy: Because she was expecting us to. She wouldn't have expected any less … I'm almost positive when she was dying that she knew mum and dad would take care of this.

Tommy: That's right. One of the things that I firmly believe is in her final moments she was thinking to herself, my dad and my family will never give up till they get to the bottom of this. So you [Gabe] can run off if you want to, but you don't know what you [are] mess[ing] with.

Cindy: I believe that in her final moment she knew that.

---

[2] Tommy Thomas, cited in Australian Associated Press, "Queensland Scuba Dive Murder Trial to Begin in US", *Herald Sun* (Victoria), 13 February 2012.

Tommy: And we couldn't give up on that ...

Cindy: I just knew as her mum, that she knew that we would fight with everything we had for justice.

Tommy: And I just think that she would have expected us to do it. And that's why we had to do it.

These comments from Cindy and Tommy, while shedding light on the reasons that have motivated them to pursue justice, contrast with the suggestions of Gabe's supporters that the Thomas family simply sought revenge and wanted Gabe punished, rather than their quest being about justice. This opposing view is demonstrated in the comments made by a family friend of the Watson's, Reverend Craig Greer, who alongside his wife performed the ceremony for Tina's funeral. In expressing his support for Gabe's innocence, Greer claimed, "I have no doubt the Thomas [family] believe everything they say … [but] I see this as vindictive grief. Somebody has to pay for what happened".[3] Reflecting upon Tina's funeral service, Greer further claimed that "Gabe hung back at the funeral … He tried not to intrude on their [the Thomas family's] grief. He knew how they felt about him".[4] Gabe's father, David Watson, similarly identified the negative view that the Thomas family held of Gabe, which he later argued demonstrated their desire to seek revenge through a second prosecution in Alabama. David claimed, "remember now, for the three or four years prior, through the newspapers [and] the blogs, the Thomas [family] … had called [Gabe] every vile, vulgar, vicious name you can imagine … [They were] against him".[5]

This more callous portrayal of what motivated the Thomas family's quest for justice is also evident in the comments of Gabe's family and civil lawyer, Bob Austin, who claimed, "nothing would have satisfied the Thomas [family] other than Gabe being sentenced to life [imprisonment], or preferably death. They would have loved it if he had been sentenced to death". Austin continued in this vein by suggesting that the Thomas family had exchanged the term "justice" for "revenge", claiming that "he [Tommy Thomas] was using that term [justice] in place of the word, revenge, [saying] you're responsible for the loss of my daughter, I want my pound

[3] Reverend Craig Greer, cited in Carol Robinson, "Gabe Watson's Family Speaks 7 Years after His Wife, Tina Watson, Drowned on Australian Honeymoon", *Birmingham News* (Alabama), 3 March 2010.

[4] Ibid.

[5] David Watson, cited in Robinson, above n 3.

of flesh back". Based on these perceptions, it is clear how the second prosecution of Gabe was seen as unjust by the Watson family.

Throughout our discussions, those who supported the view that the Alabama prosecution was unjust alleged that it was primarily driven by the Thomas family. As David claimed, the ongoing persecution of Gabe continued "because Mr and Mrs Thomas were not going to go away". However, as illustrated by the many public statements made by the Thomas family and Tommy's and Cindy's raw reflections outlined earlier, while Tina's family was relentless in their quest, they claimed they were driven not by revenge, but by the goal of attaining justice for their daughter—a process that they equated with a criminal trial and a jury verdict.

In pursing justice for Tina, a common view expressed by the Thomas family and those involved in the investigation and prosecution of Gabe has been that justice would only be attainable through the running of a criminal trial. Interestingly, the outcome of a guilty or non-guilty verdict carried much less weight in influencing their perceptions of justice than the process of running a complete trial itself. As Tommy explained to us, "the only thing that we were trying to do was get justice. It wasn't about winning anything, there was nothing to win". This perception aligns with a traditional view of justice, which involves an adversarial trial being held, having the evidence revealed and tested before an independent adjudicator, and a jury who are representative of the community determining guilt or innocence. The recognition of justice as being achieved through a contested criminal trial, and that this was the motivation for Tina's family's quest for justice, is further demonstrated by their reaction to the absence of a trial in Queensland, after which the Thomas family believed that they were robbed of the opportunity to see justice attained. Tommy explained, "the injustice is that he should have been tried in Australia". Thus, what emerged as a central component in the Thomas family's struggle for justice was not revenge, but the process of the trial, whether in Queensland or Alabama. As Tommy commented in the days leading up to the commencement of the Alabama trial, "this is our last chance to get justice, and we know it. But we're confident, and if the bulk of the evidence is presented, it doesn't matter whether it's a jury in Alabama or a jury in Australia, we're going to get a just outcome".[6]

The significant emotional hardship that the Thomas family has endured as a result of pursuing their quest for justice also strongly suggests that

---

[6] Tommy Thomas, cited in Jay Reeves, "Scuba-Diver Allegedly Drowns Wife in Australia: Gabe Watson on Trial for Tina Thomas Watson's Death", *Huffington Post* (United States), 12 February 2012.

their commitment to this case went beyond simply seeking revenge on Gabe. In April 2007, less than halfway into what would become an almost nine-year legal battle, Tommy, and Tina's sister, Alanda Thomas, identified the emotional impacts the case had already had on their family in statements to the police. In her statement, Alanda claimed, "my dad has aged considerably and his entire focus is to find out what happened".[7] Similarly, in his statement Tommy claimed:

> I think about Tina every day and miss her every day. Tina's death has practically destroyed my family. My wife Cindy is seriously ill due to Tina's death. My other daughter Alanda has health issues because of the death. I have been terribly stressed over Tina's death and the problems we have had since.[8]

The extent of the emotional impacts of this case on the Thomas family in the five-year period following these statements being made was also strongly evident in our discussion with Cindy, during which she described her fragile emotional state at various points of the investigation and upon learning that Gabe was acquitted. In describing the moment at which it became clear that a plea deal would be the legal outcome of the case in Queensland, Cindy recalled:

> The minute they [Brendan Campbell and the media advisor] were gone, Alanda jumped up bawling [and] I jumped up bawling, because we knew [there was a deal] … Brad [Flynn] grabbed Alanda and went one way, and Gary Campbell grabbed me and went the other to try and calm us down ... [but] I kept bawling.

Cindy also recalled her strong emotional reaction when she became aware that Gabe had won the right in court to exhume and move Tina's body to a gravesite approximately 188 metres (200 yards) from where she was originally buried. As Cindy explained:

> I just took off running. I always think if I run then it's not true. So I ran out the front door, and I'm barefooted and I'm running across the grass thinking, what am I doing? Where am I going? So I just ran to my next door neighbour who's my best friend, and I'm banging on the door, and I'm bawling, hysterical, and I just fall on their dining room floor … I thought, oh my God ... I actually got physically sick.

---

[7] Alanda Thomas, witness statement, 30 April 2007.
[8] Tommy Thomas, witness statement, 27 April 2007.

In an interview with the Australian ABC network's *Australian Story* program, Tommy described a similarly emotional reaction to this legal decision and his feelings on the day that Tina's body was exhumed and moved. He explained:

> The day that that happened was one of the worst days of my life. Gabe didn't come. His father showed up with his friend and the two of them just kind of nonchalantly sat around while my daughter was dug up, loaded on the back of a dump truck and moved. My thoughts, [I just] kept thinking, God, Tina. I cannot believe, if you're there and you're watching, that you're having to see this.[9]

Tommy also explained to us the emotional cost this case has had on his family, particularly Cindy, stating that, "Cindy's [been] in a really bad shape … she had some bleeding problems, she had been in hospital in intensive care and all that stuff". These significant reactions are part of the reason why Cindy was unable to attend either the Alabama trial in 2012 or the Queensland sentencing hearing in 2009. She has also developed an intense fear of seeing Gabe or his family, and has effectively become housebound. As Cindy herself described:

> I have a hard time leaving home and I don't want to be going out of the house, because I'm always thinking if I go to the store what if he's here or what if his mum or dad are here, and what if I don't see them but they see me. I don't know … I never go anywhere. I never drive my car. It's only when he's [Tommy] home and we [have] got the boys [Alanda's children] and we're going somewhere. I felt better when at least he [Gabe] was out on bail and he had that thing on his leg and he had to be home at seven. I thought, well I can go somewhere at 7pm because I know I'm not going to run into him. We did see his mother one time and I was shaking all over … And I used to not be like that. I used to go out all the time.

This painful description not only demonstrates the extent of the emotional impacts that the Thomas family have experienced throughout the duration of this case, but also supports the claim that the family have been motivated by a pursuit of justice for their daughter, as opposed to seeking revenge for her death.

The Watson family, and Gabe in particular, have also experienced emotional hardships which have consequently affected their capacity to experience a complete sense of justice even after his acquittal, given the many obstacles and perceptions of Gabe's guilt that have lingered

---

[9] ABC Television Network, "Unfathomable: Part One", *Australian Story*, 2 August 2010 (Tommy Thomas) <http://www.abc.net.au/austory/content/2007/s2971395.htm>.

throughout the case, amplified in particular by the intense media and public scrutiny that he has faced. In this regard, Austin described this scrutiny as "not intense scrutiny, intense hyperbole [and] intense fabrication ... They [the media] took things that were hearsay, and quoted them as fact. Without questioning, without reading … And there were lies told". This view was similarly expressed by Australian television journalist, Liz Hayes, who after meeting with Gabe after his acquittal reported that "it seems right from the start [that] Gabe Watson never got an even break. None of that Australian 'fair go' we like to claim as a special strand in our DNA. Instead, we dished up trial by media".[10] The impacts of this, as David explained, "on our family, on Gabe, remains to be seen".

The emotional impacts on the Watson family have also been identified by Gabe's mother, Glenda Watson. In a media interview before the Alabama trial commenced, Glenda explained that "we feel like we've been tied to the railroad tracks and run over and over … In and of itself, any one thing is horrendous, but it just doesn't stop. Tina would be just horrified if she could see the things that have gone on".[11] Similarly, in our discussion following Gabe's acquittal, David explained that:

> I had serious thoughts that I would probably retire at about age 60 ... Gabe and his middle brother would be running the company. Perfect plan right? ... I'll be 62 in a couple of months ... We've all put our lives on hold, but mostly, he [Gabe] and Kim [his wife]. Gabe hasn't been able to make a plan for eight years, because he knew Mr and Mrs Thomas were going to come after him in some way.

As described by his father, for Gabe, the last eight years have been filled with a great deal of uncertainty and accusations of guilt. Indeed, even when he was granted bail—which, as discussed in Chapter Five, is unusual in a capital murder case—Gabe was still subjected to quite stringent requirements that implied some degree of guilt. In making his determination at the bond hearing on 14 December 2010, Judge Tommy Nail stated:

> I'm going to require him to be on electronic monitor. He's got a curfew. [He] can't be out before 6am [and he has] got to be in his residence by 7pm. The only exception to that would be to go to the doctor or court or some other emergency that would be unforeseeable … And he needs to

[10] Nine Network Australia, "Deep Trouble" on *60 Minutes* (23 March 2012) (Liz Hayes) <http://sixtyminutes.ninemsn.com.au/stories/8440110/deep-trouble>.
[11] Glenda Watson, cited in Robinson, above n 3.

surrender his passport to the court. It is to be sealed and placed in the court file.[12]

Further to these conditions, Gabe was required to have no contact with the Thomas family and was not permitted to visit Tina's grave in the period leading up to, and during, the Alabama trial. In light of the ultimate outcome of the trial, in which Judge Nail stated that the evidence against Gabe was "solely lacking" and was not suggestive in any way of "an intentional killing", the restrictions placed on Gabe for the 13 months during which he was on bail, and even simply the continuation of the case as a prosecution in Alabama after his release from prison in Queensland in November 2010, can be viewed as procedurally unjust.

The toll that the case has had on Gabe was also recognised by Detective Senior Constable Kevin Gehringer in our discussions; however, these reflections illustrate the largely subjective nature of justice, whereby one person's injustice is another's justice. As Gehringer explained:

> The consolation is that from a justice perspective, Gabe's had to at least go through the anguish of knowing that at some stage we have had him in our sights as a suspect. He's had to go through the costs involved with being represented. He has had to return to Australia, he has done at least 18 months in a prison cell in Australia, and then again, he's had to have had this cloud overhanging him from when Brad [Flynn] rearrested him here [in the US], until where we are now. So from that aspect of justice ... I don't know his psyche, but I'd like to think that's caused him some grief. So that's something.

In light of Gehringer's comments, it is questionable whether the outcome of the acquittal could ever provide a full sense of justice to Gabe or the Thomas family based on their definitions and understandings of what constitutes justice. Gehringer's comments also highlight the injustice of the significant delays experienced in this case, which delayed any legal finality by almost nine years. Accordingly, the achievability of justice was significantly reduced—as is often noted, justice delayed is justice denied.

Justice is a Trial by Jury

Even in recognising the emotional costs and anguish experienced by the two families at every stage of the prolonged quest for justice in this case, as implicit in Gabe's US defence attorney, Brett Bloomston's, public comments immediately following Judge Nail's decision to grant the

---

[12] Judge Tommy Nail, bond hearing, 14 December 2010, 55-57.

defence motion, there is an argument that some form of justice was attained from the acquittal. As Bloomston claimed, "we got justice today".[13] This argument is based on the legal premise that the prosecution provided insufficient evidence to sustain a conviction against Gabe on the capital murder for pecuniary gain charge; thus, the matter was concluded at the earliest possible stage to avoid a potentially unjust trial from proceeding any further. As Bloomston explained:

> An acquittal from a judge is legally as significant as an acquittal from a jury. In fact, it is so unusual and so rare that I confirm what I've been yelling at the top of my lungs for five years: that there is no merit to this case! There never were any facts that Gabe ever did anything intentional. So personally, it's satisfying to have a judge agree with it, and a judge who's a lot smarter than I am, just because he's been practising law for 30 additional years. And Judge Nail was a prosecutor, and Judge Nail was a defence attorney, and Judge Nail's been elected to be on the bench several times. He's catching unmerciful grief for his courageous decision, and it's unfortunate, because he's a very principled guy ... His decision certainly justifies, vindicates, makes us feel a lot better [and] I think Gabe needed to hear it.

David similarly described the decision to acquit as "wonderful for all of us, it was what we had hoped for ... and I can't imagine any other decision". Even Lieutenant Brad Flynn and Gehringer recognised that the process of running a partial trial offered some degree of justice, albeit in a very limited extent and not in the traditional or procedural sense. That is, Flynn and Gehringer both perceived the matter proceeding to trial as allowing the "fight" for justice to continue, which they remarked offered some satisfaction that could to a degree be equated with justice. Falling back on the concept that justice equates with having your day in court, Flynn claimed:

> There's no doubt in my mind that if we have gotten that case in front of a jury in Australia, we would have convicted him ... Things aren't going well and it's not the way I wanted it to end up, but at the end of the day I can tell Tommy we had our day. We had our shot, and we didn't stop fighting.

Gehringer similarly explained, "at least we got to have a fight. The referee might not have been totally fair. But I always try and tell myself, don't worry about the things you can't control, just worry about the things that you can".

---

[13] Brett Bloomston, court observations, 23 February 2012.

The notion that a trial regardless of its outcome equates with justice is debatable, because even when a trial is run, the processes within and surrounding that trial may prevent it from being just. If due process is not upheld or if there is a perception of bias or inequality, the trial cannot be seen as providing any form of justice—subjectively, substantively or procedurally. This was argued, for example, in relation to the perceived bias caused by having an all-Caucasian jury determine the verdict in the 1992 Los Angeles trial of the Caucasian police officers accused of severely assaulting African American Rodney King.[14] This can also occur in the context of a trial if exculpatory evidence is withheld, if there is prosecutorial or police misconduct or overzealousness, or if a judge makes an erroneous motion—some examples of which could arguably be perceived as having occurred during the second prosecution of Gabe in Alabama. Alternatively, when it is the outcome of the trial that alone determines justice, regardless of the verdict, it is likely that some, but not all, will perceive that justice has been attained.

On this basis, Judge Nail's decision to acquit Gabe at the close of the prosecution's case could be perceived as failing to offer justice in a traditional, substantive, procedural and subjective sense, because it undermined the traditional adversarial ideal of a trial by jury, in that once a matter proceeds to trial, the jury should determine the guilt or innocence of the accused. The importance of the role of an empanelled jury, and the process of attaining a jury verdict, was highlighted by former Alabama Attorney-General, Troy King, who in the wake of Gabe's acquittal commented, "I'm very sad this morning that Judge Nail decided that his opinion mattered more than those jurors' opinions".[15] This view was also shared by the secondary victims in the case, as reflected in Tommy's comment to the media in the week following Gabe's acquittal, "we expected it to go to the jury. Had it gone, we would have been happy. It came down to one person making a decision again. That is not what justice is about".[16] In our discussions with Tommy following the acquittal, he similarly expressed a sense of injustice, claiming:

[14] Linda Skitka and David Houston, "When Due Process is of no Consequence: Moral Mandates and Presumed Defendant Guilt or Innocence" (2001) 14 *Social Justice Research* 306.

[15] Troy King, cited in Jay Reeves, "Judge Acquits Alabama Mail in Bride's Honeymoon Death", *Star Advertiser* (United States), 24 February 2012.

[16] Tommy Thomas, cited in Rachel Quigley, "'It Was Like She Died All over Again': Father of Tina Watson Speaks of Family's Hurt after 'Honeymoon Killer' is Acquitted of Murder", *Daily Mail* (United Kingdom), 5 March 2012.

> If you're promised by the legal system ... of trial before a jury, I don't believe anything should keep that promise from being delivered, and I certainly don't believe that any one man or woman serving as a judge has the right to suddenly become the jury ... Once the jury is selected and seated and you have made them sit through any of the evidence, then the jury ought to be the ones to make the decision, not the judge.

Cindy expressed a similar perspective on the unjust nature of a judicial acquittal during a jury trial. She observed:

> I never thought it wouldn't go to the jury. And I trusted the jury. I trusted his peers to hear, I thought they would hear everything. Even when the defence came up, the rebuttal witnesses, I thought once all that's out there then the jury is going to [decide] ... And I think it was wrong, I think in our country this should not be allowed, that once you've empanelled a jury and you have a trial, it should go to the jury ... If I was sitting on the jury that would make me so angry. I would have been like, what? You've been making me be here every day and sit through all this and, okay, go home, you've done your job, he's acquitted? Yeah, if I'd been on that jury that would have just angered me.

As touched upon in Cindy's comments, removing the decision from the jury can be seen as effectively silencing the jury's voice, and therefore silencing community input and involvement in the criminal justice system—an outcome which can be considered procedurally unjust. As Don Valeska claimed, "they [the jurors] sat there for two weeks and their view is, well, why didn't we get to vote on it? ... Everybody's [in the jury] supposed to have their say ... [but] they didn't get it". Tommy also identified this concern, commenting that:

> Some of the jurors were angry ... Because one of the ladies [from the jury] walked out and said that he'd [Gabe] better be damn glad that the judge acquitted him, because if she'd had anything to do with it he'd have gone to prison. But the other four jurors that they [the prosecution] talked to, Tina [one of the prosecutors] said that three of them had already said he was guilty, and the other one said that they hadn't made up their mind yet, but that he should have got a lot more time than what he did in Australia ... But there's no justice in that at all. It makes it worse, because it clearly shows that the judge should not have done what he did. I mean, it just makes it worse, because if that was true [the acquittal], there wouldn't have been anybody on the jury that would have said he was guilty.

The need for community input into decisions relating to convictions is particularly relevant in cases involving the most serious criminal offences. As a defence lawyer in an Australian study on the operation of the offence of defensive homicide in the state of Victoria noted, jury verdicts are "the one area … where the community has a real input into who it wants to call a murderer."[17] In a similar vein, the Honourable Martin Moynihan explained in his 2008 evaluation of the Queensland civil and criminal justice systems that "a jury brings to bear the combined knowledge and experience of 12 citizens and reflects community wisdom and values";[18] thus, without this input, there may be a reduced level of confidence in the "justness" of an acquittal decision. This is particularly so when that decision is made after a jury has already been empanelled and begun to hear the evidence. As Gehringer explained:

> For the judge to then intercede that it wasn't sufficient for it to go to the jury, again, it's one man's opinion or one man's decision, as opposed to 12 members of the jury, members of the community. And to me, that's supposed to be the whole role of our justice system, that it's not left up to one person, it's left up to a body of people. And as tough as those burdens of proof are, and the fact that you have to have the majority of all those 12 people, it's still just left me, personally from an investigation point of view, that again, all the evidence didn't get to be presented. And the jury just weren't given that opportunity.

By silencing the voice of the jury, Judge Nail's decision to acquit also arguably undermined the opportunity for Tina "to have her day in court"—an assurance offered by Judge Nail during the Alabama bond hearing.[19] In considering the combined effect of this perceived failure of justice and the plea bargain decision made in Queensland, former Alabama Attorney-General Troy King concluded that the case had "been through two justice systems, neither of which delivered their day in court."[20]

Injustice in the Timing

Further concerns arose in relation to the justness of the acquittal decision in light of Judge Nail's comments about the strength of the evidence in the context of a civil case, and his admission that "I don't

---

[17] Asher Flynn and Kate Fitz-Gibbon, "Bargaining with Defensive Homicide: Examining Victoria's Secretive Plea Bargaining System Post-Law Reform" (2011) 35 *Melbourne University Law Reform* 905, 924.

[18] Honourable Martin Moynihan AO QC, *Review of the Civil and Criminal Justice System in Queensland* (Queensland Government, 2008) 30.

[19] Judge Tommy Nail, bond hearing, 14 December 2010, 44.

[20] Troy King, cited in Jeremy Gray, "Ex-AG Critical of Watson Decision", *Birmingham News* (Alabama), 25 February 2012.

think anyone knows for sure what happened in the waters down there". As Valeska explained:

> In our opinion, he should have let it go on to the jury because our burden to get to the jury is very small. Any evidence taken in the most favourable light to the state, means you get to the jury. That doesn't mean the jury's going to believe it, but he hadn't heard the defence. But just to throw it [out] was disappointing and bizarre and to then say in his comments that ... you proved a good civil case ... [and] well, something went down under there, under the water. I mean it seemed to me, if he hadn't believed our case, he would have just said, listen, there's absolutely nothing [here]. You haven't proved anything.

Judge Nail's comments, particularly pertaining to what happened underwater, were also identified as problematic by Bloomston, who claimed, "the only problem I have with Judge Nail's statement to the lawyers on [his] ruling is [that] he said, we may never know what happened underwater to Tina [and that] left everything open". Perceptions that the judge's comments left significant elements of the case in an ambiguous and unfinished manner are particularly significant in light of the timing of the motion being granted. Because the decision was made at the close of the prosecution's case, there are no potential avenues for the prosecution to appeal Gabe's acquittal. This could arguably be seen as poetic or ironic justice, given the argument that prosecuting Gabe for capital murder in Alabama was in breach of international double jeopardy protections. However, in light of Judge Nail's unusual comments about the case, some participants expressed the view that the timing of the decision was unjust, particularly because Judge Nail had the capacity to reserve his judgement to a later stage of the trial, and because the defence would have also been able to lodge a second motion at the close of both side's cases. As Valeska explained:

> When the defence asked for him to throw out the case, he [Judge Nail] could have said, well, I'm not real thrilled with the state's case, but I'll just see what you have. Then after they [had] put their case on, they could have asked him to do it again and he could have ruled once the defence rested. He could have said, okay, I've heard both sides, it's not going to the jury, so we'd have been out, and I'd explained that to Tommy from the first time we met. If he let it go to the jury, if the jury had voted not guilty, then it would have been over. If they'd have voted guilty, right then, he [Judge Nail] could have thrown it out. And then he had 30 days more to make a ruling ... But with all those options that he had, we were just stunned, shocked, because there was no reason in our opinion for him to do it right then.

Perhaps the most problematic aspect of the timing of the acquittal, in terms of the outcome providing justice, was that it occurred prior to the defence presenting any evidence and the prosecution being given the opportunity to provide a rebuttal to the defence. Consequently, the timing of the acquittal decision meant that none of the defence evidence was transparently laid out, examined or tested within an open court, before all the relevant parties. As explained in the previous chapter, while a reserved judgement would have prohibited Judge Nail from considering the evidence presented by the defence in his decision over whether to grant an acquittal, the transparent testing of the evidence within a criminal trial could have provided a more complete ending to the almost nine-year duration of this case. Importantly, it could have provided a more satisfying avenue of closure for both the Watson and Thomas families.

Closure and finality are integral components of justice, in that in order for justice to be achieved or demonstrated, there must be an end, a final outcome. As Flynn explained in the context of this case, before learning of the acquittal decision:

> We've been through such a crazy up-and-down journey, and it seems like for every door that was closed in our face, another window would open and there was always—every time we thought we were done, something else would happen and we'd be back in the game again. And I guess the thing is, the finality of this [trial] is knowing that this is it, this is done. There are no more options. This is it. This is our one and only, our last chance.

The finality of the Alabama trial, as outlined by Flynn, has been granted in an official legal sense, in that the acquittal has ensured an end, because the prosecution cannot appeal the conviction and Gabe cannot be prosecuted for any alleged involvement in Tina's death again, in either Alabama or Queensland. As Valeska commented outside the courthouse immediately after the acquittal decision, "this case is over forever".[21] But in an emotional and tangible sense, neither closure nor finality was offered by the acquittal, because many unanswered questions pertaining to the evidence and guilt remain.

The importance of needing closure after Gabe's acquittal has been readily identified by all of those most involved in the case. In discussing his perspective on the finality of the legal aspect of this case, Gabe explained in his interview with the US ABC network's *20/20* program following his acquittal that "it's time for everybody to get on with their

---

[21] Don Valeska, cited in Tuck Thompson, "Gabe Watson Freed Due to Lack of Evidence at Alabama Murder Trial", *The Courier Mail* (Queensland), 25 February 2012.

lives".[22] He went on to comment that he hoped his life would not be dictated by what has happened, but by what he chooses to do in the future. This view was shared by his father, David, who stated in an interview outside the courthouse immediately after Gabe's acquittal that "the rest of his life will determine his legacy. Gabe is a good kid".[23] A similar view was expressed by Bloomston, who claimed, "this will be the end of this case",[24] and said that he hoped for Gabe's sake that "it will be put behind [him]".[25]

Gehringer also acknowledged the importance of moving on from the case, but in doing so he focused primarily on the unavailability of any further avenues for legal action as the reason for needing to move on, as opposed to the acquittal providing him with a sense of justice or closure. Interestingly, concerns regarding the absence of closure and its impact on whether a second chance for justice could be obtained in this case were evident in our discussions with all of the participants involved in the case, whether representative of the defence or prosecution. As Gehringer explained:

> We've got to move on from the case. We've got to move on ... [get] closure. I suppose it is closure because I know now there are no other avenues to pursue it. There's no right of appeal. So as far as our justice system is concerned, there's nothing. And that's obviously going to be harder on Tommy and the family as opposed to us as investigators.

As noted by Gehringer, the possibility for the Thomas family to obtain closure from the acquittal was minimal, as it failed to align in any way with their hopes for and understanding of justice. As Tommy claimed, "we don't have any closure, how could we?"[26] In expanding on these feelings, he explained that the case:

> is done now, this is the end of it … There is nothing else that we can do about it … We are just going to do the best that we can do. For the past eight years, we had to take it a day at a time, and we have to do that still

[22] Gabe Watson, cited in Carol Robinson, "Interview: Gabe Watson Looks to Leave Shadow of his Wife's Honeymoon Death and His Murder Trial" on *Birmingham News* (Alabama) (3 March 2012) <http://blog.al.com/spotnews/2012/03/interview_gabe_watson_looks_to.html>.
[23] David Watson, cited in Reeves, above n 15.
[24] Brett Bloomston, cited in Nikki Battiste, "Honeymoon Murder Trial Charges Dismissed by Judge", *ABC news* (United States), 23 February 2012.
[25] Ibid.
[26] Tommy Thomas, cited in Quigley, above n 16.

> now. He isn't the first murderer to go free and he certainly won't be the last.[27]

Similarly recognising the inability of the acquittal decision to provide a complete sense of closure to those involved in this case, David expressed some concerns, not for his own family but for the Thomas family. He explained:

> I would love for it to be [the end]. But I don't know them that well. Can they move on? I think that's the key, if they can let go of this. I don't think they'll ever change their mind about what they think Gabe did, so I don't know, we'll just have to wait and see.

One of the primary ways in which this outcome failed to offer closure to Gabe is the fear that the Thomas family might still pursue some type of public campaign against him. This concern was identified by David, who explained, "I don't know if we're through with them [the Thomas family] yet. I'm sure they'll search for something that they can do [to Gabe]".

Initially, our participants spoke of the potential for the Thomas family to continue the pursuit of justice through a civil court. This perception was formed largely due to Judge Nail's comment that "there is a sufficient [evidentiary] basis there if I was trying a civil negligence case",[28] thus highlighting the strength of a civil action. As Gehringer claimed:

> I know there's been a little bit of talk about [that] there still might be a civil pursuit in relation to the death aspect of it. So whether Tommy pursues that, I don't know, or whether he can [financially]. And I suppose if there is that avenue and he does decide to pursue, well, then it's probably not over.

The civil action identified by Gehringer falls under s 6-5-410 of the *Code of Alabama* whereby a civil lawsuit can be brought against an individual whose misconduct or negligence resulted in the death of an individual. To be successful, the plaintiff must be able to demonstrate that they depended upon the deceased for emotional or monetary support, and that the conduct of the individual accused of the wrongful death was the "proximate" cause of the death—that is, that the individual's conduct was the direct or legally sufficient contributing factor that caused the person's death. The decision is made by a jury comprising members of the community, and if they find in favour of the plaintiff, the jury must also determine an amount for punitive damages based on the "enormity of the

---

[27] Ibid.

[28] Judge Tommy Nail, court observations, 23 February 2012.

wrong" committed by the responsible individual. The money must be considered sufficient to punish the individual and to deter others from committing similar misconduct. While pursuing this case in the confines of a civil court before a jury of eight could potentially have offered the Thomas family some form of justice that fits within their procedural and subjective definitions of the term, this avenue has been closed. The statute of limitations for pursuing a civil action in Alabama is two years. As stipulated in s 6-5.410 (d) of the *Code of Alabama*, "the action must be commenced within two years from and after the death of the testator".

Thus, in terms of being able to sue Gabe for wrongful death and continue their pursuit for justice in this manner, the Thomas family have again been thwarted by the extensive delays in the *Watson* case. They can, however, continue their probate lawsuit against Gabe to seek ownership of Tina's body, which as Cindy explained to us would provide at least some sense of justice and closure: "It's the body of our child ... We just want her body back. ... I'm her mother. At this point, I just want her body back". However, this would not provide the same degree or sense of justice that underpinned the Thomas family's persistent journey through two criminal justice systems, over almost nine long years.

Acquittal in the Court, but not in the Public Realm

Another question that might be asked—albeit, less likely—when a decision to acquit is made, is whether this outcome has provided justice for the accused. In light of the problems that we have identified in relation to the *Watson* case and the lingering questions of guilt that persist in the public realm, the answer to this question is not as straightforward as may first be perceived. While Gabe was acquitted solely at the judge's discretion in Alabama, and while he was able to have a murder charge withdrawn and plead guilty to the less serious offence of manslaughter by criminal negligence in Queensland, there are still significant doubts as to whether justice—procedurally, subjectively or substantially—was wholly attained from the perspective of Gabe and his supporters. As David explained, "eight and a half years, it just seems like it was yesterday. In hindsight, it's passed just literally in the blink of an eye. That part's over. But it's gone on for an eternity. Gabe is the one we have to worry about, and how it's affected him".

Given the subjective nature of justice, it is often difficult to discern who has and who has not attained it, just as it is difficult to provide a definitive definition of justice. In discussing the acquittal decision, David highlighted it as a positive outcome, maintaining that this "was the right conclusion for all concerned", because Gabe "was vindicated". A similar view was expressed by Gabe in his interview with the US ABC network's *20/20* program after his acquittal, when he claimed, "with Judge Nail making the ruling that the evidence didn't even meet the little, bitty bump they had to get over to even get it to the jury, to me ... at least in a legal sense, it was a powerful statement".[29]

But despite the claims from Gabe and his father that the acquittal has "vindicated" him, another significant way in which the acquittal can be seen as failing to provide closure or a complete sense of justice is that there remains a strong perception within the public realm that Gabe is guilty—a perception that was strengthened by the judge's comment that "I don't think anyone knows for sure what happened in the waters down there and they probably will never know". This is evident in the commentary of an Alabama attorney, Richard Jaffe, who publicly stated the day after Gabe's acquittal that the decision will make life for Gabe "challenging". He explained, "it will be a challenge. There will always be people that will be convinced that he got away with murder, and that he's guilty, so he will be challenged ... [Even just] in knowing that many people think that you're guilty".[30] On this basis, despite Gabe's and his father's claims, a judicial acquittal, at least in the public realm, may be viewed as less powerful and less suggestive of vindication in terms of proving innocence than a jury verdict of not guilty.

A prominent example of the impact of lingering questions of guilt surrounding Gabe is the American Lifetime Production Company's telemovie of the *Watson* case, *Fatal Honeymoon*. The telemovie, which first screened in the US on 25 August 2012, claims to be based on a "true story", yet it raises significant suspicions over Gabe's involvement in Tina's death. Recognising the negative ramifications of the telemovie for perceptions of Gabe's character, prior to viewing it, Bloomston publicly commented that it would be unlikely to provide an accurate account of Tina's death, or of Gabe. He claimed:

> Just based on the previews … it's going to be derogatory. It's going to be negative towards Gabe. Gabe is not looking to sue anyone or to relive or rehash any of this ... Certainly this production has cast Tina's family with very high-profile actors and we believe their version of the case is what we'll hear most of.

---

[29] Gabe Watson, cited in Robinson, above n 22.

[30] Richard Jaffe, cited in Stephanie Salvatore, "What's Next for Gabe Watson?", *CBS 42* (United States), 24 February 2012.

Bloomston's concerns were confirmed in a review of the telemovie, which noted that:

> It's clear that, down in the murky depths of the ocean, it's hard to prove what really happened, even if everything seems to point toward this guy murdering his wife ... It was good to shed light on the story, since the alleged murderer mostly got away with his crime.[31]

This persistent view of Gabe's guilt is also evident within various comments posted online in response to media reports of Gabe's acquittal. On 2 March 2012, in response to an article written by Carol Robinson for the *Birmingham News*, one person commented that "the judge ruled the state did not present enough evidence to continue with [a] prosecution, but he DID NOT pronounce Watson not guilty. A huge difference!!"[32] Similarly, the following two excerpts are representative of a large portion of the comments posted online in response to an article written by Jay Reeves for the *Huffington Post*:

> All of my friends are divers and we've always thought he was guilty. I was gob-smacked that the judge acquitted him ... The judge disallowed a lot of the evidence against him. I think most folks really believe he is guilty, but it's impossible to prove what anyone was thinking. He got away with murder.[33]

> The practice of law in the state of Alabama leaves much to be desired, to say the least. Frankly, it's downright embarrassing; a disgrace. As I followed this trial, I was repeatedly amazed at the trial judge's rulings about the admissibility of evidence. He made numerous errors concerning hearsay rules, and virtually sabotaged the prosecution's case from day one. Of course the judge's acquittal was a 'serious indictment' of the prosecution's case, and showed their evidence was weak. That's because the prosecution was blocked from presenting the most pertinent, relevant,

---

[31] Suzanne Saturday, "Fatal Honeymoon Review" on *TV Megasie* (8 August 2012) <http://tvmegasite.net:8080/prime/reviews/2012/fatalhoneymoon.html>.

[32] Emphasis in original, Chazz50_1, "Interview: Gabe Watson Looks to Leave Shadow of his Wife's Honeymoon Death and His Murder Trial: Comments" on *Birmingham News Alabama.com* (2 March 2012) <http://blog.al.com/spotnews/2012/03/interview_gabe_watson_looks_to.html>.

[33] My Red Pony, "Gabe Watson Acquitted: Judge Acquits Husband in 'Honeymoon Scuba Death': Comments" on *Huffington Post Blog* (23 February 2012) <http://www.huffingtonpost.com/2012/02/23/gabe-watson-acquitted_n_1296452.html>.

> and explosive evidence, by the same judge, using some of the most bizarre reasoning, logic, and rulings I've ever heard in a court of law.[34]

Additionally, even in response to the favourable depiction of Gabe and the acquittal decision on the Australian Nine Network's *60 Minutes* program, accusations of his guilt were still prominent among the subsequent comments of the audience. As the following online posting made in March 2012 illustrates:

> Gabe Watson's name has now been cleared. His reputation however will always precede him. Even after watching your story of a [sic] innocent man wrongly accused, I still seem to have some lingering doubts as to the level of truth in the story he told. I've told my fair share of BS [bullshit] in my time and somehow I guess you just get to know what it sounds like.[35]

The perception of Gabe "getting away with murder" was also prominent in the wider public realm in both Alabama and Australia after the acquittal decision, whereby on various occasions we would be asked, "But did he do it?" In one instance, an Alabama attorney commented, "everybody that I know thinks he is a creepy guy at the very least, and [mostly] they think he did it". The attorney further noted that "I would like to think that it had to be somewhat justifying to them [the Thomas family] to see everything [the case played out] in the paper". Implicit within this comment is an interesting reflection on the subjective nature of justice: while it is unjust that Gabe continues to be perceived by many as a murderer after being acquitted by a judge, there may be some justice offered to the Thomas family by the existence of this perception. In discussing this concept, Tommy stated that while "there is no real justice in that", it did offer some degree of gratification. He explained:

> There is a part at least, you know, that validates some of what we've done in these last eight years. The thing to me is there's nothing going to make it better, never will, and I don't know if there's any justice in any of this. But I think there's a lot of people in this world that know that he's another murderer that got away, and if we hadn't have done anything, he would have just gotten away.

---

[34] G8R8U2, "Gabe Watson Acquitted: Judge Acquits Husband in 'Honeymoon Scuba Death': Comments" on *Huffington Post Blog* (23 February 2012) <http://www.huffingtonpost.com/2012/02/23/gabe-watson-acquitted_n_1296452.html>.

[35] Nine Network Australia, above n 10, "Comments" (Wlarkham).

This continuing perception of Gabe's guilt after his acquittal was also acknowledged by Bloomston, who explained that "Birmingham's a small city. I'd go out and people [would] come up to me and go, your client's definitely guilty. I'd say, give me five minutes and I'll tell you why [he's] not". Bloomston suggested that in order to combat people's perceptions of Gabe's guilt, he "had to try to educate people as much as possible". But herein lies the central problem of the acquittal in terms of its ability to offer a complete form of justice, transparency or closure: because no defence was ever offered, the opportunity to demonstrate—transparently, and within the confines of the rules of law—that Gabe did not kill Tina was revoked. Thus, the opportunity for the defence to "educate people as much as possible" as to what they believed happened on the fatal dive, and thereby show that Gabe was not guilty of murder, was not, and arguably cannot ever be, provided.

The inability of the trial to provide an avenue for any of the defence evidence to be tried and tested means that the acquittal not only failed to provide a publicly transparent, final outcome that clarified what happened to Tina on 22 October 2003, but perhaps more importantly also "hasn't provided any closure to the Thomas family", as Bloomston explained. Accordingly, from Bloomston's perspective, the acquittal has not offered the Thomas family the knowledge of what he believed "really happened to Tina underwater". Instead, he claimed that the outcome means that the Thomas family will continue to believe that Gabe murdered Tina. This view of Gabe was very clear in our discussions with Tommy and Cindy after the trial, wherein even in acknowledging Gabe's acquittal they still described him as a "murderer". In discussing their attempts to reclaim ownership of Tina's body, Tommy explained:

> Gabe's lawyer said we'll return her body but only on the grounds that you will not speak to the media ever again about this case. And when my probate attorney called and told me that, I told her to call him back and tell him that I was not trying to start a negotiation because I did not make deals with murderers. And that's the way we left it ... Even today, he didn't get convicted, but I'm not willing to make deals with murderers.

This view is perhaps not surprising given that the defence was not required to present any evidence to counter the Thomas family's opinions of Gabe's guilt. As a result, a commonly held view by members of the Thomas family, those involved in the investigation and prosecution of Gabe and a significant portion of the general public is that Gabe "did not walk out of that courtroom innocent",[36] because he was not labelled innocent by a jury—an important distinction for many of our participants. As Cindy explained:

> He can't even go on TV and say I'm innocent, he was not found innocent; the judge has acquitted him. So for the rest of his life, an innocent man doesn't want to live with that for the rest of his life, not if he's got a brain, a sociopath probably, yeah, but not an innocent man. They don't want that over their head. They don't want people looking at them. They want all the evidence out there and that jury to come back with innocent.

The persistence of these opinions, despite the acquittal, also supports one of our primary arguments, that where traditional legal processes are not followed, procedural justice cannot be attained. As Gehringer explained:

> Tina, Tommy, his family, they weren't given that opportunity to find out what that body of people, the jury, thought. So it's left, on the day it happened. Even though we'd tried to prepare ourselves for a negative finding, if the jury had come back with a not guilty, again, to me personally, I could have lived with that a lot better ... But in this case, yeah, again, it's just being deprived of that opportunity has left me feeling that the justice system has let us down in this particular instance. And let Tommy down, and the family down, and obviously Tina ... I know the whole justice system is geared [so] that they'd rather [that] 99 per cent [of the] guilty go free than one innocent go to jail. So I guess you could look at it, that this is applicable to this scenario. I'm certain that Gabe is one of those 99 guilty that in this instance has escaped justice.

In addition to the emotional impacts, one US legal commentator identified the practical implications for Gabe arising from persistent public perceptions of his guilt, including limited future employment opportunities. As the commentator explained, "the challenge is that unless you have employment, and he [Gabe] may, with his family, there's always that opportunity, that chance that a future employer would be hesitant to hire him".[37] Bloomston also recognised the potentially negative implications of the acquittal decision, not only for Gabe, but also for the Thomas family. In so doing, he acknowledged that prior to making the motion for a judgement of acquittal, he had questioned whether he should have postponed his request in order to proceed with running the defence case to allow the evidence to be tested, and what he perceived as the "truth"

---

[36] Cindy Thomas.
[37] Richard Jaffe, cited in Salvatore, above n 30.

surrounding Tina's death to be revealed. As Bloomston explained, Judge Nail's statement that "we may never know what happened underwater":

> left everything open, [there was] still no closure, and [Carl] Edmonds [the defence diving expert] said, I could have ... let the Thomas family know, this is what happened to Tina underwater. And I'm thinking to myself, my God, I should have put on a defence ... We had a great defence lined up ... But I had to make the motion ... I hate that it hasn't provided any closure or helped the Thomas family.

We'd Do It Again

Despite the strong perceptions of guilt that remain in light of the acquittal decision, Gabe and his supporters have expressed the view that such perceptions, particularly among the Thomas family, would have remained regardless of whether the outcome of the trial were an acquittal by the judge or a not guilty verdict by a jury. As Austin explained:

> They [the Thomas family] fussed, because the judge didn't let it go to trial. If he'd let it go to trial … I don't know … I can't help but think, what if he had let it go to the jury, what would the Thomas [family] feel? ... I don't think it mattered what had happened ... Nothing would have satisfied the Thomas [family].

Similarly, in his interview with the US ABC network's *20/20* program after the acquittal, even in acknowledging that he wanted a jury to find him not guilty, Gabe suggested that this decision would itself have been criticised. He claimed that "people would have just said the jury didn't understand this or that".[38]

While there are reasons to support Gabe and Austin's opinions, in that some people, particularly the Thomas family, might still have believed Gabe was guilty of murder even if a jury had returned a not guilty verdict, the fact that this decision was removed from the jury and the evidence supporting Gabe's version of events was not revealed or tested under the rules of evidence applied at trial, means that the ability of the acquittal to offer a complete form of justice was limited from the perspective of all parties involved. Furthermore, both Cindy and Tommy acknowledged that had a not guilty verdict been returned by the jury, it would have at least allowed them the opportunity to move forward. As Tommy explained:

---

[38] Gabe Watson, cited in Robinson, above n 22.

> At the end of the day, if there's a grand jury or a coronial inquest or whatever, that determines there's sufficient evidence that a jury should make a determination, then at the end of the day, there should be no acquittals during a trial. There should be a jury empanelled, and once that jury is empanelled, the trial should go until the jury makes a decision, whatever that is. And if the jury decides, ok, there's insufficient evidence; well, at least we've got 12 people that said, there's insufficient evidence. If a jury decides they're guilty, then we've got 12 people that have said there's sufficient evidence and he's guilty. And the other part of that ... is if you've got a hung jury, and if you've got a hung jury, and in our case, to me, a hung jury would have been better than a judge saying we're going to acquit the guy. Because a hung jury, at least we would have had people going, he's guilty, we'd have had some going, yeah, I might think he's guilty too, but I'm not sure. But at least that leaves, that would have left us going, okay, it was a strong case, it just wasn't strong enough.

Tommy further claimed, "if we had seen this through [to] the end, there would have been one of two outcomes. He would have either been found guilty, or we would have had a hung jury ... And that's where you get left with this sick and empty feeling".

As reflected in the raw emotions expressed by the Thomas family, and illustrated by our analysis from earlier chapters, it is clear that neither the Alabama or Queensland handling of the *Watson* case provided justice for the Thomas family, because the outcomes were determined by individuals representing the criminal justice system, without the input of community representation or norms into the process. This is evident in the statement Cindy and Tommy posted on the "Justice for Tina Thomas" Facebook page on the day of Gabe's acquittal, which read, "A JURY of his peers with ALL the evidence: that is all we ever asked for Tina. That is all we ever wanted".[39]

As explained at various stages throughout this book, Gabe's acquittal represents the conclusion of the *Watson* case within the context of the criminal justice system. Thus, the quest for any form of procedural justice has effectively ended, yet again by the decision of one authoritative individual—Judge Tommy Nail. Significantly, the many obstacles that have plagued this case from its commencement in October 2003, right through to the acquittal in February 2012, have painted a dark picture of a victim's family's journey through both the Queensland and Alabama criminal justice systems. In reflecting on her reaction to Judge Nail's

---

[39] Emphasis in original, Tommy and Cindy Thomas, "Justice for Tina" on *Justice for Tina Facebook Page* (23 February 2012) <http://www.facebook.com/pages/Justice-for-Tina-Thomas/164788116916236>.

decision, Cindy graphically depicted this dark picture when she stated, "when the judge acquitted [Gabe], it was like she [Tina] died all over again. It's like she's died four times … [First] when she died. Then when she got moved [exhumed] … Then when what happened in Australia happened. And now this".

Yet despite their loss of faith in the integrity of both the Queensland and Alabama criminal justice systems, when asked the difficult questions about whether pursuing the case in Alabama was worth it, and whether they would pursue their quest for justice if they had their time again, both Cindy and Tommy firmly agreed that they would. As Cindy claimed:

> Once we realised what had happened, I mean, once it started coming together and evidence started coming up and the more we'd find out, yeah, we had to fight for her, because no one else would … Would we do it again? … Oh yeah, because she was expecting us to.

In a similar vein, Tommy explained:

> You know that's a hard question to answer right now. I mean, maybe next year [2013] you could ask me that and I could answer a little better. The only thing I'll tell you is if I had to do it all over again I would have done exactly the same thing, except for maybe a couple of little differences … But was it worth it? If I had to do it over, I'd do it again. I don't know if that makes it worth it or not, but I'd be at the same place. Our ordeal through most of this, and this is what maybe a lot of people don't understand, it wasn't about him [Gabe], it was about finding out what happened to Tina, and then if he killed her, hopefully seeing justice done … That's what it was about.

CHAPTER ELEVEN

A SECOND CHANCE FOR JUSTICE

> The case shows the best and the worst of the justice system.[1]
>
> —Australian Media Reporter

The law's response to the death of Tina Thomas has undoubtedly raised questions over the adequacy and integrity of the Queensland and Alabama criminal "justice" systems. At each stage of the nearly nine years during which Gabe Watson was investigated and faced two prosecutions for his involvement in the death of Tina Thomas, the discretionary decisions of the legal stakeholders involved were in part influenced by broader financial stresses confronting both jurisdictions. These decisions have fuelled significant doubt over the capacity of either legal system to provide justice from either the public perspective or the perspectives of those most intimately involved in the case.

As evident throughout our analysis of the *Watson* case, the concept of justice is obscure. In a subjective sense, it is almost impossible to define. As Philosopher Michael Novak claims, "the minute one begins to define ... justice, one runs into embarrassing intellectual difficulties".[2] This difficulty of defining what is meant by the term "justice" has been demonstrated in each chapter by the reflections and opinions of our participants, and is perhaps best captured by Gabe's father, David Watson, who claimed:

> To get justice. Getting justice … This phrase, "getting justice for people", gee whiz. I'm not sure I even know what it means ... Mr and Mrs Thomas will tell you they didn't get justice. So I don't know how you could say we got justice and they didn't. I think it's from your perspective, your point of view.

---

[1] Australian Media Reporter, court observations, 23 February 2012.

[2] Michael Novak, "Defining Social Justice" (2000) 29 *First Things Online* <http://www.firstthings.com/article/2007/01/defining-social-justice-29>.

In examining the subjective nature of justice, three overriding themes have consistently arisen in the *Watson* case: first, justice equating with the running and completion of a jury trial; second, the cost of attaining justice; and finally, the importance of the processes involved in attaining justice. It is these three key themes that we return to in order to examine our primary research question: in light of the decision of the Queensland Office of the Department of Public Prosecutions (ODPP) in 2009 not to prosecute Gabe for murder in Australia, could the law's second response to the death of Tina Thomas provide a second chance for justice?

Justice and Juries

Within the legal context, a traditionalist's view of justice is framed on perspectives of retribution and deterrence, whereby offenders are held accountable for their wrongdoing, in order to punish and prevent further violations of the law by both the individual and the broader society. However, a common theme to emerge throughout our discussions with those involved in the case was the notion that justice is equated with the running and completion of a jury trial, as opposed to the imposition of a specific verdict or punishment. As Tina's father, Tommy Thomas, explained, "facing the evidence before a jury in a criminal trial ... that's the only way that we could get justice". The ability to attain justice from a trial was thus inherently linked with the importance of the role of the jury within the trial, in terms of offering community input and evaluation of the evidence, as well as providing a voice that represents social norms and expectations of human behaviour and justice.

The acknowledgement that the jury trial is equated with justice is well established in legal research. As highlighted by the former Chairman of the US Securities and Exchange Commission and retired Federal Court Judge, Jerome Frank, the jury plays a fundamental role in providing justice. As Frank explains:

> Law and justice every so often do not coincide. Everyone knows it ... We want justice and we think we are going to get it through "the law", and when we do not, we blame "the law". Now this is where the jury comes in. The jury, in the privacy of its retirement, adjusts the general rule of law to the justice of the particular case. Thus the odium of inflexible rules of law is avoided and popular satisfaction preserved. That is what the jury trial does. It supplies that flexibility of legal rules which is essential to justice ... And that flexibility could never be given by a judge trial ... The jury, and

the secrecy of the jury too, are the indispensable elements in popular justice.[3]

This importance of a trial by jury was also recognised by academic and former police officer from the state of New South Wales (Australia), Brian Mills, who claimed that "the right of an accused person to be judged by their peers at their subsequent trial is seen by many as an article of faith".[4] Indeed, as discussed in Part One, the absence of a jury trial was one of the key reasons why the Queensland plea bargain in 2009 was perceived as not providing a just outcome. As Detective Senior Constable Kevin Gehringer commented, "if we'd gone to trial in Australia in 2009, I would have been a happy man".

Despite this recognition of a trial equating with justice, it is interesting that the Alabama capital murder trial of Gabe Watson was also not perceived as offering justice from the perspectives of many of our participants, predominantly on the basis that it was not considered to be a "complete trial".[5] As Alabama Assistant Attorney-General and lead prosecutor in the capital murder trial, Don Valeska, described it, "he [Judge Nail] was going to give Tina her trial, well she got, I guess he could call it a trial, but she only got half a trial as far as we're concerned". The reason for this perception is primarily because the trial was stopped before all of the evidence could be exposed and tested before the jury. Thus, the absence of the voice of the defence and of a jury verdict again equated to an absence of justice.[6] As former Chairman of the US Securities and Exchange Commission and retired Federal Court Jerome Frank further noted, "the jury do justice ... Use of the jury [means] you can eat your cake and have it too. You can ... preserve your legal rules and principles unswerving and unyielding ... and you can have a jury's decision".[7] In light of these absent voices, the Alabama capital murder trial, while initially identified by many as providing a second chance for justice to be achieved, was ultimately perceived as severely failing to offer exactly that. This sentiment is captured in Gehringer's reflections following the acquittal decision:

---

[3] Jerome Frank, *Courts on Trial: Myths and Realities in American Justice* (Princeton, 1973) 128.

[4] Brian Mills, *The Criminal Trial* (Federation Press, 2011) 32.

[5] Detective Senior Constable Kevin Gehringer.

[6] Austin Sarat, "Vengeance, Victims and the Identity of Law" (1997) 6 *Social and Legal Studies* 163, 164.

[7] Frank, above n 3, 128.

> It's still a case of justice hasn't been served, and that just gets down to the fact, again, that it's come down to a single person's decision, as opposed to a jury ... So in this case, it was the judge who had the ultimate authority to cut it short and not allow it to go to the jury. And as we all know, in this instance, it appears as though the judge has erred, because he himself has said there was prima facie evidence there and throughout the trial, he'd said there were matters that were for the jury to decide on, and yet they were deprived of that at the end.

As implicit in Gehringer's claims above, where justice is "removed, abstract and impersonal, [there is] no justice at all".[8]

The Price of Justice

The cost of achieving justice has been an ongoing and unwelcome factor impacting on the law's response to Tina's death in Queensland and Alabama, with the police investigation and both prosecutions of Gabe struggling to operate within the constraints of the limited resources available in each jurisdiction. As explored in Part One, the influence of resource constraints and efficiency motivations in Queensland at the time of the ODPP's decision to engage in a plea deal with Gabe, arguably eradicated any possibility of justice being attained within that jurisdiction. Additionally, and as discussed throughout Part Two, the economic climate within which Alabama's justice system was operating leading into and during the capital murder trial meant that the prosecution was unable to utilise the necessary level of resources and funding required for justice to be procedurally, substantively or subjectively achieved. As Dr Susan Easton and Professor Christine Piper explain, "justice appears as a neutral word—the 'pure' end product of a positive moral process. The even handed figure with the scales … Yet in practice, justice is inextricably linked with money".[9]

In the Queensland context, the influence of financial constraints was perhaps most problematic in relation to the ODPP's decision not to proceed to a contested murder trial. As outlined in Chapter Two, the cost to the Queensland Government of running the coronial inquest in 2007–08 was estimated by Coroner David Glasgow to be "hundreds of thousands of dollars". On average, it is estimated that running a trial in a superior court

---

[8] Sarat, above n 6, 175.

[9] Susan Easton and Christine Piper, *Sentencing and Punishment: The Quest for Justice* (Oxford University Press, 3rd Edition, 2012) 428.

in Australia costs around $10,000 per day.[10] An analysis of the court systems in the state of Victoria (Australia), estimated that the use of a Supreme Court, in terms of the costs of the facilities alone, equates to approximately $645 per hour—a figure that does not include the prosecution's preparation costs or the accused's expenses.[11] It is difficult to concretely state how long Gabe's murder trial would have lasted had it gone ahead in Queensland in 2009. The average duration of a criminal trial across Australian jurisdictions, particularly a complex homicide trial, has significantly increased over the past 40 years. As Justice John Dunford from the New South Wales Supreme Court in Australia explained in 2004:

> When I was a judge's associate in 1959, the usual length of a murder trial was one to two days. When one trial involving two accused went for nine days, the length of the trial was regarded as newsworthy and it was, if I remember correctly, something of a record. Now a murder trial that finishes in less than two weeks is a rarity.[12]

Over ten years prior to Justice Dunford's comments, Detective Superintendent Jim Litster of the South Australian Homicide Squad extended the average duration well beyond even the rarity of two weeks, to maintain that "some years ago, murder trials would average about four weeks in duration, but now it is common for trials to take between six and ten weeks".[13] In the context of the *Watson* case, Tommy recalled Assistant Director of Public Prosecutions and lead prosecutor of the case in Queensland, Brendan Campbell SC, explaining to him that "a criminal trial over there [Queensland] would have lasted a couple of months". This is not unusual in Queensland. As explained in Chapter Three, when the state government provided additional funding to the Queensland ODPP in 2009 to enable it to prosecute a "couple of high profile and complex cases

---

[10] Robert Moles, *A State of Injustice* (Networked Knowledge, 2009) <http://netk.net.au/soi/SOI16.asp>.

[11] PricewaterhouseCoopers, "Review of Fees Paid by Victoria Legal Aid to Barristers in Criminal Cases" (2008) <http://www.vicbar.com.au/webdata/generalfiles/PriceWaterhouseCoopers.pdf> 24.

[12] Justice John Dunford, "Looking Forward: The Direction of Criminal Law" (Speech delivered at *Criminal Law Conference*, Sydney, Australia, 24 July 2004) <http://www.lawlink.nsw.gov.au/lawlink/supreme_court/ll_sc.nsf/pages/SCO_speech_dunford_270704>.

[13] Detective Superintendent Jim Litster, "The Police Perspective: Homicide in South Australia", in Heather Strang and Sally-Anne Gerull (eds), *Homicide: Patterns, Prevention and Control* (Australian Institute of Criminology, 1992) 133, 141.

that are above and beyond the normal workload of the DPP",[14] one of these cases, which involved running the complex manslaughter trial of Jayant Patel, lasted for 58 days. Thus, based on the estimates of Brendan Campbell (two months), the duration of the coronial inquest (24 days), the estimated duration of the Alabama capital murder trial (25 days) and the duration of the similarly complex *Patel* manslaughter case (58 days), it is likely that an Australian-run trial would have cost the Queensland Government, for the use of the court facilities alone, somewhere between \$92,880 and \$600,000. Importantly, this estimate does not include the prosecution expenses, the costs of having international witnesses attend to give evidence, any additional investigative costs associated with running the prosecution, or any of the accused's expenses.

It is not known how much the sentencing hearing or having to run an appeal hearing following Gabe's initial sentence cost the Queensland Government, but the resources saved from not running a trial were estimated by several of our participants to be between one and two million dollars. As our analysis in Part One suggests, this saving appears to have been a substantial motivation underpinning the Queensland ODPP's decision to bargain its way out of prosecuting Gabe for Tina's murder.

In May 2012, the US *Alabama13* news network reported that the total cost of Gabe's capital murder trial was approximately \$100,000.[15] This figure was based on data obtained from the Office of the Attorney-General in Alabama and from Gabe's US defence attorney, Brett Bloomston. It was reported that approximately \$45,990 of the total amount was spent on witnesses (for travel, hotels and meals), additional investigative expenses and the prosecution itself, while the secondary costs, including the travel costs and expenses of the prosecutors, were estimated at approximately \$10,483.[16] As a result of the acquittal, the state was also responsible for covering some of the defence costs, including the expenses associated with bringing six expert witnesses to Birmingham to testify, which were estimated to exceed \$45,000.[17]

Interestingly, while the *Alabama13* news network was critical of this \$100,000 cost to tax payers for a "failed murder prosecution",[18] this figure

[14] (Former) Premier Anna Bligh, cited in Gabrielle Dunlevy, "Queensland's ODPP Gets \$8 Million Boost", *Sydney Morning Herald* (New South Wales), 21 July 2008.
[15] Jon Paepcke, "Fact Check: Gabe Watson Case Cost State Nearly \$100,000", *Alabama13News* (Alabama), 21 May 2012.
[16] Ibid.
[17] Ibid.
[18] Ibid.

is significantly lower than any of the estimates that we obtained in relation to the likely costs of running a murder trial in Queensland. While one of the primary reasons for this significant difference is likely to be the duration of the Alabama trial, where only six and a half trial days and one day of jury selection and pre-trial arguments were run, there are several problematic implications of this costing difference. As discussed in Part Two, the limited funding available to the Alabama prosecution prevented it from being able to present its full array of witnesses and evidence collected throughout the police investigation and used four years earlier in the coronial inquest. This consequently became a strong contributing factor to the prosecution not surpassing the first stage at which an acquittal could be granted by the judge. As recognised by New South Wales Police Commissioner Andrew Scipione, "criminal trials follow months and sometimes years of laborious investigation. If justice is to be served, it is crucial that the painstaking work of building a case is matched by its strong and credible presentation at trial".[19]

In only being able to present a minimal portion of all of the available evidence and witness testimony—evidence and testimony that would have been available and most likely used in a Queensland trial in 2009—limitations on the cost of the prosecution critically undermined the strength of its case and the viability of the Alabama trial in providing a just outcome. This was most apparent in the inadmissibility of key prosecution evidence as a result of missing witnesses, including the police dive re-enactment video and an email sent by Gabe to Mike Ball Dive Expeditions (Mike Ball) approximately five months prior to his and Tina's honeymoon. As such, the inability to present the full evidence collected would suggest that the Alabama trial failed to represent the "painstaking" work undertaken by either the police or the prosecutors in building the case. Instead, it represented the inability for justice to be fully attained in an economically starved climate, further supporting our argument that the Alabama trial did not provide a second chance for justice.

Importantly, and as explored in Parts One and Two, the influence of monetary constraints on the achievability of justice extended beyond the criminal justice institutions and agencies involved, to Gabe, in being able to finance his defence, and to the Thomas family, in being able to advocate for the case to continue. As Gabe explained in his interview with the US ABC network's *20/20* program following his acquittal:

> We've spent an insane amount of money. It was every penny Kim [his wife] and I could get our hands on, and every penny the Watson family had

---

[19] Andrew Scipione, cited in Mills, above n 4, v.

> been able to sock away for retirement. Not only did all this throw my future plans out the window, it did the same for my parents. That eats at me. And I can see the physical and emotional toll it's taken on them.[20]

The Thomas family have also experienced significant financial burdens in travel and legal expenses across the almost nine-year duration of the case, reflecting the cost to the secondary victims that is often forgotten, but one which is becoming a more integral part of the pursuit and attainment of justice in modern times. As Tommy explained, "this has cost us a fortune … It's not just plane fares, you've got to eat and hotel rooms and all this other stuff … It's expensive". He further explained that:

> [Gabe]'s been sprouting off about how much it's been costing him, and that's great, but I made four trips to Australia before he made his first, and I made that one with him! ... My concern though, where I was going with that is … it's about broke us [financially]. What about people that this happens to that don't have anybody with a [financial] means to go this far?

As noted by Professor Jerold Auerbach 20 years prior to Tina's death, "in the twentieth century it is justice, the secular equivalent of salvation, that is sold for a fee ... How much justice can you afford?"[21] This concept has also been captured more recently by Professors Paul Robinson and Michael Cahill, who noted that "in the real world, we simply cannot achieve justice always and everywhere: limitations of time, knowledge, and money prevent us".[22]

Unfortunately in the *Watson* case, it appears that the price of justice has impacted significantly on both the Thomas and Watson families, as well as on the capacities of both the Queensland and Alabama criminal justice systems to provide an adequate form of justice. Indeed, the financial burden of this case on the Queensland Government and the US State of Alabama has been a significant factor that has hindered the case's progression and the legal processes used. Of significance, however, is that where the Queensland ODPP took measures to minimise the financial burden of the case through the use of a plea deal, and where the Alabama prosecution was restricted in its resources and the resultant condensing of

[20] Gabe Watson, cited in Carol Robinson, "Interview: Gabe Watson Looks to Leave Shadow of his Wife's Honeymoon Death and His Murder Trial", *Birmingham News* (Alabama), 3 March 2012 <http://blog.al.com/spotnews/2012/03/interview_gabe_watson_looks_to.html>.

[21] Jerold Auerbach, *Justice without Law* (Oxford University Press, 1983) 7.

[22] Paul Robinson and Michael Cahill, *Law without Justice: Why Criminal Law Doesn't Give People What They Deserve* (Oxford University Press, 2006) 25.

its witness list, the Thomas and Watson families did not minimise their quest for justice, despite the costs and ongoing financial (and emotional) burdens it placed on them. Yet, in spite of their persistence, in light of the problematic influence of resources and financial pressures evident throughout all stages of this case, the cost of the struggle for justice, for Tina and for Gabe, emotionally and financially, proved somewhat futile.

Processing Justice

Beyond discussions of justice equating with a jury trial, and concerns surrounding the financial costs of attaining justice, the third key theme that has emerged from our analysis is that perceptions of whether justice is achieved depend not only on the outcome of a process, but also on how that outcome is reached. This concept is referred to as the "fair process effect",[23] whereby individuals are generally willing to accept even unfavourable outcomes, if the legal processes leading to that outcome are considered to be fair. As Australian High Court Justice John Heydon explained, "the concepts of justice, and miscarriage of justice bear two aspects: outcome and process. They are different, but related … It is the process itself that is judged".[24]

From the defence perspective, this can be demonstrated by Gabe's US defence attorney Joe Basgier's perception of the capital murder trial, whereby he claimed that the processes and outcome provided evidence of the just nature of the Alabama criminal justice system. As he explained:

> Do I think justice was achieved in the case? ... I've been waiting for someone to ask me a question like that. I thought that this case was a great opportunity to test the American system of criminal justice. To see if it works the way it's supposed to. We have a lot of safeguards built into the system to make sure that a defendant's constitutional rights are met, and to make sure that an innocent person isn't convicted. And some of those safeguards didn't go in our favour at the beginning of the case, but we got to the most important one, which was, after the state had presented their evidence, they had not proven their case. They didn't prove the elements of the crime that they needed to prove. And the system stepped in and stopped it. So I think that's a good thought, and a good thing to take away from it, is [that] our system of justice worked.

[23] Linda Skitka and David Houston, "When Due Process Is of No Consequence: Moral Mandates and Presumed Defendant Guilt or Innocence" (2001) 14 *Social Justice Research* 305.

[24] *Patel v The Queen* [2012] HCA 29 24 August 2012 at 258.

In the context of a criminal trial, if the procedures leading up to and during the trial are perceived as fair—for example, the police investigation is considered just, the accused has access to due process protections, there is no perception of misconduct by criminal justice agencies, and the judge is not perceived as making biased decisions—then regardless of whether or not the outcome is favourable to an individual, there is a perception of justice in the process being achieved. As explained in a report prepared by the Commissioner for Victims and Witnesses in England and Wales, this "procedural justice viewpoint holds that fair, decent and appropriate treatment are key factors in determining approval, and can be more important than actual results".[25] As such, when the processes leading up to and within a trial are not considered just, even a favourable outcome cannot be perceived as offering justice. Within this framework, the contentious discretionary decisions that were made at crucial moments within the *Watson* case have consequently undermined the opportunity for the law, and the processes through which justice is achieved within the law, to be attained.

On this basis, in contrast to Basgier's claims, we believe that the resolution of the *Watson* case by a plea bargain in Queensland failed to provide justice, and that the capital murder trial in Alabama was never capable of providing a second chance for justice. As Tommy maintained:

> Australia and the US both have probably the best justice systems … [The judge] is there to make sure that things are done by law, but they are not there to become the jury in the case, and … that's my biggest problem with it. And see, the problem with that is that applies to both countries, because Judge Nail decided to become the jury here, Brendan Campbell decided to become the jury in Australia. And there's no justice in that. I can't … I just don't know what else to say about it. There's no justice in it.

A similar view was expressed by David in noting that even though the acquittal outcome was certainly favourable for Gabe and his family, he no longer "trusts" that the justice system and the legal processes within it are capable of providing justice. As David claimed:

> I don't trust any of them now, the Australian or US legal systems ... I've learnt a lot more than I ever wanted to know. I have greatly diminished faith in the honesty and integrity of the legal system in both countries ...

---

[25] Commissioner for Victims and Witnesses in England and Wales, *Victims' Views of Court and Sentencing: Qualitative Research with WAVES Victims* (Ministry of Justice, 2011) 6.

> Ultimately, it worked out the way it should have, but the process was totally unnecessary.

From a police perspective, Lieutenant Brad Flynn also expressed his disappointment with the legal processes involved in the case, particularly in terms of how they allowed for the polarisation between good and bad and the roles of the defence and the prosecution to prevent a just outcome from being attained:

> We had prepared ourselves for the possibility of what might happen in court and stuff, but it doesn't make it any easier to sit and watch seven years of your life go down, you know, go down the toilet. It's hard, but you play by the rules and unfortunately other people don't and that's kind of, I guess that's justice to some people. And the defence can get up there and say, spew stuff that's just ungodly amounts of lies and untruths and stuff, and we have to get up there and tell the truth. And I guess it's just another chapter in the battle of good versus evil. I guess that's just how it is. We're the good guys and I'm not, I didn't sign on for this job to know that every day was going to be a holiday and I would win every case I did, and it's hard. It's hard to see somebody walk out that in your heart you know that they're guilty.

Among the Australian participants, the failure of the legal processes to provide procedural justice was perhaps best captured in Gehringer's comments. He recognised the potential for the system to be just, but maintained that individuals working within the system could actively prevent the attainment of just outcomes—a situation that he believed happened in both Queensland and Alabama:

> The system we've got, if it's run out, I don't know of a better system, or I can't think of a better system. So I think the system itself is ok as a whole, but it's obviously where it falls down is individuals have authority within that system to circumvent it or to cut it short ... So I guess in this case, yes, the justice system has let us down.

In the Australian context, as explored throughout Part One, the inability of the plea bargain resolution to provide procedural justice can be viewed as the definitive moment when justice became unattainable in the legal system's response to the *Watson* case in Queensland. The resounding failure of the plea deal to offer justice has been understood in relation to three key areas: first, the conduct of the Queensland prosecutors involved in the case, namely Brendan Campbell; second, the absence of clarity, transparency or accountability surrounding when and why the plea bargain agreement was reached; and third, the questionable development of a very favourable agreed summary of facts which was withheld from the police investigators and quite possibly, given Brendan Campbell's admissions relating to Gabe's knowledge of the plea deal prior to leaving the US, unjustly used to inform the sentences that Gabe received. Importantly, these potentially unjust processes occurred within a resource-starved climate in which the Queensland ODPP was in deficit, and the Supreme Court failed to meet any of the national criteria applied to measure its effectiveness and efficiency levels. As identified by Professors Paul Robinson and Michael Cahill, "from this tension between doing justice and limited resources, springs the prosecutor's reliance on plea bargains"[26]—a highly appropriate comment in relation to the Queensland resolution of the *Watson* case.

Further to the questionable justness of the legal processes through which this case was resolved in Queensland, as discussed throughout Part Two, the Alabama capital murder trial also did not have the capacity to provide justice because its processes were fraught by perceptions of unfairness and injustice from the outset, through to its finalisation. This was evident even before the commencement of the trial, as the second prosecution of Gabe was viewed by some as breaching Australian and US international treaty agreements to protect an accused from double prosecutions. Furthermore, and as explored in Chapter Five, throughout the trial, questions were raised as to its legitimacy in being able to provide a just process due to a perception of bias in the judge's attitude towards the case—a perception that was fuelled by the various comments Judge Tommy Nail made, both with and without the jury being present, regarding what he saw as the shortcomings of the prosecution's case.

Importantly, as explored throughout Part Three, the processes through which the outcome of the Alabama trial was reached also led to perceptions of a lack of justice, because it breached traditional and procedural norms. The acquittal not only prevented a traditional jury trial conclusion, which in turn revoked the jurors' civil duties and right to return a verdict, but also meant that the defence evidence was not publicly revealed or tested within the confines of the rules of evidence. As Valeska stated, "all these professors and schools that write books on evidence, [well] evidence is what the judge says it is at 10:30 on the morning on the day that he threw the case out, because I can't stop the trial and appeal". The acquittal thus prevented the public and both families involved in the case from having the opportunity to see justice being conducted in its natural form. Consequently, and in a similar vein to the plea bargain

[26] Robinson and Cahill, above n 22, 72.

resolution in Queensland, the outcome of the Alabama trial left many questions regarding the case unanswered, including questions of justice and of Gabe's guilt.

In considering all of these processes and in drawing on our analysis throughout the three parts of this book, perhaps the most pertinent and overarching issue preventing a second chance for justice was that the full evidence obtained in relation to the death of Tina Thomas was never revealed, tried or tested within the confines of a criminal court. Thus, a negotiated manslaughter conviction resulting from a plea deal in Queensland and an acquittal for murder by a judge in Alabama are at odds with the concept of traditional and procedural justice. For this reason, from all perspectives, the only way justice could likely have been obtained, at least in a procedural sense, was for a trial to have been run in Queensland in 2009. A trial at this point in time would have avoided the additional two-year delay and the ongoing financial burdens attached to the case, as well as the persistent public conjecture surrounding Gabe's guilt or innocence, because the evidence of both the prosecution and the defence would have been revealed and tested within the confines of a court of law. A fully informed jury could then have determined Gabe's level of culpability, finding him guilty or not guilty of murder, or the statutory alternative verdict of manslaughter, which included the option of manslaughter by criminal negligence. While under a procedural justice framework, the jury's verdict in terms of establishing guilt or innocence would not have been the significant factor determining a just outcome, its delivery by a panel of members representative of the community, as opposed to a decision made by a single legal representative, would have created a basis for a just outcome to be attained in the *Watson* case.

Our Verdict: Justice or Injustice?

As Professor Austin Sarat explains, "what is unjust is what conflicts with the public's sense of justice";[27] but within the *Watson* case, there is no public consensus as to Gabe's guilt or innocence, and limited public consensus as to whether the plea bargain and sentence in Queensland and the acquittal in Alabama were just outcomes. Indeed, within the public realm, the mixture of views on whether justice was attained is evident even within the following small sample of comments posted on an online forum discussing Gabe's acquittal in February 2012:

---

[27] Sarat, above n 6, 176.

> I will NEVER believe that this clown is innocent. Nothing he said at the time or since makes the slightest sense. How do you leave a buddy in distress? That's the POINT to having a buddy! How could you not just inflate her BCD [buoyancy control device] and take her to the surface? Or at least put your occy in her gob, hold on tight and inflate your own? Don't start me on this boofhead.[28]

> He did kill his wife, just not on purpose.[29]

> The thing that has always amazed me about this case is how many really, really experienced divers said "yeah that could happen" and how many not so experienced divers, and the general public, said, "he's a murderer". Sanity has prevailed, finally.[30]

> Hindsight is always such a wonderful thing, but it would have been truly interesting if the case had gone to full trial in Australia to see if the defence would have exposed several of the alleged inconsistencies ... Having accepted the negligent manslaughter charge, we will never know. A lot of learning and facts have now been lost.[31]

Mirroring these divergent views, among our participants there were also contrasting opinions, some adamantly asserting that justice was not achieved in either jurisdiction, and others advocating that it was. Following the Alabama trial, Basgier even suggested that the title of this book should be "Did this trial end up providing justice? Yes".

In light of these contrasting views, we finish our analysis by returning to the question with which we started: was justice achieved? Perhaps our response to this question and our analysis of the *Watson* case can most appropriately be encapsulated by the following comment from Austin: "What is justice? I don't know what it would have taken for justice to have prevailed". As argued throughout this book, we believe that procedurally and substantively, justice did not prevail in the *Watson* case in either Queensland or Alabama. But subjectively, did justice prevail? That's for you to decide.

---

[28] Emphasis in original, DrPete, "Gabe Watson Acquitted" on *DiveOz Discussion Forum* (24 February 2012) <http://www.diveoz.com.au/discussion_forums/topic.asp?TOPIC_ID=26328>.

[29] Lesley, "Gabe Watson Acquitted" on *DiveOz Discussion Forum* (24 February 2012), above n 28.

[30] Trev Jackson, "Gabe Watson Acquitted" on *DiveOz Discussion Forum* (24 February 2012), above n 28.

[31] Mike, "Gabe Watson Acquitted" on *DiveOz Discussion Forum* (27 February 2012), above n 28.

REFERENCE LIST

Legislation and Policy

Alabama Rules of Criminal Procedure
Alabama Rules of Evidence
Australian Constitution
Code of Alabama 1975
Constitution of the United States
Coroners Act 1958 (Qld)
Coroners Act 2003 (Qld)
Criminal Code 1899 (Qld)
Director of Public Prosecutions Act 1994 (Qld)
Director's Policy (Qld)
Extradition Act 1988 (Cth)
Federal Rules of Criminal Procedure 1986 (US)
Federal Rules of Evidence (US)
International Covenant on Civil and Political Rights 1966
Justices Act 1886 (Qld)
Mutual Assistance in Criminal Matters (United States of America) Regulations 1999
Penalties and Sentencing Act 1992 (QLD)
Universal Declaration of Human Rights 1948
Victims of Crime Assistance Act 2009 (Qld)

Cases and Court Documents

A*l-Kateb v Godwin* [2004] HCA 37
Ballenger v State (1998) 720 So 2d 1033
Brown v State CR-07-1332 (2010)
Defence Motion for Judgement of Acquittal, 23 February 2012
Harnage v State (1972) 274 So 2d 333
Heath v Alabama 472 U.S 82 (1985)
Inquest into the death of Christina Mae Watson known as Tina Thomas (COR 124 of 2003) (13 November 2008–20 June 2009)
J.M.A v State 74 So 3d 487 (2011)
Patel v The Queen [2012] HCA 29 (24 August 2012)

Royals v State (1951) 56 So 2d 368
R v Carroll [2002] HCA 55 at 22
R v Maxwell (1995) 184 CLR 501
R v Nydham [1977] VR 430
R v Watson [2009] QSC 438
R v Watson; ex parte A-G (Qld) [2009] QCA 279
Sanabria v United States 437 U.S. 54 (1978)
State of Alabama v David Gabriel Watson CC-2010-3334 (2010)
United States v Lanza 260 U.S 377 (1922)
United States v Martin Linen Supply Co. 430 U.S. 564 (1977)
Woolmington v DPP [1935] AC 462

References

ABC Television Network, "Unfathomable: Part One", *Australian Story*, 2 August 2010 <http://www.abc.net.au/austory/content/2007/s2971395.htm>.

Aguirre, Holly, "'He is a Coward": Cousin of Wife in Scuba Drowning Rips Bizarre Antics of Cleared Husband", *The Daily* (Australia), 26 February 2012.

Atfield, Cameron and Amy Remekis, "Patel Case Returns to Court", *Brisbane Times* (Queensland), 31 August 2012.

Auerbach, Jerold, *Justice Without Law* (Oxford University Press, 1983).

Australian Associated Press, "Watson a 'Coward' but Not a Killer", *The Age* (Victoria), 22 April 2011.

—. "Queensland Scuba Dive Murder Trial to Begin in US", *Herald Sun* (Victoria), 13 February 2012.

—. "Doctor Thought Gabe Watson Was Trying to Help Wife on Scuba Dive", *The Australian* (Australia), 17 February 2012.

Australian Bureau of Statistics, *Criminal Courts 2007-08* (2009) <http://www.ausstats.abs.gov.au/ausstats/subscriber.nsf/0/2EBE86273 2FDD915CA2575670016BDE7/$File/4530_2007-08.pdf>.

Baldwin, John and Mike McConville, *Negotiated Justice: Pressures to Plead Guilty* (Martin Robertson, 1977).

Bancroft, Lundy, *Why Does He Do That? Inside the Minds of Angry and Controlling Men* (Berkley Trade, 2002).

Bantin, John, "Dive Computers on Test: Which Do You Trust?" on *DiverNet* (8 May 2012) <http://www.divernet.com/Diving_Gear/group_tests/158650/dive_ computers_on_test.html>.

Battiste, Nikki, "Honeymoon Drowning Witness: Husband's Version 'Not Plausible'", *ABC News* (United States), 16 February 2012.

—. "Honeymoon Murder Trial Charges Dismissed by Judge", *ABC News* (United States), 23 February 2012.

Battiste, Nikki and Alice Gomstyn, "Gabe Watson Defends His Behaviour at Wife's Grave", *ABC News* (United States), 29 February 2012.

Bellemare, Daniel, "Accountability, Independence and Ethics in Prosecution Practice: Public Confidence and Accountability in the Exercise of Prosecutorial Discretion" (Speech delivered at the *International Society for Reform of Criminal Law: 18th International Conference*, Montreal, Canada, 10 August 2004) <http://www.isrcl.org /Papers/2004/Bellemare.pdf>.

Bentley, Amanda, "Great Barrier Reef Honeymoon Death: Diver's Jail Sentence 'Ludicrous' and 'Embarrassing'", *Sydney Morning Herald* (New South Wales), 5 June 2009.

Bibas, Stephanos, "The Need for Prosecutorial Discretion" (2010) 19 *Temple Political and Civil Rights Law Review* 369.

Birmingham News, "Former Alabama AG Troy King Defends Decision to Pursue Gabe Watson Case", *Birmingham News* (Alabama), 24 February 2012.

Blackstone, Sir William, *Commentaries on the Law of England* (Clarendon Press, 1789).

Calligeros, Marissa, "Killer's Return to US in Doubt", *Brisbane Times* (Queensland), 21 September 2009.

Celizic, Mike, "Outrage over Sentencing in Honeymoon Drowning", *MSNBC News* (United States), 5 June 2009.

Chazz50_1, "Interview: Gabe Watson Looks to Leave Shadow of his Wife's Honeymoon Death and His Murder Trial: Comments" on *Birmingham News Alabama.com* (2 March 2012) <http://blog.al.com/spotnews/2012/03/interview_gabe_watson_looks_to.html>.

Commissioner for Victims and Witnesses in England and Wales, *Victims' Views of Court and Sentencing: Qualitative research with WAVES victims* (Ministry of Justice, 2011).

Cook, Bree, Fiona David and Anna Grant, *Victims' Needs, Victims' Rights: Policies and Programs for Victims of Crime in Australia* (Research and Public Policy Series No 19, Australian Institute of Criminology, 1999).

Corns, Chris, "Retrial of Acquitted Persons: Time for Reform of the Double Jeopardy Rule?" (2003) 27 *Criminal Law Journal* 80.

Daily Mail, "Honeymoon Killer Who Drowned Wife is Deported to US to Face Murder Trial after 18 Months in Australian Jail for Manslaughter", *Daily Mail* (United Kingdom), 25 November 2010.

Dawson, Myrna, "Rethinking the Boundaries of Intimacy at the end of the Century: The Role of the Victim–Defendant Relationship in Criminal Justice Decision Making over Time" (2004) 38 *Law and Society Review* 105.

Dixon, Judith, "Rights of Victims" (Speech delivered at the Prosecuting Justice Conference, Melbourne, Australia, 18–19 April 1996) <http://www.aic.gov.au/events/aicupcomingevents/1996/~/media/conferences/prosecuting/dixon.ashx>.

DrPete, "Gabe Watson Acquitted" on *DiveOz Discussion Forum* (24 February 2012) <http://www.diveoz.com.au/discussion_forums/topic.asp?TOPIC_ID=26328>.

Druckerman, Shana, Nikki Battiste and Edward Lovett, "Honeymoon Killer: Gabe Watson Breaks Silence on Details of Wife's Death" on *ABC News 20/20* (2 March 2012) <http://abcnews.go.com/US/honeymoon-killer-gabe-watson-breaks-silence-details-wifes/story?id=15819106>.

Duhs, Ted, *Crucial Errors in Murder Investigations* (Bond University Press, 2012).

Dunford, Justice John, "Looking Forward: The Direction of Criminal Law" (Speech Delivered at *Criminal Law Conference*, Sydney, Australia, 24 July 2004) <http://www.lawlink.nsw.gov.au/lawlink/supreme_court/ll_sc.nsf/pages/SCO_speech_dunford_270704>.

Dunlevy, Gabrielle, "Queensland's ODPP Gets $8 Million Boost", *Sydney Morning Herald* (New South Wales), 21 July 2008.

Dzur, Albert, "Why American Democracy Needs the Jury Trial" (2011) 5 *Criminal Law and Philosophy* 87.

Easton, Susan and Christine Piper, *Sentencing and Punishment: The Quest for Justice* (Oxford University Press, 3rd Edition, 2012).

Edmonds, Carl, "The Honeymoon Death Chronicle" on *DAN Divers Alert Network–Asia Pacific* (6 August 2012) <http://www.danasiapacific.org/main/honeymoon_chronicle.php>.

Flynn, Asher, "Non-Transparent Justice and the Plea Bargaining Process in Victoria", in Marie Segrave (ed), *Australian and New Zealand Critical Criminology Conference Proceedings 2009* (Australian and New Zealand Critical Criminology Network, 2009) 88–100.

—. "Victoria's Legal Aid Funding Structure: Hindering the Ideals Inherent to the Pre-Trial Process" (2010) 34 *Criminal Law Journal* 48.

—. "'Fortunately We in Victoria Are Not in That UK Situation': Victorian and United Kingdom Legal Perspectives on Plea Bargaining Reform" (2011) 16 *Deakin Law Review* 361.

—."Bargaining with Justice: Victims, Plea Bargaining and the *Victims' Charter Act 2006* (Vic)" (2012, forthcoming) *Monash University Law Review*.

Flynn, Asher and Kate Fitz-Gibbon, "Bargaining with Defensive Homicide: Examining Victoria's Secretive Plea Bargaining System Post-Law Reform" (2011) 35 *Melbourne University Law Reform* 905.

Flynn, Asher and Nicola Henry, "Disputing Consent: The Role of Jury Directions in Victoria" (2012) 24(2) *Current Issues in Criminal Justice* 167.

Frank, Jerome, *Courts on Trial: Myths and Realities in American Justice* (Princeton, 1973).

Freiberg, Arie and Robert Seifman, "Plea Bargaining in Victoria: The Role of Counsel" (2001) 25 *Criminal Law Journal* 64.

G8R8U2, "Gabe Watson Acquitted: Judge Acquits Husband in 'Honeymoon Scuba Death': Comments" on *Huffington Post Blog* (23 February 2012) <http://www.huffingtonpost.com/2012/02/23/gabe-watson-acquitted_n_1296452.html>.

Goodey, Jo, *Victims and Victimology: Research, Policy and Practice* (Pearson Longman, 2005).

Gray, Chief Magistrate (Victoria) Ian, "Shades of Gray" (2012) 86 *Law Institute Journal* 18.

Gray, Jeremy, "Ex-AG Critical of Watson Decision", *Birmingham News* (Alabama), 25 February 2012.

Handler, Jack, *Ballentine's Law Dictionary: Legal Assistant Edition* (Delmar Publishers, 1994).

House of Commons Debates, Vol 88, Col 2105 (1 December 1925).

Jackson, John, "The Adversary Trial and Trial by Judge Alone", in Michael McConville and Geoffrey Wilson (eds) *The Handbook of the Criminal Justice Process* (Oxford University Press, 2002) 335–52.

—. "Gabe Watson Acquitted" on *DiveOz Discussion Forum* (24 February 2012) <http://www.diveoz.com.au/discussion_forums/topic.asp?TOPIC_ID=26328>.

Jacobson, Anders, "How Does a Dive Computer Work" on *Anders Jacobson's Blog* (25 January 2005) <http://www.jacobsen.no/anders/blog/archives/2005/01/25/how_does_a_dive_computer_work.html>.

Johns, Rowena, "Victims and Plea Bargaining: Victims of Crime—Plea Bargains, Compensation, Victim Impact Statements and Support Services Briefing Paper" (Briefing paper, Parliament of New South Wales, 2002) <http://www.parliament.nsw.gov.au/prod/parlment/publications.nsf/0/578C6F10C6D98565CA256ECF00083B4>.

Kindelan, Katie and Nikki Battiste, "Gabe Watson's Father 'Relieved' after Son's Murder Case Dismissed", *ABC News* (United States), 24 February 2012.

King, Martin Luther Jr., *Letter from Birmingham Jail*, 16 April 1963.

Koch, Tony, "Queensland DPP Overworked and Underpaid", *The Australian* (Australia), 17 May 2008.

Krauss, Rebecca, "The Theory of Prosecutorial Discretion in Federal Law: Origins and Developments" (2009) 6 *Seton Hall Circuit Review* 1.

Lesley, "Gabe Watson Acquitted" on *DiveOz Discussion Forum* (24 February 2012) <http://www.diveoz.com.au/discussion_forums/topic.asp?TOPIC_ID=26328>.

Lind, Allan and Tom Tyler, *The Social Psychology of Procedural Justice* (Plenum Press, 1988).

Litster, Detective Superintendent Jim, "The Police Perspective: Homicide in South Australia", in Heather Strang and Sally-Anne Gerull (eds), *Homicide: Patterns, Prevention and Control* (Australian Institute of Criminology, 1992) 133–43.

Marriner, Cosima, "DPP Defends Decision to Drop Bride Murder Charge", *Sydney Morning Herald* (New South Wales), 10 June 2009.

Mather, Lynn M, *Plea Bargaining or Trial: The Process of Criminal Case Disposition* (Lexington Books, 1979).

McConville, Mike, "Development of Empirical Research Techniques and Theory", in Mike McConville and Wing Hong Chui (eds), *Research Methods For Law* (Edinburgh University Press, 2007) 207–29.

McConville, Mike and Chester L Mirsky, *Jury Trials and Plea Bargaining: A True History* (Hart Publishing, 2005).

McConville, Mike and John Baldwin, *Courts, Prosecution and Conviction* (Oxford University Press, 1981).

McFadyen, Michael, "Tina Watson's Death" on *Michael McFadyen's Scuba Diving Website* (2012) <http://www.michaelmcfadyenscuba.info/viewpage.php?page_id=791>.

Michael, Peter and Stefanie Balogh, "Gabe Watson Faces Murder Change over Wife's Scuba Death", *The Courier Mail* (Queensland), 21 June 2008.

Mike, "Gabe Watson Acquitted" on *DiveOz Discussion Forum* (27 February 2012) <http://www.diveoz.com.au/discussion_forums/topic.asp?TOPIC_ID=26328>.

Miller, Lisa, "Watson Facing Alabama 'Lynch Mob'" on *ABC 621 Brisbane* (2 December 2010) <http://www.abc.net.au/news/stories/2010/12/02/3082507.htm?site=brisbane>.

Mills, Brian, *The Criminal Trial* (Federation Press, 2011).

Mitchell, Peter, "Gabe Watson Murder Trial Delayed", *Sydney Morning Herald* (New South Wales), 8 April 2011.

—. "Witness Thought Watson Was Helping Wife", *Sydney Morning Herald* (New South Wales), 17 February 2012.

Moles, Robert, *A State of Injustice* (Networked Knowledge, 2009) <http://netk.net.au/soi/SOI16.asp>.

Moynihan, Honourable Martin AO QC, *Review of the Civil and Criminal Justice System in Queensland* (Queensland Government, 2008).

Murray, David, "Dad Attacks Police Inaction on Tragic Anniversary: I Know How My Daughter Died", *Sunday Mail* (Queensland), 22 October 2006.

My Red Pony, "Gabe Watson Acquitted: Judge Acquits Husband in 'Honeymoon Scuba Death': Comments" on *Huffington Post Blog* (23 February 2012) <http://www.huffingtonpost.com/2012/02/23/gabe-watson-acquitted_n_1296452.html>.

National Centre for State Courts, *Alabama Overview* (2012) <http://www.ncsc.org/information-and-resources/budget-resource-center/states-activities-map/alabama.aspx>.

Nine Network Australia, "Deep Trouble" on *60 Minutes* (23 March 2012) <http://sixtyminutes.ninemsn.com.au/stories/8440110/deep-trouble>.

Novak, Michael, "Defining Social Justice" (2000) 29 *First Things Online* <http://www.firstthings.com/article/2007/01/defining-social-justice-29>.

O'Brien, Melanie, "Society is Entitled to but One Satisfaction: *Ne Bis In Idem* and Jurisdiction Questions in the Gabe Watson Case" (Speech delivered at *Crime, Justice and Democracy Conference*, Brisbane, Australia 26-28 September 2011) <http://crimejusticeconference.com/wp-content/uploads/2012/05/Conference-Proceedings-Crime-Justice-and-Social-Democracy-An-International-Conference.pdf> 61-79.

Paepcke, Jon, "Fact Check: Gabe Watson Case Cost State Nearly $100,000", *Alabama13News* (Alabama), 21 May 2012.

PricewaterhouseCoopers, "Review of Fees Paid by Victoria Legal Aid to Barristers in Criminal Cases" (2008) <http://www.vicbar.com.au/webdata/generalfiles/PriceWaterhouseCoopers.pdf>.

Queensland Courts, *Coroners Court* (2012) <http://www.courts.qld.gov.au/courts/coroners-court>.

Queensland Police Service, "Investigation into the Death of Christina Mae Watson Nee Thomas whilst Scuba Diving off Townsville—22nd October 2003—Operation Charlie Oswald", *QPS Report* (Townsville) 27 August 2004.

Queensland Supreme Court, "Annual Report", *Supreme Court Website* (2009) <http://www.courts.qld.gov.au/__data/assets/pdf_file/0004/84775/sc-ar-2008-09.pdf >.

—. "Annual Report", *Supreme Court Website* (2010) <http://www.courts.qld.gov.au/__data/assets/pdf_file/0005/84776/sc-ar-2009-10.pdf >

Quigley, Rachel, "'It Was Like She Died All over Again': Father of Tina Watson Speaks of Family's Hurt after 'Honeymoon Killer' is Acquitted of Murder", *Daily Mail* (United Kingdom), 5 March 2012.

Rapke, Jeremy QC, "25th Anniversary Speech Delivered by the Director of Public Prosecutions" (Speech delivered at *Victorian Office of Public Prosecutions 25th Anniversary Presentation,* Victoria, Australia, 27 October 2008) <http://www.opp.vic.gov.au/wps/wcm/connect/Office+Of+Public+Prosecutions/resources/file/eb493844164f1f3/25th_Anniversary_Speech_delivered_by_DPP-2727Oct08.pdf>.

Rappaport, Elizabeth, "Capital Murder and the Domestic Discount: A Study of Capital Domestic Murder in the Post-Furman Era" (1996) 49 *Southern Methodist University Law Review* 1507.

Rawls, Phillip, "King Wants to Abolish Parole", *Tuscaloosa News* (Alabama), 22 October 2007.

Reeves, Jay, "Scuba-Diver Allegedly Drowns Wife in Australia: Gabe Watson on Trial for Tina Thomas Watson's Death", *Huffington Post* (United States), 12 February 2012.

—. "Judge Acquits Alabama Mail in Bride's Honeymoon Death", *Star Advertiser* (United States), 24 February 2012.

Riesling, Greg and Ray Henry, "Honeymoon Killer Deported: Man Convicted in Wife's Death Sent Back to US", *Huffington Post* (United States), 25 November 2010.

Roach, Kent, "Four Models of the Criminal Process" (1999) 89 *Journal of Criminal Law and Criminology* 678.

—. "The Attorney General and the Charter Revisited" (2000) 50 *Dalhousie Law Journal* 1.

Robinson, Carol, "Gabe Watson's Family Speaks 7 Years after His Wife, Tina Watson, Drowned on Australian Honeymoon", *Birmingham News* (Alabama), 3 March 2010.

—. "Interview: Gabe Watson Looks to Leave Shadow of his Wife's Honeymoon Death and His Murder Trial" on *Birmingham News* (Alabama) (3 March 2012) <http://blog.al.com/spotnews/2012/03/interview_gabe_watson_looks_to.html>.

Robinson, Paul and Michael Cahill, *Law without Justice: Why Criminal Law Doesn't Give People What They Deserve* (Oxford University Press, 2006).

Salvatore, Stephanie, "What's Next for Gabe Watson?", *CBS 42* (United States), 24 February 2012.

Samuels, Gordon, *Samuels' Review of the New South Wales Director of Public Prosecutions' Policy and Guidelines For Charge Bargaining and Tendering Of Agreed Facts* (New South Wales Parliament, 2002).

Sarat, Austin, "Vengeance, Victims and the Identity of Law" (1997) 6 *Social and Legal Studies* 163.

—. "Going to Court: Access, Autonomy and the Contradictions of Liberal Legality", in David Kairys (ed), *The Politics of Law: A Progressive Critique* (Basic Books, 3rd Edition, 1998) 97–114.

Saturday, Suzanne, "Fatal Honeymoon Review" on *TV Megasie* (8 August 2012) <http://tvmegasite.net:8080/prime/reviews/2012/fatalhoneymoon.html>.

Sebba, Leslie, *Third Parties: Victims and the Criminal Justice System* (Ohio State University Press, 1996).

Shearer, Ivan, *Extradition in International Law* (University Press, 1971).

Skene, Kathleen, "Six Months Extra Jail", *Townsville Bulletin* (Queensland), 19 September 2009.

Skitka, Linda, "Exploring the 'Lost and Found' of Justice Theory Research" (2009) 22 *Social Justice Research* 98.

Skitka, Linda, Christopher Barman and Elizabeth Mullen, "Morality and Justice: An Expanded Theoretical Perspective and Review", in Karen

Hedtvedt and Jody Clay-Warner (eds), *Advances in Group Processes* (Vol 25, Emerald Group Publishing, 2008) 1–27.

Skitka, Linda and David Houston, "When Due Process Is of No Consequence: Moral Mandates and Presumed Defendant Guilt or Innocence" (2001) 14 *Social Justice Research* 305.

Solomon, Peter, *Criminal Justice Policy: From Research To Reform* (Butterworths, 1983).

Steering Committee, Australian Federal Government, *Report on Government Services* (2009) <http://www.pc.gov.au/gsp/rogs/2009>.

—. *Report on Government Services* (2010) <http://www.pc.gov.au/gsp/rogs/2010>.

Storr, Will, "New Investigation into Honeymoon Death of Tina Watson", *The Sunday Mail* (Queensland), 28 August 2010.

Strang, Heather, *Repair or Revenge: Victims and Restorative Justice* (Clarendon Press, 2002).

The Australian, "Queensland Did Its Best to Ensure Justice Was Done over Gabe Watson, Said Bligh", *The Australian* (Australia), 24 February 2012.

Thibut, John and Laurens Walker, *Procedural Justice: A Psychological Analysis* (Erlbaum, 1975).

Thomas, Hedley, "Early Error Blinded Police on Dive Death", *The Australian* (Australia), 11 December 2010.

Thomas, Tommy and Cindy, "Justice for Tina" on *Justice for Tina Facebook Page* (23 February 2012) <http://www.facebook.com/pages/Justice-for-Tina-Thomas/164788116916236>.

Toulson, Andy, "Diver on Honeymoon: Husband Rocked by Tragic Death", *Townsville Bulletin* (Queensland), 24 October 2003.

—. "Gabe Watson Deserved Murder Trial", *Townsville Bulletin* (Queensland), 29 May 2010.

Townsville Bulletin, "Seeking Answers: Frustrated Parents Tom and Cindy Thomas", *Townsville Bulletin* (Queensland), 16 September 2006.

Tyler, Tom, Robert Boeckmann, Heather Smith and Yuen Huo, *Social Justice in a Diverse Society* (Westview Press, 1997).

Tyler, Tom and Steven Blader, "The Group-Engagement Model: Procedural Justice, Social Identity and Co-Operative Behavior" (2000) 7 *Personality and Social Psychology Review* 249.

Thompson, Tuck, "Legal Stoush over Gabe Watson Honeymoon Scuba Trial", *The Courier Mail* (Queensland), 20 December 2011.

—. "Gabe Watson 'Hung Out and Asked for Hugs' on Other Dive Boat as Others Tried to Save Tina's Life", *The Courier Mail* (Queensland), 16 February 2012.

—. "Gabe Watson Freed Due to Lack of Evidence at Alabama Murder Trial", *The Courier Mail* (Queensland), 25 February 2012.

United States President's Commission on Law Enforcement and the Administration of Justice, *Taskforce Report on the Courts* (National Institute of Justice, 1967).

Velasco, Eric, "Diver Testifies to Doubts about Gabe Watson's Story of Wife's Drowning, Another Backs Parts of Account", *The Birmingham News* (Alabama), 16 February 2012.

—. "Watson Acquitted of Wife's Murder: Charges Dropped in '03 Honeymoon Drowning", *Birmingham News* (Alabama), 24 February 2012.

Vogel, Mary, "The Social Origins of Plea Bargaining: An Approach to the Empirical Study of Discretionary Leniency" (2008) 35 *Journal of Law and Society* 201.

Watson, Duncan, "The Attorney General's Guidelines on Plea Bargaining in Serious Fraud: Obtaining Guilty Pleas Fairly?" (2010) 74(1) *Journal of Criminal Law* 77.

Weatherup, Malcolm, "Government Delivers Unexpected Budget Adjustment for Office", *Townsville Bulletin* (Queensland), 22 July 2008.

Willis, John, "Sentencing Discount for Guilty Pleas" (1985) 18 *Australian and New Zealand Journal of Criminology* 131.

Wright, Martin, "The Rights and Needs of Victims in the Criminal Justice Process", in Hendrik Kaptein and Marijke Malsch (eds), *Crime, Victims and Justice: Essays on Principles and Practice* (Ashgate, 2004) 141–54.

APPENDIX A

CHAPTER OVERVIEWS

In exploring questions surrounding the attainment of justice in the *Watson* case, this book is divided into three parts that follow the case from its commencement on 22 October 2003 in Queensland, Australia, to its legal conclusion in Alabama, US, over eight years and four months later on 23 February 2012.

Part I: Justice in Queensland

Part One: Justice in Queensland commences with an examination of the Queensland legal system's response to the case, in relation to how Tina's death was handled and finalised by the criminal justice agencies involved. It is divided into four chapters.

Chapter One: *Operation Charlie Oswald*

Chapter One examines some of the main issues that arose from the police investigation into Tina's death, with a particular focus on two of the key criticisms that have been levied at the police handling of the case: the "flawed" testing of Gabe's dive computer, and the suggestion that the lead police investigators had predetermined that Gabe was guilty of murder, rather than allowing the evidence to lead them to a homicide investigation and to perceiving Gabe as a suspect. Aside from the criticisms of police bias and questions around the involvement of Tina's family in colouring police perceptions of Gabe's guilt, concerns pertaining to the justness of the police investigation largely stem from the police not having tested Gabe's dive computer in its totality, which subsequently resulted in an erroneous finding. While significant and accurate pieces of evidence that highlighted inaccuracies and inconsistencies in Gabe's versions of what happened to Tina underwater were obtained from the dive computer tests, it has been suggested that the one flawed test result which appeared to provide Gabe with an opportunity to separate Tina and himself from the majority of the dive group is the primary piece of evidence that ultimately persuaded the police that Gabe was guilty of murder. On this basis, it is argued by members of the Watson family and Gabe's defence team that the police developed tunnel vision, which led them to focus their investigation solely upon Gabe as a murder suspect. As a consequence, the seemingly flawed testing created a possible injustice, or at least a perception of injustice, in the police investigation.

This chapter explores our discussions with the police involved in *Operation Charlie Oswald*. In contrast to the views of Gabe's Australian and US defence teams, and some media commentators, we argue that the police's views on Gabe's involvement in Tina's death were established after several years of investigation and were primarily based on a substantial body of evidence. Indeed, the analysis in this chapter suggests that the erroneous finding from the dive computer was not the primary factor that convinced the police to pursue a homicide charge against Gabe. Rather, this finding appeared to form only one small piece of a very large body of evidence that was collected over several years, and it was only in considering the evidence in its totality that the police were led to the belief that Tina's death was a premeditated act of homicide committed by Gabe.

In examining the two key criticisms questioning the justness of the police investigation, Chapter One also provides a unique insight into the complexities of the police investigation into Tina's death, and the stages at which the three police officers primarily involved in the case—Detective Senior Constable Kevin Gehringer, Detective Sergeant Gary Campbell and Lieutenant Brad Flynn—became confident that a murder charge against Gabe would be the likely outcome of their investigation.

Chapter Two: Delaying Justice? Prolonging the Police Investigation

Chapter Two further explores the questions of justice and integrity that have been asked in relation to the police investigation and the Queensland coronial inquest into the cause and circumstances surrounding Tina's death. Specifically, this chapter considers how the existence of delays and an initially unsupportive internal environment at the Queensland Police Service (QPS) undermined perceptions of justice, particularly in relation to the processes used by the police to investigate Gabe's involvement in Tina's death, and the processes and outcome of the coronial inquest.

In light of the problematic financial climate that existed within the Queensland criminal justice system throughout (and continuing beyond) the duration of the police investigation, a prominent criticism of the Australian handling of the *Watson* case has arisen from the ideal that "justice delayed is justice denied". Questions have been asked about the duration of the police and coronial investigations into the death of Tina Thomas, and the processes involved in these investigations, particularly given the accusations of police tunnel vision examined in Chapter One. Indeed, the belief that the police had predetermined that Gabe was guilty of Tina's murder is considered one of the reasons why their investigation was protracted over an extensive timeframe, on the basis that there was limited evidence to support their hypothesis, and several years were needed to gather sufficient proof. Without question, throughout its five-year duration there were several obstacles that prevented the police from being able to complete their investigation within a shorter timeframe. However, our analysis in this chapter reveals that none of the obstacles that impacted on the duration of the investigation were inherently linked to an absence of evidence. Rather, within a complex cross-jurisdictional, multi-agency investigation, the obstacles arose from a problematic climate of inefficiency, an absence of available funding and, at least in the initial stages of the investigation, a seemingly unsupportive senior management within the QPS, which essentially constrained and blocked aspects of the investigation from being conducted efficiently.

Chapter Two also considers the geographical complexities inherent to the police investigation, which included the requirement for witness statements and evidence to be gathered from various individuals and locations around the globe. On this basis, our analysis demonstrates that it is not surprising that some delays unique to this case arose which would not have existed had the investigation been conducted solely within Queensland, or even within the proximity of Australian borders. Thus, as this chapter explains, it is not the fault of the police investigators per se that the investigation into the death of Tina Thomas was protracted over almost five years.

Chapter Three: "Dealing" with Gabe

Chapter Three provides a rare insight into the *Watson* plea deal and offers an in-depth overview of the resource-starved climate that existed within the Queensland ODPP and Supreme Court at the time when the plea deal with Gabe was reached. This chapter thus examines what impact financial considerations might have had in motivating the ODPP's decision to enter into a plea bargain with Gabe rather than to run an expensive and resource-intensive trial. In drawing attention to the questions of justice surrounding the plea deal, Chapter Three considers whether the resolution of the case in this manner could be perceived as offering substantive, procedural or subjective justice.

Specifically, Chapter Three critically examines a number of key issues surrounding the motivations underpinning the decisions of the ODPP which raise significant scepticism about the legitimacy of the deal made between Gabe and the ODPP. While plea bargaining certainly has benefits in terms of guaranteeing a conviction and the sparing of significant resources, the process can also be extremely limited in being able to offer a just outcome for the key parties involved, including the accused. Unfortunately, given the reluctance of the ODPP to publicly comment on the deal beyond its brief public statement made in 2009, these questions around the justness and motivations underpinning the deal have remained unanswered, until now.

Chapter Four: "Bargaining" with the Thomas Family

In building on the analysis presented in the previous chapter, Chapter Four examines concerns surrounding the conduct of the lead prosecutor involved in the Queensland handling of the *Watson* case, Assistant Director of Public Prosecutions, Brendan Campbell SC, leading up to and following the plea deal, and also considers the implications of his conduct in relation to his statutory obligations to victims, both primary and secondary. Chapter Four also provides a unique insight into the timing of the deal, to analyse whether the plea bargain could or did provide justice in a procedural, substantive or subjective form. In drawing attention to the questionable outcome of the plea deal, this chapter also explores the favourable descriptions of Gabe's character presented by various members of the Queensland judiciary and how these images differed significantly from those presented by Tina's family and best friend. By considering how Tina, the victim, was missing—lost, ignored or deemed irrelevant—from almost all stages of the case's legal progression in Queensland, this chapter raises questions over whether justice for the Thomas family could ever have been attained in light of the diminished role of the victim, particularly as plea bargaining was ultimately used to resolve the case. In examining these issues, Chapter Four offers a conclusion to Queensland's handling of the case and considers whether the resolution by a plea bargain provided justice, or whether it meant that no form of justice—subjective, substantive or procedural—could be attained from any perspective, outside that of the Queensland ODPP.

Part II: Justice in Alabama

Part Two examines the Alabama legal system's response to, and handling of, the *Watson* case, focusing specifically upon the second prosecution of Gabe for capital murder for pecuniary gain. The four analysis chapters examine the key issues that arose prior to and during the February 2012 capital murder trial, which worked to prevent the trial from providing a second chance for justice from any perspective, or in any greater manner than that of the Queensland plea bargain.

Chapter Five: Prosecuting Gabe ... Again

Chapter Five examines some of the unique legal tensions that emerged from the contentious decision to prosecute Gabe in Alabama. It explores the three primary questions of justice and injustice that have been raised in relation to the decision to prosecute Gabe, concerning the motivations for the prosecution, the questions surrounding jurisdiction, and the issue of double jeopardy. On the one hand, the motivations underpinning the decision to initiate a second prosecution have been attributed to a quest for justice, after the perceived unjust resolution of the case in Queensland. Yet, on the other hand, the decision to run the trial has been criticised as a purely political, vote-grabbing exercise, made by a struggling Attorney-General—former Alabama Attorney-General Troy King. Further to the issue of motivation, this chapter explores questions surrounding the legitimacy and capacity of Alabama proceeding with a prosecution (and Australia doing little to prevent it), because the crime occurred and was already resolved in a separate, international jurisdiction.

Beyond questions of jurisdiction and double jeopardy, Chapter Five also considers how the logistics of running the trial in Alabama prevented it from being able to offer a just outcome for any party. This analysis explores the impact of the economic situation in limiting the number of witnesses on the prosecution's witness list and contributing to further delays in the case, which resulted in the trial being rescheduled by nine months. This chapter also considers how the basic differences between Queensland and Birmingham contributed to the failure of the trial to provide justice. In examining these issues, Chapter Five highlights some of the significant problems that arose prior to the second prosecution commencing which ultimately impacted on its capacity to ever provide a second chance for justice.

Chapter Six: Murder for Money: Proving the Motive

Chapter Six further examines some of the factors that impeded the second prosecution of Gabe from providing substantive, procedural or subjective justice, with a particular focus on the prosecution's requirement to prove a problematic pecuniary gain motive. One of the key factors that emerged within our discussions relating to the viability and likely success of the second prosecution of Gabe centred on the question of motive, or more specifically, the much stronger proof requirements on the Alabama prosecution than those that would have existed had a trial been run in Queensland in 2009, where proving motive would not have been an essential element of murder. Consequently, had the Queensland ODPP proceeded to trial, it would not have needed to prove beyond reasonable doubt Gabe's state of mind—that is, the alleged reasons for Gabe committing the offence—in order for him to be found guilty. In contrast, the prosecution of Gabe in Alabama not only had to establish beyond reasonable doubt that he killed Tina, but also had the more complex task of proving beyond reasonable doubt that he did so for a particular reason. Informed by a procedural justice framework, Chapter Six thus analyses the murder for money motive that was presented by the Alabama prosecution, and considers some of the difficulties that existed for the prosecution in endeavouring to establish Gabe's state of mind in allegedly planning and committing Tina's murder.

In questioning the justness of the motive requirement, this chapter also examines concerns surrounding the legitimacy of proceeding with the pecuniary gain charge, given that several of our participants identified a number of potential motivations in addition to financial gain that may have formed the basis for Gabe's alleged criminal conduct. Chapter Six also considers some of the critical questions of justice that arose in relation to Judge Nail's conduct throughout the Alabama trial. In particular, it examines the questions that were asked about his decision to deny the admission of testimony that Queensland Coroner David Glasgow had previously described in his inquest findings as significant, legally admissible and providing the basis for Gabe's financial gain motive.

Chapter Seven: The Fatal Dive

Chapter Seven expands on some of the key limitations of the Alabama trial identified in the previous two chapters, by focusing specifically on the prosecution's presentation of evidence relating to how Gabe intentionally killed Tina. Questions, conjecture and opinions surrounding what happened between Tina and Gabe underwater at the *Yongala* dive site have understandably been of central importance to the legal processes and outcomes in the *Watson* case, as well as to the perceptions of guilt or innocence by diving experts, the media, the general public and those intimately involved in the case. Outside the police investigation, understanding or making sense of the circumstances surrounding the fatal dive was perhaps of most significance, in a legal respect, to the capital murder trial in Alabama, as the prosecution was required to prove beyond reasonable doubt that with premeditated intent Gabe deliberately killed his bride of 11 days during the dive.

In reviewing key pieces of the evidence presented by the prosecution, Chapter Seven examines how a lack of available resources and financial support limited the ability of the prosecution to prove this central part of its case. This chapter suggests that, as a consequence of these limitations, the dive evidence presented at the trial represented only a small proportion of the total volume of material that had been collected as part of the police investigation and that which had been presented years earlier at the coronial inquest in Queensland. Working under stringent financial constraints, in its attempt to establish Gabe's guilt, the prosecution had to carefully select which witnesses it could justify flying to Alabama, and consequently which witness testimonies it would have to forgo. As argued throughout this chapter, the impact of financial pressures and restricted resources yet again raised doubt over the capacity of the Alabama trial to offer a process in which a procedurally or subjectively just outcome could be obtained.

Chapter Seven considers the extent to which the prosecution's construction of the circumstances surrounding Tina's fatal dive met the prima facie requirement on the prosecution to prove that Gabe killed Tina, and whether the judicial acquittal at the conclusion of the prosecution's case can consequently be viewed as a just outcome. Additionally, this chapter explores the degree to which a lack of resources and financial support, as well as the ongoing influence of delays, hindered the achievability of justice—subjectively, substantively and procedurally—in the Alabama trial.

Chapter Eight: Judging the "Character" of Gabe

Chapter Eight examines one of the key issues that could be perceived as preventing the Alabama trial from providing justice: the depiction of Gabe's character. Specifically, this chapter considers how portrayals of an individual's character can infiltrate perceptions of guilt, innocence and justice. While much of the negative character evidence pertaining to Gabe was not admissible in the Alabama trial, Chapter Eight considers how negative depictions of his character in the media have influenced perceptions of his guilt or innocence regardless, and how this in turn has impacted on the capacity for any outcome from the trial to be considered just.

This chapter also examines how, even in light of the acquittal judgement in Alabama, there remain lingering questions within the public realm pertaining to Gabe's guilt—questions that have permeated this case throughout its almost nine-year duration. Interestingly, as Chapter Eight discusses, one of the key influences upon these perceptions has been the debate surrounding two simplistic questions: Was Gabe capable of killing his wife? And did he have the character of a killer?

Part III: Achieving Justice

The third and final part critically examines the outcome of the February 2012 capital murder trial and provides an in-depth analysis of whether a second chance for justice was or ever could have been attained from running the second prosecution of Gabe in Alabama. Part Three is divided into three chapters.

Chapter Nine: Gabe's Acquittal

Chapter Nine focuses entirely on the final day of the February 2012 capital murder trial. It provides an overview of the defence's motion for a judgement of acquittal, the prosecution's response and Judge Nail's decision to acquit Gabe. In providing insight into the contentious decision to acquit Gabe, this chapter draws upon the defence's written motion for the judgement of acquittal, court observations and the perspectives of those most involved in the case to explore the premise behind Judge Nail's decision. In doing so, this chapter provides a basis to then analyse (in the final two chapters) the "justness" of the decision to acquit Gabe from a procedural, subjective and substantive viewpoint.

Chapter Ten: (In)Justice for Tina? (In)Justice for Gabe?

The acquittal decision was a key turning point in the *Watson* case, and arguably the definitive moment at which the Alabama trial can be seen as not providing justice under a procedural justice framework. Chapter Ten explores the achievability of justice via the acquittal outcome in a procedural and subjective sense, from the perspectives of the Watson and Thomas families, as well as those most closely involved in the investigation, prosecution and defence of Gabe in Queensland and Alabama. In doing so, this chapter considers whether the acquittal and the legal processes leading to the finalisation of the case in this manner provided any form of justice equal to, beyond, or below that offered by the plea bargain resolution reached in Queensland in 2009.

In considering the implications of the acquittal, particularly the absence of the voices of the defence and the jury, Chapter Ten expands on earlier arguments by demonstrating how one's understanding of justice is ever changing, difficult to define, and shaped by personal and subjective viewpoints. Thus, this chapter suggests that perceptions of justice and injustice in the acquittal outcome were influenced by a combination of the legal processes and outcome, representations of Gabe's character, and expectations around morality and normality. As a result, Chapter Ten considers how the acquittal failed to provide closure, even for those supporting Gabe's innocence, and explores the implications that arise from there forever remaining speculation around Gabe's intentional or unintentional involvement in Tina's death.

Chapter Eleven: A Second Chance for Justice

Chapter Eleven, the final chapter, provides an overview of the key arguments and decisions that prevented justice from being attained in this case—an outcome that we suggest is primarily due to the decisions made by individuals on behalf of the justice system: namely, Assistant Director of Public Prosecutions and crown prosecutor in charge of this case in Queensland, Brendan Campbell SC; and Judge Tommy Nail, who elected to acquit Gabe without any input from the jury. In concluding our analysis and overall discussion of the *Watson* case, this chapter highlights the subjective nature of justice, and questions whether in any way, justice prevailed or could have prevailed from either the Queensland or Alabama legal responses to the death of Tina Thomas.